Secu
21st

Security and Migration in the 21st Century

ELSPETH GUILD

polity

First published in 2009 by Polity Press

Polity Press
65 Bridge Street
Cambridge CB2 1UR, UK

Polity Press
350 Main Street
Malden, MA 02148, USA

ISBN-13: 978-0-7456-4442-4
ISBN-13: 978-0-7456-4443-1(paperback)

A catalogue record for this book is available from the British Library.

Typeset in 11.25/13 pt Dante
by Servis Filmsetting Ltd, Stockport, Cheshire
Printed and bound by MPG Books Group, UK

For further information on Polity, visit our website: www.politybooks.com

Contents

Acknowledgements

As the relationship between migration and security became increasingly complex in the new millennium, so the need for a fresh look at how the two concepts intersect appealed to me. When Louise Knight, Senior Commissioning Editor at Polity Press, invited me to write this book, the offer was irresistible. I would like to thank Louise and her colleagues at Polity for their unflagging support and encouragement. I appreciated this enormously. I must also thank the European Commission, Directorate General Research, for the generous financial support which it provided in the form of a Framework VI project, 'CHALLENGE', which permitted me the time to research this book and think through its consequences.

Many chapters have benefited substantially from the feedback I have had following their presentation at various conferences and seminars, most importantly from CHALLENGE partners at the twenty-two universities and institutes which have participated in the project over the past five years. In addition, I would like to thank Lund University, the London School of Economics and Kings College London for providing me with key opportunities to present my work beyond the scope of the CHALLENGE project, and to receive valuable in-put on it.

I would like to thank Professor Didier Bigo for his tremendous generosity, reading and commenting on many chapters, and Professor Kees Groenendijk for his wise advice on many aspects of my research. My intellectual debt to the two of them is very deep indeed. I must also thank most sincerely Professor R. J. B. Walker for illuminating so many aspects of political philosophy for me and encouraging me to complete the project. There are too many others to name, whose help and constructive criticism has assisted me greatly throughout the project.

1

Understanding security and migration in the twenty-first century

What is security? What is migration? Both these questions open hundreds of doors into many different disciplines, theories, practices and landscapes. Security as a term can be found in so many different settings and with so many different meanings that a flourishing academic discipline, security studies, has developed, within which the search for definitions is essentially contested. Anyone trying to get a mortgage will be focusing on a very different idea of security from the ones I will examine in this book. Similarly, the concept of migration can be found in multiple environments which point in completely different directions. For instance, Jacques Perrin's 2002 film, *Le peuple migrateur*, translated into English as *Winged Migration*, achieved an Oscar award nomination in the Best Documentary category but does not include any humans. It is about birds.

Human migration has given rise to an academic discipline – migration studies. Like security studies, it comes within the wider framework of international relations. The focus is on the state as the key actor regarding migration, which is a cross-border activity carried out by individuals. The state may be the state of nationality or origin of migrants or that of their destination. The emphasis in the discipline is on the state and the acts of the state around flows of people.

Both migration studies and security studies as subcategories of political science and international relations tend to reach out towards other fields – human geography, law, history, anthropology, etc. But both remain nested in international relations. It is not surprising, then, that the work of academics in security and migration studies can be classified fairly satisfactorily using the main schools of thought of international relations and political science (Williams 2008). Like security studies, migration studies has some difficulty in determining the scope of its object. Bigo has shown that security studies depends on the enlargement of the insecurity envelope (Bigo 2006). Like blowing up a balloon, the greater the insecurity concerns presented by political actors, the bigger the security issues, and hence the remit of security studies, become. Migration studies has a similar tendency – the bigger the migration flows, the wider the scope for migration studies. As migration flows diminish in some areas (for instance, the forced migration flows to Europe in the beginning of the 2000s), the development of other fields such as security studies provides new points of reference both for political actors (concerns about refugees and terrorism) and for academics (Baldaccini & Guild 2007). In effect, what happens is that foreigners, described in various different ways (migrant, refugee, etc.), become caught in a continuum of insecurity (Bigo 2002). As the foreigner becomes compressed into state-determined categories, those categories are normatively defined, including by reference to insecurity. Political actors may focus on the 'problem' and 'burden' of asylum seekers one year, then the same or other political actors may rail against economic migrants as the source of insecurity the next. Many insecurity discourses are promoted at any given time – the capacity of one set of political actors successfully to impose their view of the most important one(s) depends on a wide variety of other factors. However, the ease with which the category of the foreigner may be added to an insecurity discourse, with the effect of heightening the perceived seriousness of the threat, remains constant.

In this book I will analyse the intersection of the two fields from the perspective of international political sociology – examining the individual and his or her movement; how the state frames and categorizes him or her as an individual and a migrant, citizen or indeterminate; and how that intersects with the construction of the individual[1] as a security threat. This immediately provokes resistance; the state is not omnipotent. There is a clear correlation between the state-centric approach in migration studies and with that of mainstream security studies. Security studies tend to be dominated by a statist approach heavily influenced by realists, neo-realists and liberals (and neo-liberals). The term 'critical security studies' was coined to encompass a move away from these traditions and to examine again the meaning of the political in the definition of security and its study (Krause & Williams 2003). Central to critical security studies is a challenge to the doxa or belief that the academic experts know what the subject of the discipline is, that is to say what security is. Similarly, in this book I will challenge the supposition on which migration studies is based: that we know what migration is and which actors are entitled to determine the political in respect of migration. While critical migration studies has, as yet, not emerged as a separate approach, nonetheless this is the category which this book promotes. Building on critical security studies, I will examine both the subject matter of security (whose security, who is entitled to determine the politics of security) and that of migration (whose migration, who is entitled to determine the politics of migration). The insecurity continuum can be ruptured by the individual challenging his or her categorization: as a foreigner (for instance, I will examine the case of David Hicks in chapter 2), or by moving from the category of 'terrorist' to that of refugee (I will consider these cases in chapter 6). Similarly, it can be ruptured by a political decision no longer to treat a category of foreigners as foreign – for instance in the European Union (EU), nationals of one Member State who work and reside in another (I will consider this category in chapter 7).

In the intersection of migration and security, this book moves away from a state-centred focus in which it is the actions of the state alone which define what is political, to an approach which examines the individual and his or her concerns: how does the individual fit into a set of state structural frameworks and become categorized as a threat to security and to state control of migration? These two quite different types of security issues become conflated in much of the discussion: migrants who have escaped the control of the state are defined as security threats because the remit of the state is reconfigured. But even using the concept of migration itself is to think like a state. Individuals do not perceive themselves as migrants or otherwise except by virtue of the coercive prompting of state administrations. Even communities do not live the differentiation of some individuals from others except with a strong state push (for instance as regards the exclusion of undocumented migrants from health services in the UK, proposed in 2008: the general medical association representing doctors refused to participate, maintaining that doctors are not immigration officers).

Before developing further my own approach through international political sociology, it may be useful, briefly, to review the main schools of international relations and position the main academic work on migration and security within them. Starting then with the realist tradition, this framework is based on the idea that there is a monopoly of knowledge which is real and held by academics. According to this point of view, the state and its duty to control both security and migration are self-evident and matters of objective truth. While at its heart pessimistic, the realist approach provides explanations based on the accumulation of power by states for their own exploitation. In the migration field, Weiner represents this school most unambiguously in examining the issues around migration as essentially about state security and self-interest, in respect of which the capacity of individuals to move without state authorization represents a fundamental challenge and threat (Weiner 1997). Against this rather raw approach, liberalism is well represented in migration studies, in particular by those scholars who approach migration regimes in liberal democracies through the contradictions. While on the one hand they acknowledge the public discourse of some actors which is virulently anti-migrant, on the other they examine the generally liberal outcomes in democratic states' migration regimes (Cornellius, Martin & Hollifield 1994). In the Marxist tradition, the focus places migration within a framework of economic struggle. The way in which states treat migration as part of their economic strategies and the struggles around the exploitation of migrant workers are central to this approach. In *The Age of Migration*, Castles and Miller's central element, which informs the whole work, is the relationship of migration with capitalism and the organization of labour: 'the consequential decline of working class parties and trade unions and the erosion of local communicative networks" resulting from migration create the conditions for virulent racism (Castles & Miller 2003). The work of Robin Cohen also comes within this general group, looking, as it does, at how the preferences, interests and actions of global capital intersect with labour migration (R. Cohen 2006).

Migration as a threat to social cohesion and the right of communities to determine their membership is central to a Communitarian approach to the field. Attention is focused on the sub-state level of community and the relationship of community with the state – how do the state's activities in allowing migration flows affect community coherence (Kymlicka 1995; Etzioni 2004)? One of the difficulties with this approach as applied to migration is that it leads towards a crystallization of the idea of community which excludes change. Constructivist theorists have taken a substantial interest in the migration–security nexus, in particular through the works of Buzan, Waever and Kelstrup. The identities and interests of international actors become central in international relations. They examine the ways in which social construction of interests transforms individuals into foreigners who are perceived as a threat, as opposed to citizens (Waever, Buzan, Kelstrup & Lemaitre 1993). Sassen represents one of the most interesting voices in the constructivist/normative framing of migration. Focusing on the relationship of structure and agent and how the mechanisms work by which institutions are produced by certain sets of practices, conceptualization beyond the state becomes easier. There is, however, a strong normative setting directed at how practices are regulated or produced by norms. Her point of departure is globalization – of which the movement of immigrants is one manifestation – placed not so much in the state setting as in that of the city (Sassen 2006). Because of the strong focus on the construction and impact of norms there is a tendency towards the aspirational in this trend. Here the work of Rubio-Marin fits, examining migration from the perspective of civic membership and exclusion (Rubio-Marin

2000). While this approach is richer than the strictly state-centric ones, its focus on the impacts of globalization generates criticism that it is partial. Critical theory, in particular through the work of Habermas on citizenship, provides another prism of analysis in the field of migration. Its focus on a critique of domination bringing together social and cultural analytical tools, has proven attractive as a way to engage belonging and movement in a normative societal setting (Habermas 1992). This has opened a new debate on belonging and exclusion, primarily developed at the intersection of theory and philosophy (Follesdal 2001; Mertens 2008). However, it is through feminist theory that the focus of migration studies shifts substantially towards the individual, primarily women and their position as migrants in patriarchal statist structures (Ehrenreich & Hochschild 2002), though the public policy debate is still very much present (Vargas 2003).

More recently, international political sociology has focused on the relationship of the individual with power and authority, in particular through the constitution of power and authority: how do individuals become categorized as migrants or not. Here it is the role of individuals and their resistance to state political actors which is the subject of investigation: what are the challenges to the state's categorization of the individual? Bigo and Huysmans, coming from critical security studies, develop the analysis of migration and security through the sociology of power and its constitution (Bigo 2002; Huysmans 2006). I have chosen this framework in which to examine the nexus of security and migration. In particular, I avoid analysing the constitution of authority and power as an exclusively state attribute which is then applied to flows of people. Instead I look at the individuals and their struggles to achieve authority and voice against the overarching framework promoted by political actors, in particular in liberal democracies. By refusing to accept the disappearance of the individual into an undifferentiated flow of people which is then directed (or not, as the case may be) by state actors or processes, I seek to reveal the construction and deconstruction of assumptions about migration, identity and security. My contention is that the assumptions about groups of persons – in the case of migration, flows or stocks of migrants – are easily manipulated by political actors. When the flow is disaggregated into the individuals with their individual struggles and objectives in aspiring to constitute authority, a very different analysis is possible, though this is often one which is disturbing to statist approaches and presuppositions. As Stanley Cohen has so seminally shown in criminology, it is through the deconstruction of the mechanisms of authority in state-centric and media discourses that we can understand how society operates (S. Cohen 2003). His choice of asylum seekers and refugees as one of the groups through which to update his thesis in the introduction to the third edition of *Folk Devils and Moral Panics* is symptomatic. The vitriolic discussion about forced migrants and migration promoted by a variety of political and media actors can have real social consequences; Cohen points to the stabbing of an asylum seeker in Glasgow following attacks on 'bogus' asylum seekers in the media. The acts and aspirations of individuals count when analysing migration – both within the state and within the migration flow.

Critical security?

Security cannot be reduced to one element. Rather it can only be understood in relation to power – either more power provides more security (the Cold War scenario in which more military technology was considered essential to security) or security is based on relationships among actors and thus not a commodity at all (Williams 2008). Critical security studies began the investigation into the object of security studies – the meaning of security itself. It is within this rich discipline that the questions I pose about security are best situated (Krause & Williams 2003). One thing which is generally accepted about security is that there is a tension between collective security and security of the individual. While, in the name of collective security, measures are taken which have direct and immediate impacts on the security of the individual, the safeguarding of security for an individual may constitute a challenge to the dominant framing of the requirements of collective security. This is particularly so when the individual concerned is a foreigner (Huysmans 2006). In liberal democracies, measures taken in the name of security are taken for the good of the collectivity, that is the individuals who are entitled to voice within the community. That these measures may reduce the security of any one individual is inevitable. For example, decisions about the allocation of police resources will result in some individuals having better access than others. Changes to social benefits rules will result in great social security for one individual but not necessarily for another.

A tension also exists regarding the composition of the collectivity which is entitled to security. Depending on the way in which we are using the term 'security' and in respect of which set of relationships, some individuals will be fully included but others less so (Fierke 2007). For instance, the state sanction of social relationships through marriage is intended, among other things, to provide financial security for the economically weaker partner on the realization of specific events (such as death, divorce, etc.). The struggle of same-sex partners to enjoy this state sanction and the security which goes with it has taken up substantial amounts of parliamentary time in many liberal democracies. The question of inclusion or exclusion from the relationships of security varies depending on how one is using the term 'security' and for what purpose. Security is, then, most frequently about inclusion, exclusion and choices about sacrifice (Walker 2009). Decisions of this kind are the result of struggles around the constitution of legitimate authority.

Similarly, there is a tension between internal security and external security. The political debates on what types of security individuals should enjoy within the state, whether these be in the form of social security benefits or the length of detention before charge (which was a very hot issue in the UK parliament in 2008), take place within highly structured constitutions which constrain the variations possible. The institutions engaged in security within the state are multiple – for instance social affairs and health ministries concern themselves with limiting the risk of pandemics killing many people, the police and criminal justice departments occupy themselves with the question of crime: what it is, who commits it and how they should be punished. The more widely the concept of security is defined, the more state activities fall within its remit. External security, on the other hand, is more limited. In its classic form it is concerned with the physical integrity of the state – ensuring that the state is not overrun by some other state. The institutions most engaged with this form of security are the military and the foreign ministries. However, the boundaries between these two types of security are by no means as clear as first appears (Bigo 2001). Separatist and nationalist movements within parts of states may challenge the physical integrity of the state more fundamentally than any foreign country. Interior ministries may play an increasingly important role in foreign affairs – making extradition agreements with other countries so that the reach of national criminal law can extend into other states and catch individuals, or readmission agreements whereby states will accept back into their territory foreigners who have passed through it on their way somewhere else.

In this book I will be most concerned with the relationship of security, in many of its different forms, with the individual who is not defined as intrinsically belonging to the collectivity: the foreigner. Among the fields of security which will be central in this book are:

- sovereign, state or national security – the state's right to determine its borders, who crosses them and what the consequences of crossing a border are;
- security, policing and crime – what a crime is and how it relates to the foreigner;

- security categorization and identity – the state's power to define the identity of its citizens and thereby exclude others who are not accepted as such;
- welfare and social security – the allocation of resources to protect the individual.

Undoubtedly, for many readers, security is associated with war, strategic studies and international relations. However, my understanding is wider than this conventional one. By bringing into the security equation history, sociology, law and other disciplines which themselves have long and quite independent definitions of 'security', it is possible to attempt a deeper and more comprehensive analysis of the relationships involved (Fierke 2007). The definitional problems are part of the changing field of security studies which, until the great failings of the field at the end of the 1980s when the end of bipolarity came as a considerable surprise to most in the international relations discipline, was monopolized by military sector analysis. The addition of the concept of human security added a new range of issues to the international relations security agenda. For the moment, this security divides into three main streams: the natural rights / rule of law approach to human security, as based on internationally acknowledged human rights guaranteed by state institutions designed to deliver rights without discrimination; the humanitarian perspective, embraced by a number of UN agencies, whereby the deepening of the role of the international community and its engagement in fields which have traditionally been reserves of state sovereignty is based on the humanitarian imperative to pursue or prevent, in particular, war crimes and genocide; and economic, environmental and social issues which affect individuals and their wellbeing.

It is not surprising that 1989 constitutes a moment of transition for security studies, as the fall of the Berlin Wall, the end of bipolarity and the unanticipated transformation of the politics of protection left many professionals exposed. The end of the Cold War was in itself an important de-securization move (Waever 1995). The traditional understanding of security studies as engaging primarily the military and strategy was in decline (Buzan 1991). At the same time, and as a result of the same sequence of events, internal security was discredited in the former Soviet Union as obviously incapable of maintaining the status quo of the political system, no matter what powers they had. In many former Eastern Block states such as Romania, which is also perhaps the most important example, internal security was the object of such popular rage that the internal security files themselves were destroyed (Deletant [1995] 2006). By 2007, many in Hungary and Poland may have wished the same had happened there as many figures who had been held up as opponents to the communist regimes were gradually being revealed through the investigation of the national archives as, in fact, having been complicit with those regimes (Deak 2006).

The de-legitimization of security institutions both in international relations and in internal affairs was central to the transformation of borders in Europe. The dissolution of a series of previously (apparently) impenetrable borders (most notably the Berlin Wall itself) and the creation of a whole series of other borders – such as those of the three Baltic States, or in the fragmentation of the former Yugoslavia in a bloodbath – for many, changed the relationship of sovereignty and security. The challenges of the 1990s to sovereignty and security, and the relationship between the two, in Europe resulted in a tremendous shift in where both are claimed and how they are exercised, not least with the creation of new borders and the re-establishment of states which had not been on the international scene for a century or more, but also with the massive expansion of the European Union, itself a challenge to traditional views about sovereignty and security.

The variety of possibilities as to the meaning of 'security' leads us back to our initial question: what is security? It appears that this question may well be unanswerable in the abstract as it involves, rather than a positive state of affairs or situation, a negative, the lack of something – though it is doubtful that the lack is that of insecurity (Bigo 2002). One of the difficulties in examining security and migration is the fact that mainstream security studies not only began to distance itself from international relations studies in the 1990s but also entered into a debate with critical security studies around the meaning of 'security'. The move away from classic international relations studies, which claims fixed boundaries between the international and the internal, has been hastened through the development of concepts such as international political sociology, which reject as a false dichotomy the internal–external divide and demand cross-fertilization among different disciplines in order to analyse political violence, transnational mobilization or indeed migration (Bigo & Walker 2007).

The weakening of the classical international relations grip over security studies which came with the end of bipolarity also permitted security studies to start re-discovering sociology, history, politics and law and, through a multidisciplinary approach, to examine other institutions, internal and external, and other power relationships in order better to understand the meaning of boundaries (Bigo & Walker 2007). Security studies also began to develop a different vocabulary which includes key concepts such as risk and uncertainty (Beck 1996), (in)security (Dillon 1996), ethnic conflict (Kaufman 2006), human security (Hampson et al. 2002) and environmental change (Dalby 2002), etc. It claimed as legitimate subject matter fields as diverse as the international arms trade (Hartung 1995), peace operations (Pugh & Cooper 2002), private security (Avant 2006) and transnational organized crime (Kyle & Koslowski 2001). Among the subjects into which security studies began to venture was that of population movements, in which the activities of well-established international organizations such as the United Nations High Commissioner for Refugees, as well as ones in the process of transformation following the end of bipolarity such as the International Organization for Migration, became the subject of analysis (Bali 2008).

Critical migration studies

This brings me to the second question which this book addresses: what is migration? Even when one focuses exclusively on human beings (as opposed to birds, whose migration brings up the largest number of references in many internet searches), there are still many ways of defining the notion. The first key boundary in migration studies is that between movement within a country and movement across international borders. Migration within state borders has traditionally been a preserve of geographers. As the example of China in the twenty-first century reveals, this type of migration can be far more significant in terms of numbers than migration across international borders (Fan 2007). Another discipline, anthropology, while increasingly engaged in migration studies, is less inclined to accept that national sovereignty in the form of borders is of central importance (Vertovec & Cohen 2002). However, it is migration across international borders which has become the core concern of those working in migration studies,[2] including many geographers who are engaged in relevant research (Rajaram & Grundy-Warr 2007).

In mainstream migration studies, as the focus is on the state and its action regarding migration flows (King & Black 1997), the question of how the state constructs the individual as a foreigner attracts less attention (R. Cohen 2006). The political struggles around the state's claim to categorize the individual are invisible. In this book, I want to focus on the notion of migration which includes: (a) the state as the determiner of international borders, and (b) state sovereignty as encompassing the claim of states to an entitlement to control movement of persons across borders. In this regard,

I coin the term 'critical migration studies' to describe the process of deconstructing the state's claims in the face of resistance by individuals. Rather than accepting at face value the state's claims regarding migration flows, struggles with the term 'migration' itself are under the microscope, not as a definitional question but through the agency of individuals.

The modern state claims a monopoly over the legitimate crossing of borders (Torpey 2000). Any border-related definition of 'migration' depends on the deployment of a claim by the state to a sovereign right to designate who are its citizens and who are not (Noiriel 2001). This requires a number of steps already to have been achieved. First the state needs to have a legal definition of who a citizen is, as opposed to those who are not. This will demand a system of registration of births and deaths (and probably marriages if citizenship is related to legitimacy of birth within marriage, as it was in Europe until the end of the twentieth century). The state will need to produce identity documents which reveal that status to its own officials, whose actions are based on this distinction, and ensure that other states recognize those documents as evidence of the status of their citizens' identity claims. All this is quite an onerous proposition and means that substantial public resources must be spent on documenting citizens.

Only once states have determined who their own nationals are does it make any sense to claim to control entry of persons to the state territory on the basis of citizenship. The reverse side of the citizenship coin is foreignness. Those who are not citizens of a state may fall into two main categories. Either they are citizens of some other country and therefore foreigners to the state in question, or they are stateless and no state at all claims them as their own. Statelessness is a particularly unfortunate status as the individual can rely on the protection of no state to confirm their existence through documents, which is the first step of legal existence and a necessary prerequisite to participation in western democracies, let alone to movement across international borders in a lawful manner (Gyulai 2007). The international community has taken various steps to reduce the occurrence of statelessness, the most important of which are through the UN Convention Relating to the Status of Stateless Persons 1954 and the follow-up Convention on the Reduction of Statelessness, 1961. The purpose of the multilateral rules which seek to reduce statelessness, according to the 1954 Convention, is to ensure that all human beings are able to enjoy human rights (rights not based on citizenship) due to a profound concern that stateless persons should be able to access fundamental rights and freedoms.

Once a citizen leaves his or her country of nationality, he or she automatically becomes a foreigner unless the individual holds the nationality of more than one country – commonly called 'dual' or 'multiple' nationality (Faist 2007). Dual or multiple nationality presents particular problems for states and possibly advantages for individuals. To some extent one can make an analogy between citizenship and ownership – the state lays a claim to ownership over the individual. Of course this analogy cannot be taken very far as it rapidly becomes absurd – the range of actions which the state can take in respect of its citizens is restrained by constitutions and, in liberal democracies where the citizen participates in the choice of government, one might justifiably make the opposite analogy, that the citizen owns the state, in order to exemplify other aspects of the state–citizen relationship. However, bearing in mind the limitations of the analogy of ownership between the state and the citizen, it is the state's responsibility in the international state system to take responsibility for its citizens, whether this means accepting them back into the national territory whenever the citizen so chooses or providing consular services to them when they are abroad (that is to say, when they are foreigners on the territory where they are physically).

When two states claim the same individual as belonging to them – dual citizenship – various problems arise, for both the state and the individual. For young people, the issue of military service can be problematic – can both states oblige the individual to complete military service (in principle they can, but there are some international agreements which seek to limit the effect of that possibility (Hailbronner 1996)). Similarly, the question as to which state has the right to extract resources from the citizen to finance itself – otherwise known as taxes – raises problems – does the citizen owe a duty to pay taxes on his or her worldwide income to both countries (a problem which keeps many accountants in employment)? Political participation in two countries also raises questions about the nature of the link between the citizen and the state. There are two main state approaches to dual citizenship: (a) tolerance – for example China, the UK and many south American countries do not impede their citizens' acquisition and use of another citizenship, nor is this an obstacle to acquiring their citizenship; (b) intolerance – Malaysia, Germany and many Nordic countries actively discourage dual citizenship, often to the point of seeking to deprive an individual of their citizenship if they become aware that he or she has acquired another (Martin & Hailbronner 2003).

The concept of migration depends, then, first on the existence of inter-state borders which are the object of sovereignty claims by states, regarding their citizens and others. Thereafter, there needs to be a possibility that the individual may travel beyond the borders of the state (or states) of which he or she is a citizen (Toyota 2007). Whether this possibility is realizable or not by any particular individual is less central (Tangseefa 2007). The cross-border movement of individuals must be accompanied both by the allocation of a citizenship status to the individual which is evidenced in some form, or otherwise discernable, and by an administrative system, at least in the country to which the individual is going, which recognizes the individual as foreign and differentiates its treatment of the individual accordingly (Sadiq 2008). Normally this means that the individual is entitled to fewer rights (and possibly subject to fewer duties, for instance in the case of military service or taxes) than citizens of the state (Guild 2004).

Foreigners, immigrants and migrants: contesting migration

From the perspective of critical migration studies, not only is the subject matter of migration studies the object of investigation, in particular through the actions and agency of individuals, but also the normative consequences of the allocation of a title must be examined. The words we use in migration studies to describe individuals and groups carry normative loads capable of modification. As Stanley Cohen analysed, the use of the term 'bogus' asylum seeker carries such a heavy normative load in British society that it contributes to an environment where physical assaults on asylum seekers take place (S. Cohen 2003). Once the individual falls into the general category of 'foreigner', the variety of possible statuses which may be applied to him or her multiply. Depending on how the individual is categorized, he or she may acquire quite different and normatively charged titles. It is in the allocation of statuses that the first indications of the relationship of the foreigner with security appear. For instance, so long as the individual is a foreigner or an alien, this definition allocates the individual as the responsibility of another state, in general terms. However, once the individual is categorized as an immigrant or a migrant, a different relationship with the host state comes into existence. Both terms are meant to define foreigners and both relate to the degree of social and economic insertion the individual plans or hopes to have. But nationals of some countries are more easily defined as immigrants or migrants than those of others. For instance, it is rare to come across US citizens being described as migrants or immigrants (except by statisticians). Moroccans or Malians in many parts of Europe are almost always described as immigrants or migrants (and often illegal, irrespective of their status). Further, the children of immigrants who have acquired citizenship of the host state are often described in European discussions as 'second generation immigrants'.[3] This discourse was particularly evident (and problematic) during the 2005 social disturbances in the suburbs of Paris, where the categorization of young French citizens as immigrants provided a mechanism to speak of ethnicity without using the term (Begag 2007). The allocation of the term 'immigrant' or 'migrant' is not neutral. In many circumstances, particularly in Europe, it is already normatively loaded with a security-related content.

The first separation which western liberal democracies make is between foreigners who are legally on the territory and those who are irregularly present. Here the force of the use of the terms 'immigrant' and 'migrant' is particularly clear: if someone is described as 'an irregular foreigner', it would be uncertain exactly what aspect of the foreigner was irregular – his or her behaviour? Dress? One would not be sure. As soon as the term 'migrant' or 'immigrant' is used, there is no longer any doubt – an image is evoked which relates to the decision of the state whether to admit, or refuse admission to, the individual. While the European Union exclusively uses the term 'illegal migrant', most international fora prefer less obviously normative terms such as 'irregular' or 'undocumented' migrants. The claim to neutrality made by many scholars in migration studies disintegrates as soon as one examines the words used to describe individuals and groups (King & Black 1997). The words 'immigrant' and 'immigration' already provide indicators about the normative position of the scholars.

This division of foreigners into legal and irregular is made exclusively on the basis of the host state's knowledge of the individual. A regular migrant is someone who has passed through the formal processes of the state and whom the state recognizes as an individual who is entitled to be on the territory. It is a state-centric division which reinforces the state's claim to a monopoly on the legitimacy of movement across borders (Soguk 2007). Most commonly, these official processes take place at borders and require the formal presentation of documents, but, as I will examine in the final chapter, particularly in the context of the European Union, this paradigm of the border as the place where the state and the individual meet is subject to change. An irregular immigrant is someone who has not fulfilled the state's rules on admission or stay. This group can be further divided into clandestine immigrants – a term usually used to describe persons who crossed the border surreptitiously, avoiding all contact with state officials who would refuse him or her entry; and irregular immigrants. This term can be used to include clandestine immigrants but also covers those who arrived lawfully but overstayed the period of time they were permitted to be on the territory, or engaged in activities which are prohibited by the immigration status which the state gave them. The most common example of this is the foreigner who arrives as a tourist, then stays on beyond the end of the permitted stay and gets a job. But an illegal immigrant is someone in respect of whose presence on the territory the state has passed a law making mere existence a criminal offence. Nonetheless, how an illegal immigrant will be treated is by no means consistent. The relationship between the state of origin and the state of illegality may mean that no action is taken.

Australia has excellent statistics on entry and exit from its territory as it has a mandatory registration system which is tied to the transport companies. According to the Australian government's publication *Immigration Compliance* (2005),[4] the country whose citizens form the highest proportion of visitors to Australia is Britain. Of those foreign nationals who stayed beyond the period permitted by their visas (delicately called 'Visitor Non Return Rates') the global average is 1.22 per cent but the average for British citizens in Australia is 1.58 per cent. Thus the country whose nationals, objectively in both numeric and percentage terms, represent the greatest risk of overstaying their visit visa in Australia is Britain. If the category of illegal immigrant were one neutral of normative content then the efforts of the Australian authorities to reduce overstaying of visit visas would be directed against British citizens. Instead, the Australian report itself obscures the issue by grouping the statistics in such a way that the category of overstayers described as 'a considerable burden to the community because of the cost of their location and removal from Australia' (p. 37) is separate from the Visitor Non Return Rates (by including all sorts of other categories of persons in the first but only visitors in the second) and thereby providing an overstaying rate which puts nationals of Kiribati at the top of the list – the result of a tiny population, in respect of which even one individual overstaying will change the statistics.[5]

Irregular migrants, overstayers and 'visitor non returners' do not remain indefinitely in their categories. As the Australian authorities note in the report (above), 'most overstayers only overstay in Australia for a few days' (p. 37). Because the status is one allocated by the host state by reference exclusively to its own rules, once the individual leaves the state he or she ceases to come within the category. The same individual may return to the state and overstay again, or go to another country and overstay there, as a result of very different rules applicable to that state. Or the individual may go to his or her country of origin and never fall into the category again. These are the options immediately available to the individual as the result of his or her own actions.

It is also open to the state to remove the individual from irregularity. This may happen in many different ways. First the state may change its rules – for instance, extend the period of time generally available for visitors to remain on the territory. Alternatively, as a result of an international agreement, nationals of the state may cease to be irregular on the territory of another state and enjoy a right of residence. This happened in the EU in 2004 and again in 2007 when, by reason of their states of nationality joining the EU, nationals of ten countries in 2004 and two countries in 2007 gained a right of residence which reduced to a very low level the possibility of them becoming irregularly present in other EU states (Bigo & Guild 2005). The state may take a decision in respect of the individual to extend his or her permission to be on the territory after a period of irregular residence, for instance on the basis of marriage to a national, or successful studies. Equally, the state may open a wide regularization programme to bring classes of foreigners irregularly on the territory into regularity (De Bruycker 2000). Finally, the state may seek to force the foreigner to leave the territory, ultimately by expulsion, a more or less expensive option depending on how far the country of nationality is from the host country.

Thus, by examining the terms 'migration', 'immigrant' and 'migrant' quite a different perspective of migration studies emerges. The state is not a monolithic entity standing before a tide of migrants flowing towards its borders. Political choices are made regularly within states, on the basis of which normative categories are created and deconstructed. There is no fixed meaning to the terms 'irregular', 'illegal', or 'undocumented' migration that a state administration cannot transform very rapidly. Therefore to understand migration one must examine the political preferences, the interests, of political actors, and individuals' forms of resistance to their categorization. Critical migration studies open this field of inquiry.

Temporal classification

Individuals who are foreigners, therefore not in a state which claims them as citizens, can be subdivided into many different categories on the basis of a number of different organizing principles. Temporality is an important one used by liberal democracies to explain the presence of the foreigner: if the individual does not intend to stay long in the state, then he or she may be classified as a visitor or tourist. This classification is made by the host state on the basis of its assessment of what the individual is planning to do on its territory. So long as that is to spend a little time and money on the territory and then leave, the requirements for being a tourist or visitor are usually met. Exactly how long is a short period of time for tourists varies from state to state. In most EU states it is three months out of every six months. In the UK it is six months at a stretch, though this is subject to reconsideration; in Indonesia, the limit is sixty days. However, states classify as temporary many other kinds of foreigners, for instance those who are providing services, or employees who are seconded to the host territory (I will examine this area in chapter 8). The definition of the foreigner by reference to how long he or she will remain on the territory permits the state to make claims about the identity of its population. So long as the individual plans to leave, and is required by his or her immigration status to leave, after a fixed period of time, there is a presumption, at least, that he or she does not become part of the population with the same entitlements to social security protection, etc., as those who do (I will return to this issue in chapter 7). Thus, for instance, students are considered to be temporary (and normally not migrants at all – subject, however, to where they come from) as they are required to return home at the end of their studies.

The other group of foreigners, as determined on the basis of temporality, are those who move to the host state with the intention of staying for a long period. This will include those foreigners the state has permitted to stay indefinitely or for what that state considers to be a long period: this group is most likely to be classified as 'immigrants' at least for statistical purposes. In the EU, long residence means five years or more (Groenendijk 2007; and see chapter 7). This is when the foreigner acquires a long residence status, and with this a sustainable claim to participation in all the security mechanisms of the state becomes more difficult to resist, in particular as regards social security (Minderhoud 2008). The ways by which foreigners acquire long residence status are extremely varied, depending on the imagination of the legislator and social pressures within states (De Bruycker 2000). Another group of foreigners who are categorized on the basis of the length of time they are likely to stay in a state are those who arrive as family members of long-staying foreigners or citizens. This category also includes those foreigners who arrived for a short stay and then changed their status. A common example, which is fairly unpopular with some western governments, is that of students who marry citizens in the host state. Foreign family members are often subject to a variety of strict requirements to prevent them becoming an expense to the state and, in the case of some European countries, notably the Netherlands and Denmark, they may be required to pass a test to show they are integrated into the host society before they have left their country of origin (Groenendijk,

Strik & van Oers 2007). It is in thinking like that of a state that individuals are classified as short- or long-stay foreigners, migrants or immigrants. Even more controversially, states' attempts to control their population by creating immigration obstacles to the arrival or residence of foreign family members (usually justified on grounds of abuse, fraud or forced marriage) bring the struggles around control of migration into the territory of protection of the integrity of the family. Migration studies' ability to engage with these issues about the state and identity is hampered by a reluctance to examine the individual's struggles and the positions of political actors (or indeed entrepreneurs).

Confounding the temporal and legal/illegal classification

Forced migration is a key category in respect of the movement of foreigners across international borders as it brings into the equation state obligations to the international community which extend beyond the immediate scope of border sovereignty. It also raises profound ethical questions about state control (Gibney 2004). The central characteristic of forced migration lies in the relationship of the individual with his or her country of nationality (or habitual residence). If that country persecutes, tortures or seeks to do either to a citizen and, as a result, the individual flees to another country in search of protection, forced migration is at issue. Thus the keys to forced migration lie in the action and intention of the country of origin towards the individual, rather than those of the host country (Goodwin-Gill & McAdam 2007). However, the struggle of the individual to gain recognition as a refugee and to escape the infernal category of 'asylum seeker' (i.e. a person who has made a claim for protection but in respect of which the state has yet to take a decision) is his or her daily existence. This limbo may go on for years, depending on the efficiency and adequacy of the state's administrative and legal procedures.

While there is no right in international law for an individual to enter any country other than that of his or her nationality, there is a duty on states which have accepted commitments under the UN Convention relating to the Status of Refugees 1951 and its 1967 Protocol (the Geneva Convention) not to expel someone to a country where he or she would be persecuted. Most of the members of the UN have accepted the obligations arising from the Geneva Convention. Refugees confound the temporal categorization of foreigners, as they may be temporary – if the situation in their country of origin is likely to change rapidly so that they can return in safety – or they may be permanent if no change occurs in their country and they remain at risk of persecution and thus entitled to remain on the territory of the host state (because that state cannot expel them without breaking its obligations under the Geneva Convention).

Forced migrants also confound the division of foreigners into lawful and irregular as their right to be on the territory of the host state arises exclusively because of the actions or threatened actions of another state – that of their nationality. Thus the right to be present on the territory does not come into existence because of the particular decision of the host state to admit or not to admit the individual, it comes from the act of a foreign state. Whether the individual arrives as a result of a clandestine entry, without documents or with a false passport and false visa makes no difference to whether or not he or she has a right in international law to protection on the territory of the host state (Crepeau & Nakache 2006). I will examine forced migration in chapters 4 and 5.

The state of nationality of the individual who claims protection against persecution or torture rarely accepts that it intends to persecute or torture its citizens thus from the very outset creating a tension regarding protection. Where a host state acknowledges the claim of the individual that his or her home state would persecute or torture him or her if returned, there is at the least an implicit criticism of the state of nationality. Very substantial differences arise as to what punishment is acceptable so as not to constitute torture or persecution. While the Geneva Convention does not define persecution, leaving the matter to national authorities, the UN Convention against Torture does define precisely what constitutes torture (see chapter 5). The participation of the international community in the definition of the right of the individual foreigner to remain on the sovereign territory of a state for an indeterminate period of time, and irrespective of how he or she arrived on the territory gives rise to not insignificant friction.

The forced migrant, by reason of his or her claim to a right founded beyond the control of the sovereign state (other than if the state withdraws from the international Convention), disrupts the border claim of the state and, by so doing, the categorization of foreigners. This claim to a supranational right to reside for protection purposes raises another key issue in critical migration studies – the capacity of the individual to reach beyond the state to a source of rights to which the state is committed, and to rely on those rights against the state's preference to expel the individual. The issues are the relationship of sovereignty to the construction of authority and the capacity of the individual to interact within this system of authorization.

Foreigners, migrations and security claims

The way in which individuals move across sovereign borders and the manner in which they are categorized by the host state have profound consequences on their relationship with different types of security. If one compares a few examples:

- citizen: this individual is the one in whose name liberal democracies carry out security-related activities; the citizen is the person entitled to security but also to participate in its definition within the state; the claim is that it is in order to protect the interests of citizens that liberal democracies take action against irregular migrants, refuse to recognize forced migrants' protection claims, and expel foreigners. The security of the citizen is the starting place for the insecurity of the foreigner.
- non-national: the most generic of terms – this individual is defined by absence – the lack of the citizen's relationship to security; the non-national is the individual yet to be identified as belonging somewhere specific other than not to the host state; the non-national is categorized into a state of insecurity, one which disappears once attachment to a state is determined. This can be a matter of friction where the individual has no documents and claims to be a citizen of one state but the host state determines that he or she is the citizen of third state. This happens most frequently where the individual asked for protection as a forced migrant on the basis of the circumstances in his or her home state but the host state believes that he or she belongs to another state where there is no reason for fear of persecution or torture.
- tourist: this category is normally classed as security-neutral, though health scares in one part of the world may transform the image of the tourist from benign to a security risk in a matter of days. Similarly, the association of political violence (so-called 'terrorism') with tourism has been developed since the 2001 attacks in the USA where a number of the attackers were in the country as tourists (Guild & Baldaccini 2006).
- Ex-pat.: these people are defined by reference to where they come from rather than where they are. This arises from the difference-in-power relationship between the country of origin, to which the individual seeks to retain a very close relationship, and the host country, which is unable (or unwilling) to seek to integrate them into the host society.
- immigrant: this category normally includes people who plan to stay a long period in the state and thus may give rise to claims to social security, perturb the identity security of the state, etc. It is also a category which attaches more quickly to some groups than others, as discussed

> above. By using the term 'immigrant' in respect of an individual, particularly outside the field of statistics, a normative claim is made about the intention of the individual to become part of the community and the willingness of the community to accept the individual or not. Inherent in the term is the idea that the immigrant should become part of the community. Increasingly in Europe this means becoming part of the community without having the right to participate in the growth, changing or transformation of its features. The risk that the immigrant will bring different values, religion, language, food, etc., is constituted as a security threat to the state (Van Selm & Guild 2005).

The different words which we use to describe the individual carry different implied understandings of the relationship of belonging and security. For the foreigner the possibility of security of residence may be irrelevant, as in respect of the tourist, or a life-or-death matter, as in respect of the forced migrant. The way in which access to security of residence is structured in liberal democracies tends to be around the perceived interests of the host state, privileging some foreigners over others, usually on the basis of the resources – economic, educational or cultural – which they bring with them. The state's assessment of these resources is not normatively neutral – for example, according to Dutch legislation, where a foreigner has a job offer which guarantees a salary above a specified amount, the individual will be given permission to work and reside. However, three categories are excluded from this rule: imams, football players and prostitutes.

The concept of migration not only involves the idea of the individual as a citizen of some country crossing borders but also excludes the movement of the citizen back to his or her country of nationality. While for the demographer such a movement may be equally significant to the movement of a non-citizen national to a state of which he or she is not a national, in legal thinking and in political terms this type of movement has gradually ceased to have central importance as the period of decolonialization gradually fades from the European memory (Guild 2004). During that period, in the former colonial powers of Europe, a lively debate took place as to whom belonging, in the form of citizenship, should apply. Movement 'back' to a state where an individual was not born nor had ever set foot, on the basis of historic citizenship, was highly contested in some countries (e.g. the UK) and a matter of faith in others (e.g. Portugal) (Nascimbene 1996). The security of the national to go to his or her country of citizenship has become well entrenched, though the social consequences of such movement may be more important than the arrival of foreigners. The case of the arrival in Germany of ethnic Germans from the former Soviet Block is a case in point (Groenendjik 1997).

The need for a new approach

The argument which I present in this book is that the construction of authority around the issues of migration and security is not (or no longer) a monopoly of state political actors but is certainly not a path to globalization with the elision of states. Thus it is not possible to understand the nexus of migration and security from an exclusively state-centred or globalist position. Two further topics are critical to any analysis of the area: (a) the individual as differentiated from a flow or stock of people, and (b) the supranational structures within which liberal democracies participate and which are capable of legitimating or delegitimizing state actions. Individuals, through their struggles around specific identities, are central to the resistance to the capacity of state political actors to construct successfully discourses about the belonging and otherness of these individuals by categorizing them into groups. The arrival of the individual on the international scene happens not just through the activities of actors such as Amnesty International, for instance, with its prisoners-of-conscience campaigns, but through individuals accessing international dispute resolution mechanisms such as the UN committees, the European Court of Human Rights, etc., in their struggles against state authorities. In doing so, states' claims to authority and legitimacy may be undermined. This is an important fact that political scientists and even sociologists often neglect.[6] The 'migrant' turns out to be a citizen after all; the 'terrorist' turns out to be a refugee in need of protection. Some political actors within states lose authority as a result, while that of others is enhanced. The relationship of individuals to both state actors and supranational actors changes the relationship between state actors and international actors. States are forced to obey the international courts and tribunals or lose legitimacy both internally and within the international community. Through the analytical tools of international political sociology discussing the boundaries of the political scene in the world today, I seek to challenge the state-centred and globalist approaches which currently dominate migration studies and to promote the development of critical migration studies in which the individual, as a construct and as a point or line of resistance, is first and foremost the subject of inquiry. It is in reaction to the movement of the individual that the state seeks to apply concepts of borders, citizenship, migration, identity, etc. It is also often against the individual that globalist approaches operate by reducing the multitude to a homogeneous reference to humanity or cosmopolitanism and accordingly becoming the spokesperson, with the result that the agency of the individual becomes invisible, wrapped up in claims about a global humanity. In the ensuing struggle, even the legitimacy of democratic state migration controls may be thrown into doubt as the individual reaches out to supranational sources of authority to support his or her claim.

In order to pursue this analysis, I will examine the relationship of the foreigner and security, as it relates to individual security and collective security and the claims around both. I will follow the individual foreigner in search of security and examine the actions of states around this figure. I pay particular attention to the way in which the individual on the move or in search of identity constitutes a source of friction between states. I follow the individual as he or she becomes visible in the international system through the claims, based on international rules, which escape the state through the engagement of international dispute resolution mechanisms. In the chapters which follow, I will develop this approach as outlined below.

In chapter 2 I examine security and the claim of an individual to identity. Here I analyse the nature of citizenship and what it means in terms of security of the individual. To do this I take the case of the so-called 'Australian Taliban', David Hicks, who spent more than five years in detention in the US military base at Guantánamo Bay. When his state of nationality, Australia, refused to seek his release, he sought to activate another identity – British citizenship – as the UK government had successfully negotiated the release of their nationals. Through an examination of the identity claim of an individual and his relationship with a state which refused to accept responsibility for him in the face of a third state's security claim, the claims of three states about the individual are thrown into disarray. While traditional migration studies are loath to accept as migration the forced migration of an individual, like David Hicks, where this is caused by a liberal democratic state in an illegal manner, the acts are as much forced migration as when the persecution comes from a totalitarian regime. The capacity of the individual to renegotiate his identity with a third state, in order to escape inhuman and degrading treatment on the basis of another state's security claim, exemplifies the importance of critical migration studies as a means of understanding the nature of state relations among themselves and with individuals.

In chapter 3 I move to the question of conflict and migration. Here I examine the internal security arguments of states which are in the process of expelling foreigners. Taking the example of the creation of supranational rights in the European Convention on Human Rights, I analyse how the right to define the individual as a security risk, at least in part, has escaped European states and become embedded in rules beyond sovereignty. This has resulted in the foreigner successfully claiming security of residence against the state's claim to the protection of public security through the expulsion of the individual. The framework of conflict and migration is between the individual and the state – the state's categorization of the individual as an immigrant liable to expulsion and the individual's resistance to that claim. The conflict between these two very unequal parties is transformed by the ability of the individual to mobilize the international commitments of the state against the state officials seeking to expel him or her. The last word in the conflict is no longer within the bounds of the sovereign state. The obligation of the liberal democratic state to comply with its international commitments brings the authority of the supranational institutions to the aid of the immigrant against the state. From the perspective of critical migration studies, this moves the focus to the individual in conflict with the state and the constraints on the state which the individual is able to mobilize through international commitments. The mantra of traditional migration studies – that states are sovereign in their border controls – must be revisited in light of the changing framework and sources of individual rights. The mantra of the no-border world in the making of globalist migration studies is equally limiting. Boundaries exist, but instead of encircling state territory, they are more and more frontiers of human rights law and jurisdiction.

In chapter 4, I move to the issue of conflict, migration and protection. Armed conflict results in displacement of individuals and the spreading of insecurity. An increasing reluctance of liberal democracies in the western world to accept spontaneous refugees on their territory has resulted in the use of border controls as a mechanism to prevent the entry of persons to whom states would then owe a duty of protection. I look at the results of these mechanisms and what they mean for security in a wide range of senses. This chapter moves to the issue of conflict in the form of violence between and within states that results in people fleeing. First, I examine how violent conflict is defined – the difference between crime and war is central here – and which institutions have the authority to decide which definition is dominant. What happens to the people fleeing violence? On the one hand, if they cross the border of sovereignty they may be entitled to security as individuals who are beneficiaries of states' obligations to refugees. On the other hand, if they cannot escape across the border they remain trapped in the local, that is to say, the state. While the state in armed conflict is rarely efficient at maintaining the sovereignty of its borders for the purposes of controlling movement of persons, in fact it is too often the actions of liberal democracies in placing obstacles and hindrances in the way of people trying to flee across international borders which deprive these individuals of the possibility of becoming refugees and entitled to international protection. The focus in this chapter is on the consequences for individuals of enforced 'sovereignty' imposed by other states on states in armed conflict, which prevents those individuals from fleeing to safety. The flip side of this enforced sovereignty is the ability of liberal democracies to avoid what they increasingly call the 'burden' of providing international protection for refugees, as the refugees never come into existence. Refugees are neither victims nor *Homo sacer*; they are struggling for their rights. Notwithstanding a political climate in many liberal democracies which facilitates their demonization, refugees are often successful in mobilizing international institutions against the preferences of state actors.

In chapter 5 I move to the question of security and torture. These two issues touch migration through international obligations on states not only to refrain from torturing individuals but also to give protection to persons fleeing torture. In this chapter I look at two examples of the claims around individuals, security and torture. First, from the UN tribunals, two claims by individuals to remain on the territory of a state because their expulsion would result in their return to torture in their country of nationality are examined against the claim of the state that their expulsion is necessary to public security. Second, from national institutions and then the UN tribunals, I analyse the extraordinary rendition of two Egyptians from Sweden in December 2001. At the centre of this chapter is the question of the assessment of state claims to international security, individual claims to personal security, and the international community's evaluation of the competing claims. Torture is among the most condemned practices in international and national conventions and laws. By taking the perspective of the individual who is returned at the hands of liberal democracies to a country where he or she is tortured, the question of the legitimacy of state action is unavoidable. Mainstream migration studies have failed to come to terms with this reality, leading to a weakening of its analytical value, while globalization theorists tend to ignore the emergence of the individual within the international state system.

In chapter 6 I examine the claims of liberal democracies that the documentation of foreigners is critical to state security. The challenge which this presents lies not only between the individual and the foreign state which seeks to allocate an identity to the individual, but also between the individual's state of nationality, which claims the right to provide security of identity to its citizens, and the foreign state (the individual's host or destination) which claims to create a separate and equally valid identity for the same individual. It is through the examination of the individual's right to identity that his or her claim to residence, protection from expulsion, and family life is accessed. It is a form of resistance to a targeted surveillance society which, in wider terms has been the subject of much research in surveillance studies and international political sociology. The relative political weakness of foreigners within liberal democracies has made them the guinea pigs for a raft of surveillance measures which may be rolled out later for the wider community. For instance, in 2008 the UK authorities implemented a biometric identity card system for foreigners, expressly stating that this was a first step towards an identity card system for the whole population. In this chapter and the following two, I will return to the issue of the security continuum, how the individual is subsumed into a category which is suspect – the category of foreigner or migrant. Because the category is suspect, its impact on other fields leads to a stigmatization – the foreigner is constructed as inherently insecure, so the state needs to know more about him or her than about its own citizens. The foreigner, as inherently insecure for the state construction, can be added to the economy, transforming normal economic relations into a source of insecurity.

Chapter 7 moves to the relationship between the economy, security and migration. The competing claims regarding the role of foreigners in economic activities in states – as a threat to security or a benefit to the state – are at the centre. The example I take in this chapter is the European Union – looking at, on the one hand, how labour migration as a threat to social security was constructed at the time of enlargement of the EU in 2004 and 2007, and, on the other, the perception of the foreigner as a potential security threat, as revealed in the EU legislation about long-term resident third-country nationals. It is insufficient to argue that labour migration reveals the class struggle in its most international form. The modalities by which labour migration is constructed as a threat or not are critical to our understanding. It is necessary to examine the practices of labour migration not only through the discourse of various political actors but also through the impact of circulars, laws and measures on individual workers, in order to get some picture of what happens on the ground. The security continuum is particularly in evidence here.

In chapter 8 globalization and the non-national are at the core. I look at the rules of the international trading system, the World Trade Organization (WTO), as they relate to the movement of persons across borders for economic purposes. Against the basic principle in favour of such movement, I examine the security arguments of states and the counter-movement which can be found in the international rules on preventing and punishing the trafficking of human beings. Here the supranational system provides a gradually developing impediment to state sovereignty as regards labour migration (called 'service provision'). The relationship of the state with the supranational system impacts directly on individuals, pushing them into the protective arms of their employers who increasingly stand in the shoes of the state in constituting the authority capable of permitting or blocking international mobility. In one sense, one part of the supranational system begins to develop mechanisms to privilege its actors, transnational companies, against sovereign claims by states that economic migration is a threat. The WTO develops tools to decrease the possibilities available to actors at the national level to use the security continuum to prevent or hinder economic migration. While the demonization of migrant workers as an economic security threat may be a useful political tool to rally resources, particularly in times of rising unemployment, resistance to this political move by international actors – for instance the WTO seeking to protect their interest group, employers – becomes increasingly evident.

This book ends with an examination of the changing nature of sovereignty as it relates to the border and the possibility for, and right of, individuals to cross it. The example I take is the European Union and the way in which sovereignty has gradually been divested from the borders and, indeed, sovereignty itself has migrated elsewhere, away from the single face of the foreigner. In the twentieth century, the most emblematic of state sovereignty symbols was the border – the black lines around territories, filled in with different colours representing different sovereign countries. In this final chapter I inquire whether this presentation of sovereignty is still valid, looking at what border controls on movement of persons actually mean and how they are carried out. I challenge the globalist–cosmpolitanist discourse which downplays the significance of boundaries and exclusion. Examination from the perspective of the individual within a supranational setting shows the surprising flexibility of controls and their separation from any obvious relationship with territory. Instead, the controls relate exclusively to the individual, or group of individuals, who carries the mirage of immigration controls around with him or her, confounding our understandings of inside and outside. The borders are engraved in the individual's passport, not in a physical place. I finish with this examination as it is the most controversial in critical migration studies, as it questions the image of what a state is and our capacity to imagine the state as a container. If the state cannot be likened to a container, with the right people on the inside and others on the outside, then clearly we need new theoretical tools to understand how boundaries organize life, without referring to an 'inside versus an outside' dichotomy.

2

Migration, citizenship and the state

The concepts of 'migration', 'migrant' and 'immigrant' all presuppose the capacity to identify who is a citizen. Without a clear category of 'citizen', 'migration' can only describe the wanderings of people, not the relationship of movement across international borders and the acquisition of rights. Without the category of 'citizen', the justifications which states put forward for treating some individuals more favourably, and others less so, tend to sound suspect to modern ears. For instance, the organizing principle of feudal societies relates to social class and the ownership of property (Gellner 1983). Thus discrimination against peasants is self-evident as they do not belong to the social class entitled to privileges of property ownership. In liberal democratic states, the organizing principle around access to goods and services is citizenship. The principle of equality among citizens, famously arising from the French revolution, has become also the dividing line between entitlement and exclusion (Heater 1999). Those who are not citizens are foreigners and this is sufficient reason for their exclusion from the territory, from benefits and, as I will discuss in this chapter, from safety.

I will start this chapter by outlining the main mechanisms by which individuals become citizens – what are the main rules states use to determine who belongs to the state and who does not? Then, instead of taking migrants as the point of reference, I will start by looking at citizens who are outside their country of citizenship. The reason for this is that there is always a moment of surprise when one must think of migrants not as some sort of non-citizen, but rather as rights holders, citizens, of another country. Foreign students often find this particularly surprising when they arrive for their studies to find themselves treated as foreigners or migrants, rather than citizens. The full force of not having citizenship rights can be quite a shock, depending on which liberal democracy one finds oneself in. So before we can think about migrants, we need to clarify who are citizens.

The relationship between the statuses of citizen and migrant is a contested one. Two states, at least, may be in conflict over the same individual

– a citizen to one, a migrant to the other. The territory on which the individual finds him or herself is only one factor in the relationship of the individual to the state. There is always negotiation between the individual and the state regarding the state's duty towards the individual. These negotiations may take a variety of shapes and forms which I will examine in this chapter.

In order to do this I will take the examples of two so-called 'migrants' and 'citizens' – the LeGrand brothers, Germans in the USA (now executed), and David Hicks, an Australian in US custody in Guantánamo Bay (now released). These men were not simply migrants to whom the state in which they were present could do as it wished – they were also citizens of other states which claimed or rejected duties of protection to them. The two cases present different pictures of the struggles of individuals and state claims to legitimacy. In the case of the LeGrand brothers, the US authorities claimed the right to treat the men as if they were citizens and to disregard the claims of their state of citizenship. In the case of Hicks, the US authorities claimed the right to treat Hicks as an enemy combatant, a status designed for those held in detention in Guantánamo Bay. The struggle of Hicks with both the Australian and UK authorities over citizenship was based on the international relations of the USA with those two states.

The ability of these men to mobilize support from their state of origin – in the case of the LeGrand brothers – and eventually from the International Court of Justice, or to claim the right of citizenship and thus protection from a third state – in the case of Hicks – provides particularly good examples of the central thesis of this book – the construction of the individual as agent in the migration process, with which state actors must engage not as with an undifferentiated group but as with individual interests and objectives.

The case of David Hicks is particularly troubling as he becomes an involuntary migrant – i.e. resident against his wishes in a country outside that of his nationality – by reason of US military forces taking him, against his will, from Afghanistan to the US base in Guantánamo Bay, where it appears fairly clear that he suffered inhuman and degrading treatment and torture. When we use the term 'forced migration', scholars refer to totalitarian dictatorships which torture their citizens or threaten to do so, resulting in their citizens fleeing to seek asylum in liberal democracies. When the state agent of forced migration is a liberal democracy which causes the forced migration with the purpose of inflicting treatment which has been challenged as contrary to fundamental human rights (Sands 2008), we are deeply uneasy. Where the illegal migration is forced by a liberal democracy

– no law permitted the US authorities to take Hicks to Guantánamo Bay, where he did not wish to go – we are even more concerned about the adequacy of the definitions we are accustomed to deploying.

State theory and international law concur on the centrality of the state's right to determine who are nationals and who are not. Max Weber's famous definition of the state as a territory and people, within which and over whom a bureaucracy has established a claim to a monopoly over the legitimate use of violence, depends on the ability to define borders and people (Weber 1964). In this chapter I will look at this right to define people within or outside citizenship and what this means for security – both collective and individual, internal and external.

The liberal democratic state is one which founds its legitimacy on the relationship between the citizens and the way in which the state is governed, tempered by constitutional and fundamental rights within the state and human rights obligations accepted through international treaties (Preuss 1998). Within liberal democracies, the claim is that sovereignty is based on the citizens collectively and exercised through their participation in the determination of the government. The duty of the state is to act for the citizen through securing rights, the content of which is determined by the government (Hardin 2003). The exercise of sovereignty in the liberal democratic state depends on a clear definition of the citizen who constitutes its source. This relationship of the citizen and the state also forms the base for excluding the foreigner from certain rights. If citizens' rights and duties are the building blocks of the sovereign state, then the inclusion of the foreigner within those rights and duties is always negotiable.

The development of human rights as inviolable and belonging to the individual, irrespective of any citizenship, changes the conception of how individual rights are formed within the state system (Gearty 2008). But this process, although ascribed roots in the ancient Greek philosophers, takes modern form with the Universal Declaration of Human Rights 1948, a founding document of the United Nations (Ishay 2004). The principle that human beings have rights beyond states is a very attractive one as it limits the power of the state, in particular the totalitarian state (Arendt 1970). The difficulty lies in delivery of these rights. Unless states embrace them and give them a status in their national law which individuals can access and which enjoys the enforcement mechanisms which apply to national law, it is difficult to secure them for individuals. The UN has provided some of the international human rights instruments with dispute resolution mechanisms – tribunals capable of receiving complaints against states by individuals, based on international human rights obligations – but the jurisdiction of these tribunals depends on a formal state Act acknowledging that it is bound and state compliance with the outcome (Scheinin, Orlin & Roasas 2000). I will return to the international tribunals in chapters 3 and 4.

Understanding citizenship

How does the state determine who are its citizens and who are not? This takes place through laws on citizenship which rely mainly on three principles. The first is *ius soli*, under which system citizenship passes to all those born on the territory of the state. This system creates a very specific relationship between the soil and the individual where birth alone on the soil suffices to ensure participation in the state as a citizen. According to the second basic principle – *ius sanguinis* – citizenship passes automatically to a child born to a parent holding the relevant nationality. This means that it does not matter where the child is born but rather to whom it is born. Citizenship is inherited from the parents. Thirdly, some mechanism is created by law to permit foreigners to acquire citizenship by some voluntary act – this is naturalization. This mechanism applies to persons who are not citizens of a state – normally the one where they live – and would like to become citizens. They are required to present themselves to the state authority and justify why they should become citizens. This can be easier or harder depending on the state. For instance, in many Arabian Gulf states, although there is a high proportion of the population who are foreigners, there are very restrictive mechanisms whereby they can become citizens – if at all.

In the USA and Canada, all those born on the territory are, by that birth alone, citizens of the state (with very limited exceptions in respect of the children of diplomats, etc.). In Europe, there is a mix of mechanisms by which citizenship is acquired – usually a combination of birth on the territory and citizenship or immigration status of the parents. For instance in Germany, citizenship passes primarily on the basis of the citizenship of the parents irrespective of where the children are born – in Germany or abroad. But a child born in Germany, and whose parents are foreigners, have a secure residence status and have resided in Germany for seven years or more, is born German. On arriving at majority, if the child has more than just German citizenship he or she must renounce the other citizenship in order to remain German.[1] The current German law dates from 2000 and promises to raise interesting problems regarding the retention of citizenship by young people as its full effects are felt.

Until the middle of the twentieth century, acquisition of citizenship by birth (i.e. automatically) was also informed by gender in many liberal democracies, including Germany and the UK, etc. The most widely used rule was that, of children born aboard, only those born to male citizens would automatically acquire citizenship. If the child was born outside the state to a female citizen, then it would not acquire citizenship automatically. These rules were gradually abandoned virtually everywhere in Europe – for instance in Germany in 1954, in the UK in 1981. However, until 2002, no provision was made in the UK to sort out the situation of children born abroad to British women before 1983 (the date of entry into force of the 1981 Act) so that they could become British. So, for instance, a child born in the USA to a British citizen mother and US citizen father on 31 December 1982 was born only a US citizen, with no entitlement to British citizenship. If the same child had been born to the same parents on the next day, 1 January 1983, he/she would have been born a British citizen as well (Fransman 1998).

Finally, in 2002, the British government changed the law and permitted people who had been born abroad to British citizen women before 1 January 1983 to register as British citizens. This registration is by right on completion of a form and the taking of an oath of allegiance to the Queen. The fact that the children of British women born abroad were excluded from citizenship until the end of the twentieth century, and that the status of those excluded from belonging before then because their relationship to the UK was via a woman (their mother) was only addressed at the beginning of the twenty-first century, indicates a fairly entrenched gender dimension to the polity and the political settlement about belonging, at least in some liberal democracies.[2]

Acquisition of citizenship otherwise than by birth (i.e. automatically), naturalization, is subject to a wide variety of requirements, most frequently a mix of length of residence, language ability, financial capacity and, increasingly in Europe, integration tests (Ryan 2009). Liberal democracies change their rules for acquisition of citizenship through naturalization more easily than the mechanisms of automatic acquisition by birth. The constitutional settlements as to who is a citizen and whose children will be citizens are less flexible with regard to automatic acquisition than as regards voluntary acquisition. Further, those who acquire citizenship by naturalization are often considered 'lesser' citizens than those who acquire the status automatically – for instance the UK law on deprivation of citizenship permits the state to withdraw citizenship from those who acquired it by naturalization and registration on a simpler basis than from those who acquired it by birth.[3]

The ill of statelessness

All people are supposed to have a citizenship, of some country or another. If a person does not have a citizenship, he or she will be stateless. This means that there is no state which accepts responsibility for the individual. The individual will be in an international no-man's-land where there is no state to which he or she can turn to seek protection, against which to seek to exercise rights, and from which the individual can claim entitlements of belonging and equality (Gyulai 2007). Within the international state system, the stateless person is a terrible headache as there is no state which accepts responsibility for the individual. This means that there is no state to which the individual can be expelled when his or her residence in another state is determined to be irregular or undocumented. These individuals belong nowhere and owe no allegiance to any state. This problem was particularly acute at the end of the First World War in Europe when the transformation of the landscape, with the creation of many new countries which chose not to extend their citizenship to all persons on the territory, resulted in people ending up stateless (Torpey 2000). The same problem reoccurred after 1989 when the Soviet Block and the former Yugoslavia disintegrated, creating a number of new states, not all of which extended their citizenship to all residents either because they considered them (often, in the former case, Russians) to have been imposed upon them by the Soviet regime or, in the latter case, on the basis of a re-emerging ethnicity. In 2006 the Council of Europe, a European regional organization comprising forty-seven states, including those most affected by the 1989 changes, opened for signature a Convention on the avoidance of statelessness in relation to state succession – a response almost two decades after the upheaval.

To deal with the problem of statelessness, the UN opened for signature, in 1954, the Convention Relating to the Status of Stateless Persons, to which sixty-two state parties had signed up by 2007. This Convention, extended by a companion Convention in 1961, sets out the rights which states must accord to stateless persons. But so far it has only attracted thirty-three state parties. The objective of the Conventions is to prevent stateless persons from falling into the category of non-persons, who are then are at risk of all forms of exploitation because of their lack of enforceable rights which derive from the ability to establish their existence as human beings. The United Nations High Commissioner for Refugees is responsible not only for refugees but also for stateless persons. It produces annual reports to the UN – but progress on statelessness seems very slow. Not many states are keen to accept even the limited responsibilities contained in the two Conventions regarding stateless persons.

The duties and obligations of citizenship

The relationship of the state to the individual is defined first and foremost by citizenship, which tells the state, the international system and the individual to what polity he or she belongs. In international law there is one key obligation on states which applies exclusively to citizens – the duty to admit to the territory of the state any citizen (and to allow citizens to leave, though this right may be qualified, for instance, by a criminal law penalty, for reasons of public health, etc.). The nineteenth-century struggles around the creation of citizenship within the state context were always somewhat fuzzy about the duties of citizenship (Bagehot 2007). In the UK, for instance, in 1918, the nationality law stated that (acquired) citizenship could be revoked for trading with the enemy prior to the grant of citizenship or disaffection or disloyalty. These last two concepts are the bottom line of the duties of allegiance.

This is so because other duties which citizens have are not defined by the status of citizenship, at least not in international law. For instance everyone must obey the criminal law or else be subject to coercive measures, but this is not limited to citizens. Similarly, citizens must pay taxes, but so also do foreigners who earn money in the state or buy goods to which sales taxes apply (hence various tax reimbursement schemes for tourists). The state, however, owes duties to the citizen, though exactly what these are depends on the national constitution and so can vary. Within the international state system, the duties of states to their citizens are the subject of the UN's Vienna Convention on Consular Relations 1963, which, at article 36 onwards, sets out the rights of states to access to their citizens on the territory of third states. Essentially, the Convention provides a right to a state via its consular officers to communicate with and have access to its citizens. The individual has a right to have his or her consular authorities informed without delay wherever he or she is arrested or committed to prison, or to custody pending trial, or is detained in any other manner. This includes the right of consular officers to visit a national, converse and correspond with him or her, and arrange for legal representation.

Even these limited rights, which are designed to provide security to the individual and the state, have come under substantial pressure. The most famous challenge to consular protection has been by the USA in respect of two brothers, Karl and Walter LeGrand, both German nationals, who were executed in the USA in 1999 following their conviction for murder. The two brothers had moved with their family to the USA at a very young age and were treated as US citizens, although they remained German nationals. Thus it was not until eight years after their conviction that the German authorities became aware of their existence (and citizenship) and sought to exercise the consular rights contained in the Vienna Convention. The US authorities refused them access. The German authorities brought a case against the USA before the International Court of Justice (ICJ – the dispute resolution mechanism available only to states and state entities to resolve questions of the interpretation and application of treaties).

The ICJ found that the US authorities had failed to comply with their obligations under the Vienna Convention to provide the German authorities access to their nationals. It held that the rights of the Convention applied both to states and to their citizens.[4] The seriousness with which the German authorities took the case was related to European developments. In July 1989 Germany ratified the 6th Protocol of the European Convention on Human Rights (ECHR) which abolished the death penalty. The 6th Protocol had been opened for signature in 1983, though it was not until the mid 1990s and into the twenty-first century that the majority of Council of Europe states signed and ratified it. By 2008 all Council of Europe states had signed the Protocol and only Russia has not yet ratified it. In 1992, the campaign to encourage European states to sign the Protocol was in full flow. The sensitivity of the German authorities to the situation of their nationals, about to be executed in the USA, fits within this wider political framework.

In the struggle over the identity of the LeGrand brothers, the USA refused the German claim that, as German nationals, they had a right to protection by the German authorities. The security of the US criminal justice system took priority over the claims of the men's country of nationality. Notwithstanding the condemnation of the US authorities over their refusal to allow consular access to foreign nationals in their criminal justice system, in particular when they are facing the death penalty, on 5 July 2008 a Mexican national was executed in Texas without having been permitted access to the Mexican authorities. The US Supreme Court rejected an application to stay the execution until he had that the benefit of consular protection in full consideration of the ICJ judgment.[5] Where there is a conflict with the US authorities regarding the security of the foreigner, even in the most extreme situation where the individual is about to lose his or her life, the US authorities are very reluctant to acknowledge the claims of other states to any role at all regarding their citizens.

Whose citizen? Whose responsibility?

In the LeGrand case, two countries claimed responsibility for the individuals and entitlements to determine their security. In the case of David Hicks, no state wanted to interfere with the US authorities' security claim. David Hicks is an Australian national who was detained from 11 January 2002 until 30 May 2007 at the US military detention centre in Guantánamo Bay.[6] He was convicted by a US military tribunal after he pleaded guilty to a charge of providing material support to terrorists.

The Guantánamo Bay detention centre was established hastily at the end of 2001 as a place where the US military could send suspected Al Qaeda / Taliban members or sympathizers, for indeterminate periods and without charge or trial (Rose 2004; Stafford Smith 2007). The Taliban regime which ruled Afghanistan until ousted by a US-led but UN-sanctioned military intervention in October 2001 was suspected of harbouring persons who had been involved in planning the attacks in the USA which took place on 11 September 2001. Many countries made representations to the US authorities for the release of their citizens (Worthington 2007). By mid 2005 the UK had succeeded in obtaining the release of all the UK nationals at the detention centre, and they were at liberty in the UK (Begg 2006).[7] David Hicks was born an Australian citizen on 7 August 1975. His mother was a British citizen who had been born in the UK. Had Hicks been born after 1 January 1983 or had his father been a British citizen (born in the UK), then he would have been born a British citizen. Had he been a British citizen then it would have fallen to the UK authorities to seek his release from the Guantánamo Bay detention centre.

The centre caused substantial problems for the US authorities. The then US Defense Secretary, Donald Rumsfeld, who was responsible for its establishment, has been heavily criticized regarding the legality of the centre and its regime (Sands 2008). When questioned about the centre, Rumsfeld stated that the persons held there would not be viewed in legal terms as prisoners of war but as unlawful combatants and as such 'they do not have any rights under the Geneva Conventions' (which regulate the position of foreign soldiers held by an enemy army) (Rose 2004). The way in which individuals found themselves in the detention centre appears to have been highly irregular according to the accounts of those who have been released and the US authorities themselves (Begg 2006; Kurnaz 2007; Sheppard 2008). This includes accounts that foreigners in Afghanistan and Pakistan were picked off the streets by criminal gangs and 'sold' to the US authorities for substantial sums of money on the basis that the individuals were 'Talibans'. The treatment which the detainees received both in their transport to the island base and while there has been characterized as torture (Sands 2008).

The detainees were originally held without the intention of bringing them to trial (Worthington 2007). Under pressure, the US authorities established a military tribunal to try at least some of them. Approximately 700 persons had passed through the detention centre by 2006 and many were still there, including David Hicks. Fuller accounts of the Guantánamo Bay debacle have been published, not least by the British non-governmental organization Reprieve, which took up the plight of the Guantánamo prisoners and has been central in representing them, primarily in the US courts.[8] What is of interest to this book, however, is what happens to the relationship of responsibility between the state and its citizens in such cases. As mentioned above, because the US authorities refused to categorize the detainees as prisoners of war, they were able to reject the application of international law rules on the treatment of such prisoners – contained in the 1949 Geneva Conventions. As a matter of grace, the US authorities did allow the International Red Cross, whose job it is to monitor the application of the Geneva Conventions, access to the detention centre. The only court which the US authorities accept as having authority over what happens in the Guantánamo detention centre is the US Supreme Court. It did not exercise its powers until 2006.[9]

If international law does not protect persons in this position and the national authorities which are holding the individual do not provide any remedy, where can the individual look for relief? Citizenship comes into the picture here – the duty of the state to protect its citizens against abuse at the hands of foreign governments, which is a counterpart of the citizen's duty of allegiance. David Hicks sought, through his lawyers, the intervention of the Australian authorities. They refused, in response to which David Hicks brought legal proceedings in Australia to seek to force his government to demand his return to Australia.

On 8 March 2007 the Federal Court of Australia accepted David Hicks' claim that the Australian government owed him some duty (though exactly what duty is not clear) in so far as the judge ordered that the matter proceed to full trial.[10] According to the decision, the Australian authorities, while acknowledging that David Hicks was an Australian national, declined to make any request to the US authorities for his repatriation. The reason for this refusal was, according to Hicks' statement of claim, 'because Mr Hicks had committed no offence against any law of the Commonwealth [of Australia] or of any of the States or Territories, or against or under the common law in the Commonwealth, and because no Australian Court would have jurisdiction to try Mr Hicks for any criminal offence for which he may be punished in accordance with any such law' (para. 23). In other words, the Australian authorities accepted or were unwilling to challenge the argument of the US authorities that Mr Hicks was a terrorist threat and could be held indefinitely without trial in the Guantánamo Bay detention centre.

Loyalty, security and the individual

Mr Hicks sought to register as a British citizen in October 2005 under the new law which permitted the children of British mothers, who had not been able to acquire citizenship from their British parent because of discrimination on the basis of gender in British nationality law before 1983, to now do so (see above). As the application is one which does not involve discretion by the state – that is to say, so long as the individual fulfils the objective criteria, he or she is entitled to register as a British citizen – the UK authorities decided that they must accept the application. Clearly, this was a bitter pill and they had no wish to accept any responsibility for David Hicks, whom they considered an Australian problem. The UK authorities wrote to David Hicks' lawyers as follows:

> The Secretary of State proposes to proceed as follows. He is considering acceding to the application for British citizenship but at the same time making an order for the deprivation of citizenship under section 40 of the British Nationality Act on the grounds that [your client – David Hicks] has done things seriously prejudicial to the vital interests of the UK. Having taken legal advice, it appears to the Secretary of State that this is the proper method under the legislation to balance the competing interests in this case, and it means that your client would have the procedural protection of being able to appeal to the Special Immigration Appeals Commission in respect of any decision that he should be deprived of citizenship. (Para. 3)[11]

Mr Hicks sought judicial review of the decision of the UK authorities on the basis that it was illegal.[12] The UK court accepted that the only reason Mr Hicks sought British citizenship was because he considered that he had a better chance of being released from Guantánamo Bay detention if he were a British citizen. The judge noted that the UK authorities had, by April 2006, successfully negotiated the release of all British nationals at the centre – effectively indicating that Mr Hicks was correct in his supposition that the UK authorities were more solicitous of the freedom of their nationals than their Australian counterparts (at least under duress from national courts – see above). The case turned on the legal measures on the basis of which an individual can be deprived of British citizenship – what are legitimate grounds and what are illegitimate? The same law which permitted Mr Hicks to register as a British citizen also permitted the UK authorities to deprive any British citizen of citizenship (however acquired) on the grounds that 'the Secretary of State is satisfied that the person has done anything seriously prejudicial to the vital interests of: (a) the United Kingdom, or (b) a British overseas territory'.[13]

The UK court found against the authorities on the ground that anything which an individual did before he or she became British could not justify deprivation of citizenship after the individual acquired it. Only acts undertaken after an individual acquired citizenship could warrant deprivation. In order to reach that decision, the court had to consider the basis on which the state can withdraw citizenship. At the heart of the argument is the concept of disloyalty and disaffection. In a decision shortly after the Second World War the UK courts had upheld, in a judgment which has been much criticized, the principle that a non-citizen can be guilty of disloyalty and hence treason.[14] However, in that case the court held that the defendant, by holding and using a British passport, asserted and maintained a claim to continued protection of the Crown and thereby pledged the continuance of his fidelity. The principle is one of reciprocal duties – on the one hand, the pledge of fidelity by the individual; on the other, protection by the state. In the case of Hicks, the UK authorities did not seek to argue that David Hicks had done anything which constituted disloyalty. Instead, they argued that the second historical legal ground for withdrawal of citizenship applied – disaffection. The court defined disaffection as wider than disloyalty. It occurs 'when an individual has by word or deed displayed active hostility to Her Majesty (as representing the United Kingdom) by showing himself unfriendly to the Government of the United Kingdom or hostile to its vital interests'.[15] The court rejected the UK authorities' argument that there could be a duty in citizenship to refrain from disloyalty or disaffection which predates the reciprocal duty of the state to protection of the citizen. The judge giving the lead opinion stated baldly: 'What none of these propositions establish [i.e. the arguments of the UK authorities] or come close to establishing, is that conduct of an Australian in Afghanistan in 2000 and 2001 is capable of constituting disloyalty or disaffection towards the United Kingdom, a state of which he was not a citizen, to which he owes no duty and upon which he made no claims' (para. 37).

UK higher courts are composed of more than one judge, and each judge is entitled to write an opinion as part of the decision. In the Court of Appeal judgment on David Hicks, all three judges agreed on the outcome but one judge added a further consideration. The other British detainees at the Guantánamo Bay detention centre were also dual nationals holding citizenship of a country other than the UK as well as that of the UK. The judge noted that the UK authorities at no time sought to withdraw their British citizenship. The lawyers for David Hicks argued that seeking to deprive David Hicks of British citizenship constituted discrimination. The UK authorities argued that they had a discretion which they were entitled to exercise on this point (i.e. whether to seek to withdraw citizenship or not) and that, in the exercise of that discretion, the Secretary of State was entitled to take into account the extent of the links, including family links, which those British citizens had with the UK. Further, as David Hicks was an Australian citizen, he was entitled to the protection of the Australian government. His links with the UK were weak, according to the UK authorities. Indeed, the UK authorities argued that the other British citizens who had been held in Guantánamo Bay had held that citizenship before they were captured and taken there. The second judge in the UK court approved of this argument, confirming his opinion that the UK authorities were entitled to distinguish between David Hicks and the other British citizens and to provide the latter with a higher level of protection. The only basis for this difference of treatment was the way in which, and the time when, David Hicks obtained British citizenship.

This would lead to the conclusion that the UK authorities are entitled to a discretion to provide greater or lesser protection to British citizens abroad depending on how they acquired their citizenship and when. However, it seems clear that the judge's reasoning was much influenced by the fact that David Hicks also holds Australian citizenship and the view that, on account of his family and social links, that country ought to take responsibility for him, not the UK.

Security, the state and David Hicks in the Australian court

When David Hicks was captured by the Northern Alliance in Afghanistan in November 2001, he was at a taxi stand, and he was handed over to the US authorities in December 2001 on the basis that he was a supporter of the former Taliban regime there. When he was detained, there was an armed conflict between the Northern Alliance and the Taliban which had been in power in the country. US forces were participating in the conflict on the side of the Northern Alliance.[16] Hicks states that he took no part in this conflict. He was taken to the Guantánamo Bay detention centre by the US authorities around 11 January 2002. As the Australian judge pointed out in his 2007 decision, the US authorities 'have never announced any intention to try Mr Hicks in relation to any offence against United States municipal law, or with any offence allegedly committed by him within the territory of the United States or within the jurisdiction of any of the civil courts of the United States' (para. 8). (As a result of international and domestic pressure, the US authorities did eventually bring charges against David Hicks.) His case was caught up in the US Supreme Court decisions on the lawfulness of the Military Commissions constituted to try persons detained in Guantánamo Bay, but this part of the history is beyond the remit of this chapter.[17] The US authorities stated that David Hicks committed a belligerent act for the Taliban in the Afghan conflict but pressed no charges against him until 2007.

The Australian authorities, which endorsed the US-led intervention in Afghanistan and later participated as well in the US-led invasion of Iraq, refused publicly to request David Hicks' return to Australia. David Hicks' family and friends began a substantial campaign to seek to persuade the Australian authorities to protect him but there was great resistance for a considerable period of time.[18] A movie on the plight of David Hicks was made and commercially released – *Hicks v Bush* – which provided additional impetus to the campaign for his release.

David Hicks brought a challenge in the Australian High Court, demanding that the Australian authorities seek his return to Australia. He claimed that his wrongful internment was the responsibility of the Australian authorities, not only the US ones. Various Australian authorities had made statements to the effect that the Australian government would not seek the return of David Hicks because, if he were brought back to Australia, he could not be prosecuted under Australian law (which begs the question whether he has committed any crime under Australian law and, if the answer is negative, why he should be convicted of anything in that country). In addition, the Australian authorities had confirmed that they had encouraged the US authorities to charge and try David Hicks, even though the rules and standards of trials before the Military Commissions which applied to those persons detained in Guantánamo Bay did not conform to international law fair trial standards by which the USA was bound, and had been repeatedly struck down for fair trial shortcomings by the US Supreme Court.

The series of challenges which were concurrently taking place before the US Supreme Court regarding the adequacy of the military tribunals proposed for prisoners in Guantánamo Bay had not reached their conclusion by the time the Australian Court was required to consider the matter. The most recent of these cases, *Boumediene* v. *Bush & others*,[19] represents an important step towards access to justice for those prisoners still in the detention centre, as it gives them access to the US civil courts. However, when the matter was under consideration in Australia, it was far from clear that the US Supreme Court would ever go this far to protect the rights of these individuals.

The Australian authorities obtained a judgment at first instance that the proceeding should be stopped because there was no reasonable prospect of success. This decision was overturned on appeal and it is that appeal judgment which is of interest here as it reveals the tensions in the relationship of security, the state and the individual, and the role of the courts in that tension.[20] The Australian authorities made two main arguments on why the court should not determine the matter. First, the Australian authorities argued, this would require the Australian court to pass judgment on the legality of acts of a foreign sovereign government, something which, under the doctrine of Act of State, courts must refrain from doing. Second, the Australian authorities argued that the issue impacts on or relates to foreign relations and gives rise to non-justiciable questions such that there is no matter on which the court can or should adjudicate – in other words, the affair is one of foreign relations and negotiation, not court justice.

David Hicks' lawyer argued that Hicks was subject to unlawful detention by a foreign power which had no intention of bringing him before a lawfully constituted court on lawful criminal charges. Further, the Australian authorities had been aware of this since his arrival in Guantánamo Bay in 2002 but had done nothing to seek his return from this unlawful captivity. He argued that Australia owed a duty of protection to him or at the least had a function to provide security to an Australian citizen overseas. He accepted that the Australian authorities had a discretion with respect to how the state's protective duty should be exercised in any specific circumstances. However, the argument was that the exercise of that discretion was subject to the law and to review by the Australian courts.

The judge disagreed with the Australian authorities about how and where the obligations owed by the state to a citizen abroad are to be determined. Notwithstanding the issue of negotiations among states, he found that the court was entitled to hear evidence and review the situation of David Hicks and the arguments of the authorities. He considered that neither the doctrine of Act of State nor the principle of non-justiciability were sufficient to justify rejecting the claim of David Hicks at that point in the proceedings. Thus he did not rule out the possibility that at some future point in proceedings, the Australian authorities might succeed in such an argument. The judge found that David Hicks' claim to the Australian state's protection against unlawful detention was justified. The Australian authorities argued that as they had no control over the detention of David Hicks, they should be under no duty as regards that detention. The judge was not persuaded – noting that the UK had succeeded in repatriating its citizens from Guantánamo Bay.

On the question of the right of an Australian judge to find the acts of foreign governments illegal, the judge was persuaded that, as deprivation of liberty is by definition unlawful until it is rebutted by evidence of lawful authority, it must be accepted in law that David Hicks' detention was unlawful (para. 53). As to the discretion of the Australian authorities regarding how and in what way they protect their citizens abroad, the judge found that the exercise of that discretion was subject to judicial control. In particular, where there is evidence that the exercise of the discretion has been tainted by irrelevant considerations such as whether the individual could be tried in Australia, it is for the judge to determine what is relevant and what is not. Further, the fact that the Australian authorities were encouraging their US counterparts to try David Hicks under a procedure which offended against the rules of fair trial, both in Australia and internationally, and failed to comply with the Geneva Conventions was not a consideration which should determine the exercise of the discretion of the authorities on how to protect the citizen.

While the judge accepted that the duty of the Australian authorities to protect their citizens abroad was not one on which an individual can rely in a court, nonetheless this does not mean that the duty has no legal consequences (para. 65). It is the scope of this legal consequence for the state which is subject to judicial control. In the end, the issue was resolved when Hicks pleaded guilty before a US Military Commission established by presidential decree.[21] An agreement was reached between the US and Australian authorities that he would be returned to Australia to serve his sentence there. He was finally released in December 2007. There is no international acceptance of the legal procedure through which Hicks was convicted (Stafford Smith 2007).

Conclusions

The relationship between the state and the citizen in liberal democracies is based on a principle of reciprocity. The state accepts the individual as a citizen on the basis of social and political settlements about belonging – such as equality between the sexes. The right to be a citizen depends on fidelity – it is a status which can be lost. Nonetheless, the international community cannot condone deprivation of citizenship from an individual unless there is another state which will take responsibility for the individual. The problem of statelessness is one which perturbs the whole international community, and the internal affairs and struggles of a state are not, in principle, to be permitted to cause new sources of friction.

When the citizen is abroad, in the international community he or she remains attached to his or her state through the duty of protection which is part of citizenship rights and practices. The activities of the individual may disrupt international relations, for instance when individuals engage in political violence on the territory of a state other than that of their nationality. The extent to which the state is obliged to provide protection to their citizens often then becomes contested. If inter-state relations depend on the individual citizen's interest in protection being subordinated to the claim of a foreign state to act in a certain way towards the individual, what protection is there for the individual? To examine this problem I have taken the example of four states with strong security claims, the USA, Australia, Germany and the UK. I have followed the movement of three individuals through the authority of these states, on the basis of citizenship claims as opposed to migration-related claims. The US authorities claimed to treat the LeGrand brothers as their own nationals, refusing Germany's claim to access to them before their execution; but the US claim regarding David Hicks is based on his status as a foreigner and consequently a right to detain him indefinitely and subject him to treatment illegal under the US Constitution. (The US authorities accepted that they have no such right to hold US citizens indefinitely in Guantánamo Bay (Sands 2008)). The UK authorities sought to avoid responsibility for David Hicks by depriving him of citizenship. By so doing, they would then have no obligation to set about trying to convince the US authorities to release him. The Australian authorities placed the interests of inter-state relations with the USA above their duty to protect their citizen, effectively subordinating his position to the wider Australian interests in good relations with a powerful ally.

In this case, the claim of David Hicks to liberty based on citizenship was rejected by the two states who were liable under the principle of reciprocity of rights and duties of citizenship. David Hicks turned to the courts to determine whether the state's lack of protection to him was lawful. In the UK case, the court thwarted the state's claim to be entitled to deprive David Hicks of citizenship but left open the option that, even with British citizenship, the UK authorities might still be entitled not to protect him in the same way that they would be required to protect British citizens who had been born as such and had strong links with the UK. In the Australian case, the judge held that the claim of sovereignty by the Australian authorities could not survive the claim of the citizen to protection. The state was answerable to the courts for the way in which it protects the citizen abroad, even where this may result in discomfort in international relations. While Hicks' problem was that he was foreign in the USA and not British enough for the British authorities, the LeGrand brothers were too American for the US authorities to allow their German counterparts to claim the relationship of citizenship rights. All three men were foreigners – migrants, voluntary or forced - in the USA (or under US control) but their dilemmas not only perturbed their states of nationality but also the USA. In all three cases, the moral and legal authority of the USA was diminished in international relations as a result of the actions of these migrants, while, in their states of origin, difficult questions of the state's responsibility to its citizens were taken out of the hands of the executive and became judicialized.

3

Migration, expulsion and the state

In the last chapter I examined the relationship of the individual to the state both as a citizen and as a foreigner. This engages many different relationships – the citizen and the state by which he or she is accepted as a national; the citizen of one state under the control of a foreign state; the individual claiming to be a citizen of a state in the face of the state's refusal to accept responsibility for him or her. The central theme of that chapter was the relation, both in power and within the international community, between states when one state claims to act in respect of the national of another state. While the USA claimed the right to treat foreigners, the LeGrand brothers, as if they were US nationals, thus refusing Germany's claim to access to them as its citizens, in the case of David Hicks not only did the USA treat him as a foreigner but the UK sought to do so as well, notwithstanding his citizenship right.[1] In the second case, the identity of the state responsible for Hicks (either Australia or the UK) was at issue. The determination of that question rested on the agency of Hicks himself in his citizenship claims and his analysis of which state was more likely to manage to convince the US authorities to release him from detention in Guantánamo Bay.

In this chapter I will focus on a different aspect of conflict between the individual as a foreigner and the state. When does the state have the right to expel a foreigner? In the previous chapter the state which had physical control over the foreigners did not want to give them to their countries of origin. Instead it claimed the power and the right to subject them, on the one hand, to the full exigencies of its criminal law (the death penalty), and, on the other hand, to a special detention regime established for foreigners considered a danger to the state's security. More commonly, states claim a right based on the requirements of sovereign security to expel the nationals of another country. Examining where this claim comes from and how it applies to the individual foreigner is the first step I will take in this chapter. Then I will look at the sources of constraints which limit the power of the state to expel the foreigner and how those constraints operate.

The objective of this chapter is to raise questions about the nature of state sovereignty. Migration studies tends to accept, without question, the sovereignty of the state vis-à-vis the foreigner, immigrant, illegal immigrant, etc. Similarly, the globalists conflate the individual into a general humanity category about which claims can be made. However, when one examines the struggles of individual immigrants with the state regarding the claim to the sovereign right to expel the immigrant on security grounds, one becomes aware of the limits of state sovereignty and the centrality of the agency of individuals. To remain respected partners in the international system, states are required to play by the rules they have signed up to – for instance the European Convention on Human Rights (ECHR). If they are European states which are members of, or aspire to membership of, the economic entity – the European Union – they are required to live up to their ECHR commitments as part of the deal to participate in the EU's internal market. In the struggle of the immigrant to remain on the territory of his or her state of residence, often he or she has reached out to the ECHR as a source of rights beyond the state but capable of providing protection against the state's security claims in favour of expulsion.

The adjudication of these claims by individuals in, for instance, the European Court of Human Rights (ECtHR) transcends the sovereign claim of the state to control its security. If the individual designated as a security risk by the state authorities successfully challenges that appellation and its consequence of expulsion, can one still say the state is sovereign in the determination of its security? This is all the more a question when the state, through its participation in other European institutions, is constrained to accept and comply with the supranational decision regarding its own security claim. While each case is about one individual, that does not mean it is no more than anecdotal. Decisions of courts like the ECtHR have the effect of being a precedent – the state is required to change its law, rules or practices on expulsion to ensure that it does not repeat the human rights breach identified by the court. Thus the individual's struggle modifies the meaning of security for the state through the intercession of a supranational court. The state is under a duty of good faith to change its national rules on security and expulsion so that no one else suffers the same threat of what has been designated 'unjustified expulsion' constituting a human rights breach. The emergence of the individual in a judicial venue beyond the state's own institutions has the capacity to change the state's appreciation of security.

Limiting sovereignty

The starting place regarding the power of the state is in the convergence of the territory (surrounded by its boundaries), the people (citizens) and the authority (government or bureaucracy) which claims a monopoly over the legitimate use of violence, which Weber defined as the state (Weber 1964), a definition which scholars have subsequently modified but, by and large, accepted (Tilly 1975; Giddens 1985). This starting place does not prevent states from banishing their own nationals or expelling foreigners.

The post-Second World War development of the UN as the mechanism of the international community for regulating conflicts rests not only on its Charter but on principles of human rights. The Universal Declaration of Human Rights 1948 was proclaimed by the UN General Assembly in December of that year and remains the cornerstone of the international move to limit the sovereign power of states (Morsink 1999). The Declaration uses six main arguments, set out in its preamble, to explain why the interference with state sovereignty is necessary. These are:

- The recognition of the inherent dignity and of the equal and inalienable rights of all members of the human family is founded on freedom, justice and peace; what is particularly important in this argument for my purposes is the principle that all people, not just citizens, are entitled to equal and inalienable rights; the foreigner is defined into the equation.
- Disregard and contempt for human rights have resulted in barbarous acts which have outraged the conscience of mankind, and the advent of a world in which human beings shall enjoy freedom of speech and belief and freedom from fear and want has been proclaimed as the highest aspiration of the common people; this reference to the Holocaust, as made possible in German law through the depriving of Jews of their citizenship, justifies the erasure of the citizen–foreigner differentiation in the allocation of rights.
- It is essential 'if man (*sic*) is not to be compelled to have recourse, as a last recourse, to rebellion against tyranny and oppression', that human rights should be protected by the rule of law; here the direct link is made between revolution and unjust laws, and the principle that the rule of law must incorporate human rights and provide expression to them for the protection of the individual.
- It is essential to promote the development of friendly relations between nations; this part of the preamble expresses the notion that good international relations depend on how individuals are treated.

- The reaffirmation of faith in fundamental human rights, in the dignity and worth of the human person and in the equal rights of men and women and the determination to promote social progress and better standards of life in larger freedom; this claim to the good faith of states is important to the construction of disadvantages for states which fail to fulfil their obligations.
- The pledge of cooperation within the UN to promote universal respect for and observance of human rights and fundamental freedoms.

The arguments in favour of the Declaration are powerful and appeal not simply to the international community but also to individuals. As a Declaration, many states have resisted strenuously any argument that it is capable of having any legal effect within their state system (Douzinas 2000). The argument is that it is a declaration of intent not a binding commitment, not least because of its wording, but also as it was declared by the General Assembly of the UN, not signed and ratified by each state. The contents of the Declaration have gradually been transposed into international human rights agreements which must be signed and ratified by states in order for their content to apply to those states (Bayefsky 2001). The two key international instruments which incorporate much of the Declaration's content are the International Covenant on Civil and Political Rights 1966 (which has two optional Protocols and 162 state parties) and the International Covenant on Economic, Social and Cultural Rights 1966 (which has 159 state parties). Together these documents are frequently referred to as the International Bill of Human Rights (Kalin, Muller & Wyttenbach 2004).[2]

The Universal Declaration takes two important steps which limit the power of states to banish their own nationals. The first is at art. 9 which states that 'no one shall be subject to arbitrary arrest, detention or exile'. While this is primarily about the operation of the criminal law, exile as a means of punishment which is related to the border of sovereignty is included. The addition of the qualifying adjective 'arbitrary' leaves open the possibility that exile which is not arbitrary might be acceptable. But that attempt to maintain exile as an option for state action is further limited by art. 13(2) which states 'everyone has the right to leave any country, including his own, and to return to his country'. The right to return indicates that the individual, if he or she so chooses, has a right of entry to the country of nationality. Thus banishment and exile are not consistent with the principles of the Universal Declaration. This does not diminish the force of the concept of exile as a politically meaningful one. The Tibetan leader, the Dalai Lama, refers to his absence from Tibet as exile in a particularly effective way which conveys a series of challenges to the legitimacy of Chinese control over Tibet (Dalai Lama 1990).

Moving from the relationship of the citizen with his or her state, what do we find in the Universal Declaration regarding the foreigner and the state's power to expel? The answer is: very little indeed. While all the rights are written in terms of everyone, rather than in terms of citizens, there is little which indicates that states intend to abandon their right to expel foreigners. Rights beyond the state limiting state choices regarding the expulsion of foreigners are oblique, in so far as they are founded in the Universal Declaration at all. The main exception is art. 14 which provides that 'everyone has the right to seek and enjoy in other countries asylum from persecution'. This wording of a right to seek asylum did not reappear again in the UN Convention Relating to the Status of Refugees 1951, or its 1967 Protocol which only provides a right not to be expelled (Kneebone & Rawelings-Sanaei 2007).

The other main source of a human right which interferes with the sovereign right of the state to expel the foreigner is found in art. 12 of the Universal Declaration: the right not to be subject to arbitrary interference with privacy, family, home or correspondence. From the principle of a right to respect for family and private life there gradually emerges a restraint on the power of states to expel the individual.

I will follow this relationship in its European context through the struggles of migrants to remain on the territory of a state when the state has determined, for security reasons, that the individual should be expelled. I will follow this relationship through the lens of the rule of law. How does the democratic state determine which migrant should be expelled and on what grounds? How can the migrant challenge that determination, claiming sources of rights which are founded beyond the state?

The most central difference between the citizen and the immigrant is the fact that the state can expel the latter but not the former. Other distinctions are also present; for instance most European states do not permit immigrants to vote in national elections. Many states place restrictions on the economic activities of immigrants, in particular those economic activities which are associated with state sovereignty (for instance membership of the army, judiciary and other institutions which exercise sovereign power). However, the inclusion and exclusion of immigrants in these fields varies substantially. What remains key in law is the power of the state to remove the residence right from the immigrant and to expel him or her.

Foreigners, expulsion and security

The question then arises, why do states expel foreigners? What is it about foreigners that pushes states to exercise their control over the territory in such a way as to engage in expulsion? The arguments are all related to security in one form or another. The first reason, and the simplest, is that the immigrant is irregularly on the territory (Bogusz, Cholewinski & Szyszczak 2004). This ground normally means either that the state never authorized the individual to enter the territory (i.e. he or she arrived clandestinely) or that, although the state authorized the entry of the immigrant, the individual either has overstayed his or her permission to reside or is engaging in activities which are not authorized by his or her status (Ruhs & Anderson 2006).

The security which is breached as a result of the irregularity of the foreigner is the power of the state to control who is on the territory. As Bigo has demonstrated (Bigo & Guild 2005), state claims to control borders and the movement of persons across borders is something of a mirage. Even the most heavily patrolled borders do not result in a complete control of individuals' entry onto the territory. For instance, the UK, which invests heavily in the principle of secure borders, has no controls on movement of persons to and from the Republic of Ireland (Ryan 2003). Nonetheless, the more states invest political capital in the effectiveness of border controls on the movement of persons, the more problematic becomes the individual who has not complied with those controls. The authority of the state is undermined by the existence of the individual irregularly on the territory. Once the claim to control all persons who cross state borders has been asserted as an important element of sovereignty, then those persons who somehow offend against that control become the object of legitimate coercion. The more important the political investment in border controls, the higher the stakes against the foreigner who has not fulfilled the conditions. While irregularity is no more than a disjunction between the state's authorization and the individual's presence, it becomes elevated to an essential element of the foreigner: the individual becomes characterized as 'illegal' and illegality in itself is a security issue (Bogusz, Cholewinski & Szyszczak 2004).

There are three common state responses to irregularity: first, the refusal (or incapacity) to invest sovereignty in border controls. This lack of control is a feature of some of the accounts of men in the US detention centre in Guantánamo Bay regarding their movements across the borders between Pakistan and Afghanistan (Begg 2006). Second, where the irregular is inconvenient or otherwise problematic – for instance the individual has a nationality in respect of which it is not expedient for the host state to expel the individual (see for instance, the example I used in chapter 1, regarding British visitors in Australia) – or where the foreigner is irregular because the state bureaucracy is incapable of dealing with applications in a timely manner (a common complaint about Spain and Italy (Calavita 2005)), the state can ignore the irregularity or regularize the stay (De Bruycker 2000). Finally, the state can pass laws which make it a criminal offence to cross the border otherwise than in the permitted fashion, or to remain on the territory without authorization (Guild & Minderhoud 2006). In this way, anyone who offends against these laws, by the manner in which they crossed the border or by staying on the territory after their permission to be there has expired, becomes an object of security in the form of a person who is breaking the criminal law. This is the most draconian way in which states determine what acts are contrary to their security (the use of the criminal law), and those who offend against those criminal laws are by definition acting against the security of the community as expressed by the state's criminal laws. It is primarily through the criminal law that the state may legitimately imprison individuals.

The second main reason why states expel foreigners is because they have committed a criminal act. This may include a so-called 'border crime', that is a crime which only a foreigner can commit because it relates to the crossing of a border and the citizen always has the right to enter his or her country of nationality. But leaving the class of border crimes apart, this ground is the one on which I will focus in this chapter. This is the most common ground for expulsion of foreigners who have lived in a state for a substantial period of time and whose residence is lawful. The struggle which will appear as a human rights issue in the field of expulsion of foreigners arises here – when does the expulsion of a foreigner who has lived for a substantial period of time and has family ties in a country constitute a failure by the state to respect the human right to family and private life of the individual? The security which is compromised in this case is that related to crime and the right to define crime. This collective security must be weighed against the claim of the individual to security of residence and thus protection against expulsion (Thym 2008).

The third common ground which states have for the expulsion of foreigners is that they are a threat to national security. I will return to this issue in chapter 5 when I look at the claims of states to the right to expel foreigners on grounds of their state security, on the basis of the actions of the individual, on the basis of the state's relations with the country of nationality of the individual, and on the basis of the state's relations with a third country which demands, in the interests of its national security, that an individual be expelled somewhere else.

In the rest of this chapter I will examine state claims to the right to expel the foreigner who is lawfully on the territory of the state. This means I will not return here to the figure of the irregular migrant (except tangentially). Instead, the purpose of this chapter is to focus on the claims by states to expel individuals whom the state has admitted. The reason for this is because it is in this claim by the state to be able to reconsider its decision to allow the foreigner to reside that the security dimension is particularly important – to what extent does the state have the right to change its mind and expel the individual? I will look at the foreigner as a security threat in the sense of the criminal law for these purposes. Three themes emerge as central to the arguments of states that the expulsion of a foreigner who has committed a crime is conducive to security. The first is that expulsion is a form of punishment which follows on from any other penalty which the individual may be subject to (Julien-Laferrière 2003; Mathieu 2006). Second, these arguments flow from the fear that the individual may commit a second crime after the completion of any other penalty which may be imposed and thus the community will be better secured if he or she is expelled. Third, assuming that the individual is likely to be a security risk in the future, the security of the host state is more important than the security of the state of origin of the individual. The spread of gang violence from the west coast of the USA to Central America has been tied to the deportation policies pursued by the US authorities from the 1980s onwards (Kanstroom 2007).[3]

I will take my examples from European experiences. The reason for this is that Europe provides a particularly interesting setting in which to examine expulsion policies. On the one hand, there is the European Union in which, by reason of the EU treaties, nationals of the participating states have a right of entry onto the territory of other Member States. Thus the elision of irregular entry with criminalization is not possible. This means that the reasons states use for expulsion must be justified more clearly on the security grounds around the activities of the individual, rather than the individual's relationship with the border (Guild 2001). Secondly, the Europe of the Council of Europe, which is much bigger than the EU (the Council of Europe includes forty-seven countries while the EU has a membership of twenty-seven), brings an important human rights dimension to the issue of expulsion of foreigners. All Council of Europe countries are obliged to ratify the European Convention on Human Rights, a human rights agreement which incorporates the main civil and political rights contained in the Universal Declaration of Human Rights and the International Bill of Human Rights. However, Council of Europe countries are further required to accept the jurisdiction of the European Court of Human Rights, which was established to adjudicate on complaints about state failure to comply with their obligations under the ECHR. So, in order for a state to be a member of the Council of Europe club, it is required to modify its sovereignty by accepting, as a source of rights for individuals, the ECHR and, further, accepting that the state institutions themselves are not final in their interpretation of those rights. The ECtHR has the final word regarding the meaning of those rights (Jacobs & White 2006). So, through examining two quite different European venues, some of the key tensions around the foreigner, the state and expulsion are revealed, as states are obliged to set out their reasons for expulsion and to defend them in light of their international obligations.

Sovereignty, security, conflict and migration

In Europe, the claim to a sovereign right to expel the foreigner has been modified in three key ways – first, twenty-seven countries in Europe[4] have circumscribed their right to expel one another's nationals and their family members through the law of the European Union (Guild 2001). Second, those same states (minus Denmark, Ireland and the UK) have adopted an EU law which regulates the situations in which non-EU nationals who have resided legally for five years or more can be expelled (Groenendijk 2007). This means that national law is no longer the exclusive determiner of the power of national officials of those twenty-seven states to take decisions to expel foreigners. Third, forty-seven European states[5] which are parties to the Council of Europe have accepted that there is a human right to continued residence for foreigners on the territory, which can only be trumped in the circumstances permitted by the ECHR as interpreted by the ECtHR (Thym 2008). I will examine each of these categories separately.

The EU nationals and their family members

The migrants best protected from expulsion in Europe are nationals of EU Member States on the territory of other EU Member States. These people enjoy a status which is called 'citizenship of the European Union' (Carlier & Guild 2006). As discussed above, it is something of a contradiction in terms to speak of a citizen as a person liable to expulsion as a citizen cannot be expelled from his or her country of citizenship. While it is true that EU citizens cannot be expelled from the territory of the whole of the Member States combined, they can be the objects of expulsion decisions made by the Member States and expelled back to the Member State of which they are nationals (Martin 1995). This paradoxical situation is the result of the fact that EU citizenship is a complementary citizenship which is additional to nationality of a Member State. Thus a Latvian national is also a citizen of the EU, but is only the latter because of the former. If the individual was not a Latvian (or other EU national), then he or she would not be a citizen of the Union.

The transfer of sovereign power to control the population on the territory from the Member States to the European Union has been most complete in respect of these citizens of the Union. Through the EU treaties, the right to cross the border, reside and exercise economic activities anywhere in the EU has been firmly conferred on the individual EU national (Martin 1995). Where a Member State seeks to interfere with this right of free movement, it is for the Member State to justify the interference and that justification must be founded on the very limited exceptions contained in the treaties (Guild & Minderhoud 2001).

The EU was created in the early 1950s as a mechanism to diminish the probability of war in Europe. The founding fathers (as they are called, and indeed they were all men) determined that the best way to achieve security in Europe was to integrate the markets of, in particular, France and Germany, so that war making would not be possible (Pinder & Usherwood 2007). The EU can be seen as a security project of sorts – the object of which was to avoid and prevent war. The mechanism to achieve the security objective was to create an internal market which would be characterized by the abolition of obstacles to the four freedoms – free movement of goods, persons, services and capital (Weale & Nentwich 1998). The abolition of obstacles to the free movement of persons, to take the example of most interest here, required the dis-application of all rules on visas, permission to enter a Member State, residence permits and work permits as regards nationals of the Member States. Nationals of the Member States were to have a right to enter, reside and engage in economic activities which the state would have (virtually) no power to control. So, the security project of the founding fathers was implemented by the massive and impressive de-securitization of movement of persons (Guild 2001). This took place through the negotiation of a treaty, the European Economic Community Treaty 1957 which was extended in 1987 to include the abolition of border control among the participating states (I will return to this issue in chapter 9).

Nonetheless, Member States retain a residual power to expel a national of another Member State back to his or her state of nationality (or to refuse them admission). Where the state establishes that the individual is a threat to public policy, public security or public health, it is entitled to expel the foreigner. These are the only three grounds on which expulsion of EU nationals (or exclusion) is permitted. Further, because the grounds are specifically set out in the EU treaties, the final decision on what they mean belongs exclusively to the EU itself. The last word on what this provision means rests with the European Court of Justice, the final arbiter on the meaning of EU law.

The loss of state power to expel foreigners (as EU nationals are on the territory of a Member State other than that of their citizenship) did not happen all at once, nor without some contestation. The history of this struggle takes place in two steps – first the attempts by the Member States to expel EU nationals on the basis of public policy, public security and public health, the three grounds specifically permitted in the treaties; and second the claim by Member States that nationals of other Member States are not covered by the scope of EU law (usually on the basis that they are not exercising economic activities or otherwise self-sufficient) and therefore cannot claim the benefit of the limitation on expulsion (Carlier & Guild 2006).

Elsewhere I have examined in some depth the path in law, regarding the limitation of the Member States' power to expel citizens of the Union, through the jurisprudence of the European Court of Justice, which consistently held that public policy and public security must be interpreted very narrowly in order to protect the right of the individual (Guild 2004). As regards the expulsion of an individual on the grounds of security because of his or her criminal activities, the test which has been established is that the existence of a previous criminal conviction can only be taken into account to justify expulsion in so far as the circumstances which gave rise to that conviction are evidence of personal conduct constituting a present threat to the requirements of public policy (Condinanzi, Lang & Nascimbene 2008). Further there must be a clear future threat to a sufficiently serious interest of society. Expulsion on general preventive grounds, that is to say an expulsion ordered for the purpose of deterring other foreigners, which is common in many Member States, is prohibited for EU nationals and their family members (and others protected by agreements with the EU, such as Turkish workers). This is particularly the case where the measure automatically follows a criminal conviction, without any account being taken of the personal conduct of the offender or of the danger which that conduct represents for the requirements of public policy. On the specific facts of different cases, one can see that the threshold is very high. For instance, an accomplice to the importation of 1,500 grams of heroin who was convicted in Germany was nonetheless protected from expulsion as the threshold to show a future propensity to offend was not fulfilled.[6] The European Court of Justice noted in particular that the convicting court had suspended the 21-month prison sentence on the basis of the level of the individual's involvement and its assessment that the offence was a one-off.

The second claim of the Member States is that they are entitled to expel individuals who are nationals of another Member State on the grounds that the individuals are no longer protected by EU law as their activities are not specifically covered by the EU rules on free movement. These rules originally only protected nationals of other Member States who were economically active. But this scope was widened to include the economically inactive in 1990. However, for the economically inactive, the EU requires that they show they are economically self-sufficient, at least to the level required not to be a drain on the social security or social assistance scheme of the host Member State (Condinanzi, Lang & Nascimbene 2008). I will return to the EU nationals as an economic threat in chapter 7. For the purposes of this chapter, what is important to the power of states to expel is that the European Court of Justice rejected this approach, instead favouring the principle that nationals of the Member States always have the right to be present on the territory of another Member State, irrespective of what they are doing, until the state can justify the ground for expulsion.

The right to protection against expulsion covers not only nationals of the Member States but also their third-country-national (i.e. non-EU-national) family members, including spouses and partners, children, parents and other relatives in the direct ascending and descending lines who are dependent on the family (Condinanzi, Lang & Nascimbene 2008). Member States are also obliged to facilitate the entry and residence of other family members who, in the country from which they have come, are dependants or members of the household of the Union citizen having the primary right of residence, or where serious health grounds strictly require the personal care of the family member by the Union citizen.

EU Directive 2004/38 codifies and extends the jurisprudence of the European Court of Justice on the question of expulsion as follows:

- Member States may restrict the freedom of movement and residence of Union citizens and their family members, irrespective of nationality, on grounds of public policy, public security or public health but these grounds shall not be invoked to serve economic ends;
- measures taken on grounds of public policy or public security must comply with the principle of proportionality and be based exclusively on the personal conduct of the individual concerned. Previous criminal convictions cannot in themselves constitute grounds for taking such measures;
- the personal conduct of the individual concerned must represent a genuine, present and sufficiently serious threat affecting one of the fundamental interests of society. Justifications that are isolated from the particulars of the case or that rely on considerations of general prevention shall not be accepted.

The protection against expulsion does not end there. The Directive also requires a Member State to take account of considerations such as how long the individual concerned has resided on its territory, his/her age, state of health, family and economic situation, social and cultural integration into the host Member State and the extent of his/her links with the country of origin. Further, after five years' residence on the territory, Member States cannot expel a citizen of the Union or his or her family members unless there are serious grounds of public policy or security. This is not defined, but clearly it must be more substantial than the protection provided to those who have lived in the country for less than five years. After ten years, the Directive prohibits expulsion except on imperative grounds of public security. Children are also protected from expulsion except on imperative grounds of public security (Hailbronner 2007).

Third-country nationals and expulsion from the EU

Leaving aside Turkish workers in the EU, in respect of whom a special regime applies which mimics that for EU citizens, third-country nationals (the general term for all persons who are not citizens of the Union) are not protected in EU law against expulsion until they have completed five years' authorized residence and obtained evidence from the authorities of this status. The EU adopted a Directive (2003/109) in 2003 which provided this new supranational limitation on expulsion of foreigners. While there are a number of excluded categories (such as students, seconded workers and others), the majority of third-country nationals resident in the EU have lived there for more than five years and are likely to come within the ambit of the Directive (Groenendijk 2007).[7]

For third-country nationals who have fulfilled the conditions, expulsion is no longer a matter of national sovereignty (Halleskov 2005). The Member States may only expel such persons if their expulsion is permitted under the terms of the Directive. The grounds on which expulsion is permitted mirror those which relate to nationals of the Member States and are as follows:

- Member States may take a decision to expel a long-term resident solely where he/she constitutes an actual and sufficiently serious threat to public policy or public security (note that public health has disappeared as a ground);
- the decision cannot be founded on economic considerations;
- before taking a decision to expel a long-term resident, Member States must have regard to the following factors:
  - the duration of residence on their territory;
  - the age of the person concerned;
  - the consequences for the person concerned and family members;
  - links with the country of residence or the absence of links with the country of origin.
- where an expulsion decision has been adopted, a judicial redress procedure must be available to the long-term resident and legal aid available to those lacking adequate resources, on the same terms as apply to nationals of the state where they reside.

A comparison of the grounds for expulsion of nationals of the Member States and of third-country nationals who have resided regularly in the EU for five years indicates few differences. The main one, however, is that nationals of the Member States gain more protection against their designation by a state as a security risk on the basis of public policy and public security the longer they live in the host Member State. For third-country nationals, the level of protection remains stable. As Groenendijk explains, the development of EU law in respect of third-country nationals has diminished some important differences between their status and that of nationals of the Member States (2007).

Human rights and expulsion of foreigners

The power of states to expel foreigners is modified by the human rights commitments which they accept. As discussed at the beginning of this chapter, international human rights obligations, arising from the Universal Declaration of Human Rights, place no specific limitations on states' powers to expel foreigners (other than in respect of refugees). This is because human rights by their nature apply to everyone – that means all human beings, irrespective of their nationality or status as citizens or foreigners. The international human rights system depends, however, on states being able to deliver on their human rights commitments, while at the same time it sets thresholds for state action which limit the exclusion of foreigners from rights within the territory.

The delivery of human rights depends on states having the capacity to ensure that rights are respected – weak states, such as Somalia, are neither able to deliver human rights protection to all persons on their territory nor effectively liable for their failure to do so. The weaker the state, the less likely its institutions are to carry out human rights obligations. The stronger that state institutions are, the greater the possibility of effective accountability in the inter-state system for human rights obligations. Among liberal democracies, strong state institutions are frequently founded on strong constitutional guarantees designed for the citizen. The differentiation between citizens and foreigners on the basis of the constitutional settlements finds expression in many fields – for instance, I will look at the economic field in chapter 7. The point here is that just because a state has strong institutions which are able to make good on human rights commitments does not mean that it will be willing to guarantee those commitments to foreigners as well as citizens. In the field of expulsion of foreigners, if one looks at the cases which have come before the ECtHR the large majority come from old, well-functioning liberal democracies in Western Europe. Far fewer cases come from the post-1989 Member States of the Council of Europe, though this is gradually changing (Sikuta & Hubalkova 2007).

Some human rights raise questions for state expulsion decisions and practices. This is particularly the case as regards the right to respect for private and family life. I will examine how this right to respect in the ECHR has given rise to limitations on how states use their powers of expulsion on grounds of security, in particular in respect of criminal convictions. Because the forty-seven states which are members of the Council of Europe are required to accept the human rights obligations of the ECHR and the jurisdiction of the ECtHR to adjudicate on complaints, including from individuals, regarding state failure to respect human rights, the arguments of states in favour of expulsion must be spelt out clearly. Further, because the ECtHR has not accepted many of the arguments of states regarding the necessity of expulsion to ensure security, a supranational test regarding the justification for the expulsion of foreigners has arisen in Europe. All Member States are required to comply with this new test, which changes the relationship of the state with the foreigner as regards the construction of who is a security risk.

The ECHR consists of the 1950 Convention and six substantive Protocols (Protocols 1, 4, 6, 7, 12 and 13). The other protocols only amended the ECHR and so do not have an independent life. Protocol 14 (not yet in force in 2009) once again amends the ECHR and the procedures specifically in relation to the ECtHR, in order to streamline its activities. The Member States are not required to ratify the Protocols in order to maintain their status as members of the Council of Europe. Thus one finds many states which have signed up to some but not all of them. Two Protocols – 4 and 7 – provide specific guarantees for foreigners.[8] A number of pre-1989 Member States, such as Greece or the UK, have not ratified them, though most post-1989 Member States have.[9]

The ECHR applies to all states which have ratified it and to all persons within the jurisdiction of the Member States. 'Persons' means exactly that – everyone, irrespective of their nationality or immigration status. The ECtHR has had no difficulty in applying human rights protections to persons irregularly present on the territory.[10] Further, the concept of jurisdiction is not limited to the territory of the Member States. Wherever state officials exercise control over individuals, that control is subject to compliance with their human rights obligations (Guild 2006). Indeed, following the lead of the ECtHR, the UK's highest court, the House of Lords, held that the ECHR applies to the detention of persons by British forces in Iraq.[11]

Few human rights are absolute (the most notable exception is the prohibition on torture which is indeed absolute). Those which permit exceptions require that they be justified on the grounds permitted in the provision itself. Thus, differential treatment of foreigners in respect of a human right, such as the right of expression, is only permissible if the state can justify the difference on the basis of the exceptions which are contained in the article itself. Further, the principle of proportionality applies – that is to say that the difference of treatment cannot be disproportionate to the legitimate aim which is being pursued. In other words, the discrimination must not exceed what is absolutely necessary to achieve the aim of the measure, which aim itself must be permitted.

The most important human right which has given rise to limitations on states' power to expel foreigners has been art. 8 ECHR, the right to respect for private and family life. The provision states that 'everyone has the right to respect for his private and family life, his home and his correspondence'. However, it is followed by a second part which states: 'there shall be no interference by a public authority with the exercise of this right except such as is in accordance with the law and is necessary in a democratic society in the interests of national security, public safety or the economic well-being of the country, for the prevention of disorder or crime, for the protection of health or morals, or for the protection of the rights and freedoms of others'. With such a health list of grounds on which to justify exceptions to the right to private and family life, one would not be reproached for thinking that states could expel just about any foreigner and find a ground on which to hang it. Somewhat surprisingly, this is not the case; the ECtHR has condemned many Member States for the attempted expulsion of foreigners, even when they have been convicted of very serious crimes (Lambert 2001).

The ECtHR has held that there are five steps which must be considered when looking at the protection of family life as required by the ECHR.

- Is there family or private life? It is for the applicant to establish whether he or she in fact has family life in the state concerned – but so long as the individuals are related, there will almost always be family life. For instance, no matter how estranged, parents and children always have some family life which comes within the meaning of art. 8; the question regarding the foreigner will be whether that is sufficiently strong a bond to displace the state's argument in favour of expulsion. As regards private life, this has been defined as the total of the relationships which an individual has in the state.
- Has there been an interference with that family or private life? So long as the state is seeking to expel the individual, there will always be an interference with family or private life.
- Is the interference in accordance with the law? Unless there is a law which permits the state to expel the foreigner, then its action will be unlawful. If one returns to the UDHR, the idea that the rule of law is central to the delivery of human rights protection is inherent in this requirement to abide by the UDHR.
- Is the interference based on a permitted ground? States usually have no trouble finding a ground among the list in the second part of the provision on which to justify an expulsion decision.
- Is the interference necessary in a democratic society? This is a question of weighing the interest of the individual against the claim of the state in

> expulsion: are there other less drastic options which the state could follow in respect of the individual rather than expulsion? The principle is that democratic societies only take action which is detrimental to the human rights of an individual if this is necessary and proportionate to the aim which the state is seeking to achieve (Hussain & Blake 2003).

In accordance with this test, the ECtHR has not infrequently found the expulsion of family members of nationals or resident foreigners to be incompatible with the ECHR. Similarly, the expulsion of persons convicted even of serious crimes, where they have strong family and private life links to the state, has been excluded. Although the ECtHR has not been willing to find a quasi-citizenship right to absolute protection against expulsion for foreigners who have been born on the territory of the state or spent most of their life there, it has been willing to find that, where an individual has lived most of his or her life in a state, there is a presumption in favour of his or her right to enjoy private life on the territory. Similarly, where a foreigner has strong family ties in a state, expulsion will often be included on human rights grounds.

The case of Mr and Mrs Boultif is exemplary.[12] Mr Boultif, an Algerian national, went to Switzerland on a tourist visa in December 1992. In March 1993, he married a Swiss national. In April 1994, he was convicted of unlawful possession of weapons. The day after his conviction, he committed a further crime of robbery and damage to property, according to the judgment 'by attacking a man, together with other persons, at 1 a.m., by throwing him to the ground kicking him in the face and taking 1,201 Swiss francs from him'. He was convicted for this crime too, after which the state began expulsion proceedings against him. The national courts agreed with the expulsion decision and Mr Boultif left Switzerland in 2000. Having exhausted all venues for relief in Switzerland, the couple brought a complaint to the ECtHR that the Swiss authorities had failed to respect their right to family life. The ECtHR went through the criteria to determine whether the expulsion of Mr Boultif was compatible with the couple's right to family life under art. 8 and concluded that it was not. Having found a violation (which meant that Mr Boultif had to be allowed back to Switzerland to live with his wife), the ECtHR also ordered the Swiss authorities to pay him 5,346.70 Swiss francs in costs and expenses.

The ECtHR accepted that there was family life (the couple were married), that there was an interference with it (Mr Boultif was forced to leave Switzerland) and that there was a law in Switzerland sufficient to order the expulsion of Mr Boultif. Its reasoning as to why that expulsion was contrary to art. 8 was as follows. (a) The requirement of a legitimate aim: the ECtHR accepted the assessment of the Swiss authorities that Mr Boutlif's crime was a serious offence. The Swiss authorities had curtailed his residence permit in the interests of public order and security. (b) Was the interference necessary in a democratic society? The ECtHR did not think so.

The ECtHR was careful to recognize the right of states to control the entry and residence of aliens and, in so doing, to expel foreigners convicted of criminal offences. However, to fulfil the requirement that this is necessary in a democratic society, the action must be justified by a pressing social need and be proportionate to the aim pursued. This requires an assessment of whether a fair balance was struck between Mr Boultif's interest to be with his wife in Switzerland and the prevention of disorder and crime. Central to the ECtHR's assessment were the obstacles which stood in the way of Mrs Boultif's possible move to Algeria. The criteria the ECtHR used in order to determine the interests are as follows:[13]

- the nature and seriousness of the offence committed by the applicant;
- the length of the applicant's stay in the country from which he or she is to be expelled;
- the time elapsed since the offence was committed and the applicant's conduct during that period;
- the nationalities of the various persons concerned;
- the applicant's family situation, such as the length of the marriage, and other factors expressing the effectiveness of a couple's family life;
- whether the spouse knew about the offence at the time when he or she entered into a family relationship;
- whether there are children to the marriage, and, if so, their ages; and
- the seriousness of the difficulties which the spouse is likely to encounter in the applicant's country of origin.

This may not be the most satisfactory or comprehensive of lists of factors to be taken into consideration. Indeed, there has been significant criticism of some of them (Dembour 2006), but what I want to focus on here is the detail of the criteria which a supranational court has given to the national authorities of forty-seven countries regarding their power to expel foreigners who have committed serious crimes and who have family life on their territory. Resolving the challenge between the security claim of the state to be entitled to expel the foreigner and the security claim of the foreigner to be able to continue to live in the state does not rest exclusively with the state institutions but escapes national appreciation on the grounds that there is a human right at stake. On the basis of that claim to a human right, the security of residence of the individual may overtake the collective security claim of the state through the intervention of judicial authorities outside the state but to which the state has undertaken obedience.

Conclusions

In this chapter I have examined the way in which interests in migration and security intersect and enter into competition with one another. The claim of states to expel foreigners who are on their territory is based in the interests of the security of the collective. The claim of the foreigner to security of residence and family life comes into conflict with the state in particular when the foreigner has been convicted of a criminal offence. In the two examples I have set out here, the state's room for manoeuvre in respect of the resident foreigner is changed because of the international commitments which the state has entered into. On the one hand, the EU prevents states from expelling some foreigners (in particular nationals of other Member States and their family members), except on very limited grounds of security which are controlled by the EU institutions. In the second example, it is the claim of the foreigner to human rights that is decisive to the determination of the security claim. The fact of being a human being modifies the obligation of the state as to how it determines the competing security interests.

Once the field of action exceeds that of national sovereignty, the position of the foreigner is also transformed. Whether on the basis of reciprocity of treatment of citizens, as the EU rules began, or generally on the basis of human rights, supra-national rules in the European area tend to increase the protection of the individual against expulsion. Not only do the laws adopted both within the EU and in human rights commitments tend to provide greater protections for the individual against expulsion, but supranational institutions responsible for the interpretation of those rules tend to give the foreigner a sympathetic hearing.

Whether in the case of the EU rules or that of European human rights norms, European states are active participants and supporters of the process. For instance, the EU states affirmed and extended the human rights contained in the ECHR by creating a European Union Charter of Fundamental Rights which includes all the ECHR ones, accepts explicitly the jurisprudence of the ECtHR and adds more rights. This is not the action of twenty-seven states which seek to avoid, undermine or withdraw from the interpretation of human rights which the ECtHR has given. Similarly, many Council of Europe states are actively campaigning to enter the EU, which will mean accepting the limitations of their sovereignty as regards the treatment of foreigners. It can be argued that the economic interests of countries in the region to join the EU far outweigh the security interests expressed by interior ministries regarding control over foreigners. Nonetheless, the acceptance of the modification of security which both the EU and the ECHR require – to privilege the security of residence of the foreigner over the state's appreciation of the needs of collective security within the state – constitutes an important dimension to our understanding of the relationship of the two concepts.

4

Armed conflict, flight and refugees

In the first chapter I examined the need to bring together critical security studies, which opens up to analysis the meaning of security, with a new approach, critical migration studies, which challenges the assumption that the subject matter of migration studies is a state-centred approach to movement of persons constructed as individuals forming groups. The globalists similarly construct humanity as an entity in respect of which they perform the role of spokesperson. By taking as the point of departure the individual, I analyse how the state seeks to define the individual as part of a group or flow framed by the state's definition of belonging or foreignness (citizenship versus other). Through the struggles of individuals reaching both within and beyond the state to escape the state's categorization, in this and the next chapter I examined conflicts around the citizen / foreigner divide and the ultimate sanction of the state against the person categorized as a foreigner – expulsion from the territory. In these two chapters, the relationship of the individual to the state's framing of his or her agency is questioned in light of the capacity of individuals to arrive as actors in supranational spaces, the importance of which is underestimated by the state-centred approaches and colonized by the globalist ones – but in generalities which miss the changing nature of actors. The capacity of the individual to defy the state's determination using tools both within and beyond the state depends not least on the liberal democratic state's sensitivity to rule of law and international opinion. The European Union presents an interesting alternative picture as regards state obedience to successful human rights challenges by individuals, in that the EU founded on international economic principles not human rights.

In this chapter I will move to the problem of forced movement – an issue which I will examine from two different perspectives in this chapter and the next. Before considering the problem for the individual of flight from death, torture and armed conflict, I will return to security studies to examine violence, in particular state violence against the individual. The key move is around the concepts of crime and war – how a situation is defined transforms the individual–state relationship: if it is crime, one set of institutional measures is appropriate; if it is war or armed conflict, another may be used which permits the state to engage in extrajudicial killing. But it is on the individual that I want to focus, so I will move from the problem of defining violence to the flight of the individual from state violence. I will look at two types of flight: flight within the state – from one village to the neighbouring one or further down the road – and flight across an international border.[1] Thirdly, I will look at the international community's response – what are the tools of solidarity with these people fleeing conflict? Once I have laid the groundwork in this chapter around the individual and flight from violence, I will return in the next chapter to the individual's struggle for protection against violence, focusing in particular on the individual's reach beyond the state to international rules to obtain safety.

Situations of current and potential armed conflict give rise to many different consequences. One of these, however, is flight. There is nothing surprising about the fact that people flee such conflict. Long queues of refugees fleeing the site of fighting are among the most enduring images of armed conflict and war. But where are they going? When they get somewhere, will they find protection from the fighting and under what circumstances? How will the decision be taken whether they can stay or whether they will be sent back to the place they came from?

As Jabri insists, the discourse of war aims at the construction of a mythology based on inclusion and exclusion (Jabri 1996). Violent conflict which involves substantial numbers of persons inevitably engages systems of inclusion and exclusion. That the identity of groups is constructed and reconstructed by political projects is certainly not a new idea in sociology, though the rapidity of the changing political projects which followed the end of bipolarity in Europe and Central Asia, and their consequences for identity, have been considerable (Toth 2006; Castells 2003; Anderson 2006). Armed conflicts among groups across the world have been reframing identity through political claims which are reinforced by armed struggle. In this changing landscape of armed struggle and identity, securing the individual is key. The individual must accept participation in the reconfiguration of identity or detach him or herself from the group claim (Zizek 2008). The legitimacy of an individual's claim to the right to security through detaching him or herself from a group and fleeing depends on how the international community views the conflict and the border. The principle of state sovereignty means that, as long as the individual is within his or her state, then the state is responsible for his or her care. Human rights abuses of nationals by their states are a ground for the international community to condemn a state and require it to explain its action in the context of the UN bodies. The principle contained in art. 2(3) of the UN Charter that all members shall settle their disputes by peaceful means has required substantial clarification and explanation, not least by the General Assembly of the UN (Noortmann 2005). But when states lose control of part of their territories which are de facto controlled by another state, that other state may find itself responsible to the international community for the delivery of human rights (Guild 2006).

To be recognized as a refugee in international law, the individual must be outside his or her country of origin and fear persecution on the ground of race, religion, nationality, membership of a social group or political opinion (the UN Convention Relating to the States of Refugees 1951 and Protocol 1967: the Geneva Convention). Protection of the individual by a state of which he or she is not a national within the inter-state system only arises with the crossing of an international border (Goodwin-Gill & McAdam 2007). If the individual is unable to get beyond the state's borders, then he or she is an internally displaced person (IDP), in respect of whom there is no international treaty to provide protection. The individual who arrives at the frontier of a state and claims protection under the Geneva Convention is frequently termed an 'asylum seeker'. This is because the individual is seeking protection but the state has yet to determine whether, objectively, on the basis of the definition of who is a refugee, the individual fulfils the requirements. The status of 'asylum seeker' is a temporary one – it lasts from the time the individual asks for international protection until the state from which he or she asked for that protection makes a decision on the case. If the decision is positive, then the individual is (and always has been since leaving his or her country of origin) a refugee. If the decision is negative, then the individual is not a refugee, and no longer an asylum seeker. At this point the individual usually becomes irregularly present on the territory of the state, unless he or she can bring him or herself within some other immigration category.

For the individual seeking security and protection, the existence of sovereign borders which are protected by the institutions of the state is critical to being able to mount a claim based on international obligations. State sovereignty is a prerequisite to providing the foreigner with protection from persecution. Without the transformation of the individual from citizen to foreigner through the crossing of an international border, he or she cannot become a refugee. The containment of armed conflicts through the sealing of borders thus has vital consequences for persons fleeing violence (Duffield 2008). However, to be a refugee, the individual does not need to be fleeing conflict, only persecution. Indeed, in the international protection system, states are not under a duty to provide protection as refugees to persons who are fleeing armed conflicts but not persecution (Goodwin-Gill & McAdam 2007).

Counting the conflicts

What are armed conflicts and how does one count them? In international law the easiest answer is war which comes in the form of a declaration of war by one state against another. This rather clear indicator has fallen out of favour since the end of the Second World War. However, whether this has been such a clear indicator of armed conflict remains questionable, as states which may be formally at war with one another may not engage in any armed conflict for long periods of time (Holsti 1996). The question 'What is an armed conflict?' has significant legal consequences. If an event or series of events is classified as an armed conflict, then international humanitarian law applies. If the violence is less than armed conflict, then it falls outside the scope of international humanitarian law (though not outside the scope of human rights law). If an armed conflict is international – i.e. engages more than one state, but including liberation wars – then international law in the form of the four Geneva Conventions 1949 and their 1977 Protocols applies. These Conventions regulate how people must be treated during the armed conflict. If one is to make a crude division regarding the individual, the Geneva Conventions 1949 and their 1977 Protocols, which regulate how armed conflict is carried out, apply within the territory where the armed conflict is taking place. The Geneva Convention 1951 and its 1967 Protocol, which set out states' duties towards refugees, apply once the individual is outside the state where the conflict is taking place. International humanitarian law, which is based on the Geneva Conventions 1949 and the 1977 Protocols, covers the following:

- wounded or sick military personnel in land warfare, and members of the armed forces' medical services;
- wounded, sick or shipwrecked military personnel in naval warfare, and members of the naval forces' medical services;
- prisoners of war;
- the civilian population, for example: foreign civilians on the territory of parties to the conflict, including refugees; civilians in occupied territories; civilian detainees and internees; medical and religious personnel or civil defence units.[2]

If the conflict is internal (i.e. not international), then international humanitarian law still applies according to the 1977 Protocols to the Geneva Conventions 1949, but in a more limited manner. It includes the armed forces, whether regular or not, taking part in the conflict, and protects every individual or category of individuals not, or no longer, actively involved in the hostilities, for example:

- wounded or sick fighters;
- people deprived of their freedom as a result of the conflict;
- the civilian population;
- medical and religious personnel.[3]

It is of substantial importance to determine whether a conflict constitutes an armed conflict within the terms of international humanitarian law, as important consequences flow, or whether the conflict constitutes only indiscriminate violence which does not reach the threshold of armed conflict. In the latter case, it is a problem of internal order, normally dealt with by the criminal justice system. The state coercive institutions which form part of that system will be competent for the resolution of the problem unless the political authorities deem them insufficient and call on other services such as the military. International human rights obligations apply whether the conflict is one of the re-establishment of order or of armed conflict (Guild 2006). The core question is whether what is at stake is war or crime. This will have very important consequences regarding the actions of combatants (Dieben & Dieben 2005; Kerr 2008). The Protocols state that, for non-state-armed actors to be covered by international humanitarian law, they must be under responsible command, which means that they are able to carry out sustained and concerted military operations. The problem is: how much organization is needed?

One way to draw the line is by using international criminal law as a guide. Looking at the statute of the International Criminal Court and the findings of the various international criminal tribunals (principally that of the Former Yugoslavia, and the Rwanda Tribunal), Barnes concludes that there needs to be protracted armed conflict between organized armed groups and governmental authorities before a conflict can be classified as armed conflict rather than generalized violence. So, length of conflict, as well as its ferocity and organizational structure, is central to its categorization. Barnes notes that, in some cases, a conflict of a few months is sufficient (Barnes 2005). This seems to be the key to the difference between armed conflict and civil unrest or political violence. As Moir points out, the problem with the definition is its flexibility. Unless there is an external body with the power to determine whether an event or series of events is violence, unrest, political violence or armed conflict, the decision falls to the state. In light of the fact that, once defined as an armed conflict, the consequence in international law is that humanitarian law applies, even beyond the cessation of hostilities up to conclusion of a peace or, in the case of internal conflicts, until a peaceful settlement has been achieved, states may be reluctant to declare themselves in a state of armed conflict as this prevents them from dealing with their opponents according to criminal law (Moir 2005).

Into this space of state sovereignty, there has been no clear intervention of the international community. Instead, a non-governmental organization (NGO), International Crisis Group, with a very impressive executive committee including Lakhdar Brahimi, Joschka Fischer and Cheryl Carolus, issues monthly bulletins on current and potential conflicts, armed and otherwise, around the world. It seeks to summarize developments in about seventy countries.[4] The information is put on its website together with further references, assessments of the overall situation, whether it is getting better or worse and alerts for readers on situations. It also produces reports and briefing papers. The idea of counting conflicts and providing an international source of information, as far as possible in fairly neutral terms, about a conflict, constitutes an interesting alternative to state information (the most widely known being the US State Department Reports on countries). Other non-governmental organizations provide invaluable information about human rights abuses around the world, most notably Amnesty International Human Rights Watch. Both of these NGOs have a global reach.

Armed conflict and internally displaced persons

The difficulties in determining what is an armed conflict have enormous implications for the individual. If an individual cannot become a refugee until he or she is outside the borders of the state of nationality, then what regime governs those who flee within a state? On the one hand, as noted above, the decision to declare a conflict as such in international law has consequences which impinge on sovereignty. Thus, unless the international community intervenes to declare an armed conflict or to place sufficient pressure on a state to make such a declaration, the tendency often is to treat the conflict as political violence, crime, etc. The individual fleeing within his or her state on account of conflict is an internally displaced person. For him or her, protection is under, first, the constitutional rules on treatment of citizens and, second, the international human rights obligations of the state. Sadly, all too often the state is either unable or unwilling to provide protection to the individuals. This may be because the state does not have the capacity – it is fighting an undeclared war with a segment of its population and has no resources for those displaced by the conflict. Or it may be because the individuals who have fled are viewed with suspicion, as more properly being the responsibility of the other group (D'Appollonia & Reich 2008). The categorization of identity as belonging to the ascendant population holding power or belonging to the group which is disputing that control on the basis of separation takes place not only within the community but also for the individual. The interaction between the two may result in protection or not. This process, as it took place in Kosovo, particularly leading up to the NATO bombing of Serbia in 1999, is compellingly described by Judah (2000).

Since the end of bipolarity after 1989, an increasing emphasis has been placed by states on containing armed conflict within the territory where it is taking place. Among other forms this has taken, it has included international attempts to limit movement of persons outside the state in which the conflict is taking place (Gibney 2006). As international law only recognizes as a refugee someone who has crossed an international boundary, persons who are not able to leave their country do not qualify. Instead, if someone flees his or her home but cannot flee the country, he or she becomes an internally displaced person. The working definition which the United Nations High Commissioner for Refugees (UNHCR) uses for internally displaced persons is: 'people or groups of individuals who have been forced to leave their homes or places of habitual residence, in particular as a result of, or in order to avoid, the effects of armed conflict, situations of generalized violence, violations of human rights or natural or human-made disasters, and who have not crossed an international border'.

Global refugee trends show a considerable drop in the numbers of refugees worldwide, from 14 million in 1996 to 11.4 million in 2007 (with a further 4.6 million Palestinian refugees under the responsibility of the United Nations Relief and Works Agency for Palestinian Refugees in the Near East (UNRWA)) according to the UNHCR.[5] In 2007, the main countries of origin of refugees were (in order of importance) Afghanistan, Iraq (which two countries between them accounted for half of all refugees of concern to UNHCR worldwide), Colombia, Sudan, Somalia, Burundi and the Democratic Republic of the Congo.

Conflict-related IDP populations have grown over the period from 17 million in 1996 to 26 million in 2007 according to the Internal

Displacement Monitoring Centre (IDMC).[6] IDPs due to natural disasters stood at 25 million in 2007. For conflict-related IDPs, the figure is now the highest since the early 1990s (when both the Soviet Union and the former Yugoslavia broke up, giving rise to substantial movements of people) and constitutes a 6 per cent increase on the previous year. According to the IDMC, the continent most affected by IDPs was Africa. The main countries affected by internal displacement in 2007 were the Central African Republic, Chad, Colombia, Democratic Republic of the Congo, Ethiopia, Indonesia, Iraq, Kenya, Pakistan, Somalia, Sudan, Uganda and Zimbabwe. There is significant, but by no means complete, overlap between the countries which produce refugees and those with substantial IDP populations. The most striking contrast is as regards Afghanistan which produces refugees but not significant numbers of IDPs (or at least not recorded ones), while Colombia produces the third-largest number of both refugees and IDPs. It is difficult to avoid one question: do the attempts by western liberal democracies to seal their borders against persons arriving irregularly not also have an effect in transforming refugee flows into IDP flows (Joly 2002; Gibney 2006)?

The IDMC report includes some very disturbing information about the treatment of IDPs: there are fifty-two countries affected by IDP populations; twenty-eight of them have new or on-going conflicts which are creating IDPs; in ten of those countries, all or most IDPs were exposed to serious threats to their physical security and integrity; in a further ten countries, they face obstacles to access to the basic necessities of life. The governments or occupying forces of twenty-one of those countries were directly or indirectly involved in deliberately displacing people; and 11.3 million IDPs remain without any significant humanitarian assistance from their governments.[7]

The challenge of IDPs is in no small measure one to both sovereignty and security within the state. There is no international Convention providing a framework for protection of IDPs (Phuong 2005). Efforts to develop an international framework started around 1992 when the UN Secretary General appointed the first Representative on Internally Displaced Persons.[8] Among the most difficult problems was establishing the legitimacy of the international community's involvement in the internal affairs of states, including in this area. The UN Representative on IDPs set about trying to broker agreement on the subject and to extend the remit of international protection in this area. The first pressing need was to provide a definition of IDPs which would stick. Eventually, and after much deliberation, the definition the UNHCR uses was agreed. A simpler definition is used by the IDMC: persons who 'have been forced to flee their homes because their lives were in danger, but unlike refugees have not crossed an international border'. The UN refugee agency, UNHCR, has become increasingly involved with IDPs since the beginning of the twenty-first century, not without controversy (Lanz 2008).

The IDMC, set up by the Norwegian Refugee Council and enjoying the support of (among others) the UNHCR and the UN Office for the Coordination of Humanitarian Affairs (OCHA), counts IDPs. It estimates that there are approximately 5.8 million IDPs in Sudan, 4 million in Colombia, 2.5 million in Iraq, 1.4 million in the Democratic Republic of Congo, and 1.3 million in Uganda. For IDPs, one of the most pressing problems is that of individual security. Inherent in the definition of an IDP is the fact that his or her movement is involuntary (Phuong 2005). The individual is forced to move from his or her home to somewhere else on account of violence, persecution or other manifestations of armed conflict. The fact that the individual is still dependent on the same state for protection creates uncertainties. The IDMC raises eight points which make these persons particularly vulnerable:

- the role of transit: IDPs by definition are escaping one place of danger; they may be in hiding, may be forced towards insecure environments, or face other circumstances that make them especially vulnerable;
- the displacement from traditional social organization: family groups may be separated or disrupted; women may be forced to assume non-traditional roles or face particular vulnerabilities;
- displacement of any kind but particularly where accompanied by a lack of security in the place of refuge may cause profound psychosocial distress;
- displacement inevitably involves some, if not a complete, displacement from sources of income and livelihood which adds to physical and psychosocial vulnerability;
- education is disrupted;
- the inability of local communities to provide reception, or competition for scarce resources with local inhabitants, may increase risk to IDPs;
- IDPs, by the fact of their flight, may be the subject of suspicions in local communities, be rejected by them or be the objects of threat by armed combatants, or other parties to conflict;
- IDPs often lack identity documents essential to receiving benefits or legal recognition; or they may have disposed of all documents as they may tie the IDP to the source of persecution.

The vulnerability of IDPs will, of course, depend greatly on local conditions. If they have fled to a secure part of the state where the authorities have sufficient resources and are able to provide protection, then their situation may be acceptable. If, however, no part of the state is secure and those persecuting the IDPs are able to act with impunity throughout the territory, then the closure of the external border is particularly problematic (Bagshaw 2007). The common problems among IDPs are disappearances, missing persons and uninvestigated deaths; detention and the use of closed camps to detain them; the lack of personal identification making claims to individual rights impossible; the inability to make claims to property to retain their belongings, not least for lack of documentation; difficulty of access to relief workers and organizations (Bagshaw 2007).

The UN first approached the increasingly pressing problem of IDPs by appointing a Representative on IDPs in 2004 who presided over the development of guiding principles designed to address the specific needs of IDPs. There are thirty principles addressed to states, other authorities and groups, international organizations and non-governmental organizations involved in matters concerning IDPs. While the principles do not have a specific legal status they are intended to be of persuasive authority (Kalin 2000 – who provides an excellent analysis of the principles and their sources in international law). There are five sections.

The first section contains the general principles: first, IDPs are entitled to equality of treatment with other nationals of their country; the principles are to apply to all authorities, groups or persons and are not to be interpreted restrictively. IDPs are entitled to humanitarian assistance and should not be persecuted or punished for having sought it. The principles should be applied without discrimination on the basis of race, colour, sex, language, religion or belief, political or other opinion, national, ethnic or other origin, legal or social status, age, disability, property, birth or on any other similar criteria.

The second section contains the principles relating to protection from displacement. The overriding concern is to avoid displacement through the provision of sufficient protection in the area. This section begins with a reminder that all authorities and international actors must respect human rights and humanitarian law. This covers protection against arbitrary displacement, which is defined as including ethnic cleansing and similar practices, and displacement as a result of:

- armed conflict;
- large-scale development projects unless justified by compelling and overriding public interests;

- disasters; or
- imposition of collective punishment.

Where authorities are considering displacement of persons, they must ensure that all other options are considered but are not feasible, and take all efforts to minimize displacement and its adverse effects. Proper accommodation must be provided, including satisfactory conditions of safety, nutrition, health and hygiene, as well as ensuring that families remain together. In situations outside of armed conflict, the authorities must ensure that displacement only occurs where a specific decision has been taken in accordance with the law, full information on the reasons and procedures has been provided to the individuals affected, free and informed consent of the displaced sought, the displaced have been involved in the planning of their relocation, law enforcement has been made available, and the displaced can access an effective remedy. In any event, displacement must not violate the rights to life, dignity, liberty and security. Specific attention must be paid to the needs of indigenous people, peasants, pastoralists and certain other groups.

The third section of the principles deals with protection during displacement. The guidance requires that IDPs be protected against genocide, murder, arbitrary execution, enforced disappearances and threats of any of these. They must not be attacked, starved, used as shields for military operations, attacked in their camps or settlements or be the object of anti-personnel landmines. The guidance reiterates that IDPs are entitled to dignity and physical and moral integrity. They must be protected against rape, mutilation, torture, cruel, inhuman or degrading treatment or punishment and other outrages upon personal dignity. They must not be subject to slavery or acts of violence intended to spread terror.

Like all other human beings, they have the right to liberty and security of person and thus not to be interned or otherwise detained. IDPs must not be recruited to participate in hostilities. They should have the right to seek safety elsewhere in their country, to leave their country to seek asylum elsewhere and to be protected against forcible return to a place where their safety or health would be at risk. IDPs are entitled to know where their missing relatives are and to have their family life protected. Also in this section is the principle that IDPs must have the right to an adequate standard of living and access to essential food and water, shelter, clothing, medical services and sanitation. Special emphasis is placed on access to medical services, which are included as a separate principle. Recognition before the law and the right to property are also included as principles, as well as the right to freedom of thought and expression, association and a vote and to communicate in their language. In this section the final principles enunciate the right to education and training.

The fourth section deals with humanitarian assistance and commences with the principle that this must be provided without discrimination and must not be diverted for political or military reasons. The duty to provide humanitarian assistance is placed on the national authorities but includes a right for international humanitarian organizations to offer assistance, consent to which must not be arbitrarily withheld. Free passage for humanitarian assistance and access to IDPs must be respected, including transport and supplies. International humanitarian organizations and other actors providing assistance (NGOs, etc.) must take into account the needs of IDPs and comply with international codes of conduct.

The final section covers the difficult issues of return, resettlement and reintegration. The principles place a duty on the competent authorities to permit the voluntary return of IDPs in safety and dignity to their homes, or to allow them to resettle voluntarily elsewhere in the country. Where IDPs choose to return, they must be protected against discrimination as a result of displacement and have equal access to public affairs and services. The competent authorities are to assist IDPs to recover their property or to provide compensation or reparation.

The list of woes which the principles prohibit sets the reader's imagination to work on just how terribly vulnerable a group this is. Clearly, the principles are designed to ban the worst practices of state authorities in respect of the excluded group known as IDPs. But a reading of the principles which is sympathetic to the plight of IDPs makes one wonder whether the better solution is to help them escape out of the country and the clutches of authorities intent on subjecting them to such appalling treatment. As is clear from the principles, the efforts of the international community to arrive at some agreement on IDPs are premised on the idea that protection is part of national sovereignty. The problem is that the principles in fact do no more than enumerate the duties which states have already accepted under international human rights commitments in respect of all human beings. The Universal Declaration of Human Rights, together with the two International Covenants – the one on civil and political rights, the other on economic, social and cultural rights – already set a threshold for the behaviour of states towards all persons, not just their own citizens, which prohibits all the acts which the principles seek to outlaw (see chapter 3).

What the principles do is to place these existing human rights obligations in an IDP setting, indicating how they apply to the specific group. However, the key problem of IDPs is the state itself which is either directly carrying out or complicit in their persecution. While the principles may be very useful, particularly in cases of natural disaster where the state authorities are not targeting the group, they are much more difficult to implement in an armed conflict where the state is not neutral in respect of the group. The classic modern case is of course that of the Rwandan genocide of 1994 (Prunier 1995). In this case, sovereignty, in the form of a hard border, may be the only recourse for the individual: if he or she can only arrive at the other side of the border, the sovereignty of the state of reception may provide some protection against their state of origin which is intent on persecuting the individual, though whether a neighbouring state is capable of providing protection may also be in question (Gentile 2002).

Armed conflict and refugees

In comparison with IDPs, refugees are much better protected in international law. The key international instrument is the UN Convention Relating to the Status of Refugees 1951 and its 1967 Protocol (commonly called the Geneva Convention). Notwithstanding some suggestions that the Geneva Convention is a Cold War instrument, it is clearly a post-Second World War development (Loescher 1993). The original Convention was limited in time, to events occurring before 1 January 1951, and states had the option of applying a territorial limit to their obligations under the instrument to refugees arising as a result of events in Europe (Goodwin-Gill & McAdam 2007). The 1967 Protocol lifted both the temporal and territorial limitations with the effect of making the Convention applicable to anyone who comes within its definition, irrespective of when or where they are. The Convention and Protocol apply to those states which have signed and ratified them.

The Convention defines a refugee as anyone who,

> owing to well-founded fear of being persecuted for reasons of race, religion, nationality, membership of a particular social group or political opinion, is outside the country of his nationality and is unable, or owing to such fear, is unwilling to avail himself of the protection of that country; or who, not having a nationality and being outside the country of his former habitual residence as a result of such events, is unable or, owing to such fear, is unwilling to return to it. (art.1A(2)).

The reason an individual needs refugee protection is that the state authorities, or actors whom the state is unable or unwilling to rein in, are deploying symbolic or actual violence to exclude the individual, as part of a group, from equality. Actors within the state are deploying mechanisms which define inclusion and exclusion in a particularly violent manner, resulting in the excluded being the object of persecution because of a characteristic – race, religion, nationality, membership of a social group or political opinion – which is constructed as a form of essentialism (Zizek 2008). The definition of the grounds on which persecution gives rise to a successful refugee claim has been the subject of substantial struggle in western democracies, reflecting identity politics in the host state. For instance, women as refugees – their agency as actors, whether domestic violence constitutes persecution, whether they can constitute a social group, etc. – has been the subject of substantial debate and legal argument (Forbes Martin 2004).

The key protection which the Convention provides to the refugee is that the state (which has signed the Convention) must not 'expel or return (*refouler*) a refugee in any manner whatsoever to the frontiers of territories where his life or freedom would be threatened on account of his race, religion, nationality, membership of a particular social group or political opinion' (art. 33(1)). The first aspect to note is that, in contrast with the IDP, the refugee does not exist until and unless he or she is outside the country of origin. Thus the border of sovereignty is the critical border between the individual's security depending on the authorities of his or her state (i.e. being an IDP) and that security depending on the international commitment of another state not to return the individual to the country of origin (being a refugee). The objective of the Convention is to turn all countries into sources of security for the individual who has the well-founded fear of persecution in his or her own state of origin. A refugee seeks asylum on the territory of a foreign state, asylum consisting of the right to remain and the rights contained in the Geneva Convention (which are more extensive than those in the IDP principles). However, the policies of many western democracies to regionalize refugee movements so that those seeking protection do not arrive at their doors creates problems of disparity among states as regards offering protection (Joly 2002).

There is an exception to this duty not to return the individual to a place where he or she might be persecuted, which is where there are reasonable grounds for regarding his or her as a danger to the security of the country in which he or she is, or where, having been convicted by a final judgment of a particularly serious crime, he or she constitutes a danger to the community of that country (art. 33(2)). Here the security of the refugee against return to persecution is subordinated to the state's claim to collective security within its borders. Nowhere has the claim to exclude refugees on the basis of their involvement with political violence been more vocal than in the USA after the 11 September 2001 attacks, though many European states have also engaged in a reconsideration of their asylum policies on this basis as well (Guild & Baldaccini 2006; Baylis 2008). The changes have taken place in three main ways: first, legislation has been changed to place more emphasis on the exclusion from protection of refugees who are suspected of having been engaged in political violence; second, refugees from certain countries are designated as particular risks; third, rights of appeal have been diminished for those refugees who are considered a danger to national security (Guild & Baldaccini 2006).

The determination of whether an individual is a refugee or not depends on the officials of the state from which the individual has sought protection. While the UNHCR is often involved in that process, it is primarily the responsibility of the host state to examine the claim to protection and to reach a decision on whether it is justified. In view of the periods of time which may elapse between the making of the claim to protection and the determination by the authorities of whether it is justified, European countries use the term 'asylum seeker' or 'asylum applicant' to describe a person who has made an application for international protection but whose application has not yet been determined (see above). The wording of the Geneva Convention is clear that the individual is a refugee from the time he or she fulfils the definition of a refugee, i.e. has a well-founded fear (Goodwin-Gill & McAdam 2007). However, no European or North American country grants asylum seekers the same rights to which refugees are entitled, notwithstanding the fact that they may be refugees. Indeed, it was with some difficulty that, in the European Union, the Member States managed to agree among themselves a set of minimum conditions for the reception of asylum seekers, which includes housing, food, medical treatment, access to education, etc. (Baldaccini 2005). This is even though the European states were arguing among themselves that changes to national rules on reception conditions for asylum seekers were displacing flows to other countries, and thus a floor below which no country could go was necessary. Agreement was finally reached in 2003 and it has been implemented with more or less success in all participating EU Member States.[9]

Two other international developments have changed the legal obligations of states to provide protection to refugees. First, there has been a widening of the international commitments to providing protection to foreigners through the inclusion of a duty not to return a person to a state where there are substantial grounds for believing that he or she would be in danger of being subjected to torture (art. 3 UN Convention Against Torture and Other Inhuman and Degrading Treatment or Punishment 1984, 'Convention against Torture'). This widely signed and ratified convention includes a strict definition of torture,[10] as well as a strict obligation on all parties never to return a person to a country where there is a substantial risk that he or she would be tortured. The Convention does not provide any exception on grounds of national security to the rule against return to torture. Thus it is more constraining on states than the Geneva Convention as regards national security. As the Convention against Torture was only opened for signature in 1984 and most liberal democracies have signed and ratified it, the conclusion must be that, notwithstanding appearances to the contrary, these countries are committed to refugee protection (Herman Burgers & Danelius 1988). In chapter 5, I will examine some of the security issues which arise in respect of the Convention against Torture and the individual seeking international protection.

Second, in the European region, the European Court of Human Rights has interpreted the prohibition on torture in the European Convention on Human Rights as including a prohibition on the return of a person to a country where there is a real risk that he or she would suffer torture or inhuman or degrading treatment. Thus, like the UN Convention against Torture, the ECHR, as interpreted by the ECtHR, also prohibits the return of a person to a country where this is a real risk. The ECHR prohibition is somewhat wider than that of the UN Convention against Torture as it also prohibits the expulsion of a person to a country where there is a real risk he or she would suffer inhuman or degrading treatment or punishment (as well as or instead of torture). This threshold is lower than that of torture. Another difference relates to the author of the torture, inhuman or degrading treatment or punishment. In the Convention against Torture, for there to be torture there must be 'the consent or acquiescence of a public official or other person acting in an official capacity' (art. 1(1)). According to the ECHR, the author of torture is not important, the purpose of the Convention provision is to protect the individual. So the fact that the individual is at risk of torture by armed groups which the state is seeking to defeat makes no difference to the right of the individual to protection in the host state, so long as the authorities of his or her state of origin are not able to protect him or her from torture, inhuman or degrading treatment (Hussain and Blake 2003).

These two instruments both extend the scope of protection of the individual as the only criterion is whether the individual would be subject to torture or, in the case of the ECHR, inhuman or degrading treatment. There is no need for the individual to show that the treatment would be because of his or her race, religion, nationality, membership of a particular social group or political opinion. Further, under these instruments, the security of the state is never a justification for the return of a person to a country where he or she would be at risk of the prohibited treatment. The individual's security always takes priority (Mole 2007).

The UK and Italian governments sought to convince the ECtHR that there should be a balancing of the risk of harm if the person is sent back to his or her country of origin against the danger which he or she represents to the community if not sent back.[11] The UK government argued, in particular, that, where an individual presents a threat to national security, stronger evidence must be adduced to prove that there is a risk of ill treatment in the country of origin. This argument was rejected by the ECtHR. It considered the argument incompatible with the absolute nature of the individual's protection against return to torture or inhuman or degrading treatment. Instead, the ECtHR reaffirmed that the prohibition means that, so long as there are substantial grounds for believing that there is a real risk that the individual will be subject to the prohibited treatment, his or her expulsion is a breach of the ECHR.

One of the key weaknesses, though, of the UN Convention against Torture and the ECHR on this point is that neither specifies what rights the individual must have while in the host state. The Geneva Convention sets out clearly the rights which a recognized refugee is entitled to (Hathaway 2005) but the other conventions do not, leaving it to the state to determine the content of the protection (subject to other human rights commitments).

Armed conflict, IDPs and refugees

What happens when we compare armed conflicts, IDPs and refugees according to where the conflict is taking place, where the situation of IDPs is particularly of concern, and the states of origin of people seeking international protection: is there any clear correlation between the three? In table 4.1, I have taken the sources discussed in this chapter – the International Crisis Group regarding conflicts, the IDMC for the IDPs, and the UNHCR regarding asylum seekers – and put them side by side. I start with the country and its total population, then provide the IDMC statistics from July 2008 on the numbers of internally displaced persons, and the UNHCR statistics on the total numbers of refugees from that country who are abroad. This column is followed by some Euro-centred statistics – how many people from these countries were eligible, and in fact applied, for asylum in the 1st and 2nd quarters of 2007 (the latest periods for which statistics were available at the time I made the comparison). In the last column can be found the country assessment from the International Crisis Group on the status of armed conflict in each of the countries. The purpose of presenting

Table 4.1

Country (by country of IDP concern)	IDPs and total number of refugees abroad (2007)[a]	Asylum seekers: applications 1st & 2nd quarter 2007 in EU[b]	Conflict: most recent report[c]
Sudan: total population, 36.23 million	Latest IDP figure: 6 million Number of refugees abroad: 523,032	Q1: 469; Q2: 377; decrease: 28% over previous year; ranking: 25th	'Darfur's New Security Reality', *Africa Report*, 134 (26 November 2007) High concern
Iraq: total population, 26.70 million	Latest IDP figure: 2.8 million Number of refugees abroad: 2,279,247	Q1: 9,369; Q2: 8,836; increase: 51% over previous year; ranking: 1st	'Iraq's Civil War, the Sadrists and the Surge', *Middle East Report*, 72 (7 February 2008) High concern
DR Congo: total population, 57.54 million	Latest IDP figure: 1,400,000 Number of refugees abroad: 401,914	Q1: 1,054; Q2: 1,080; increase: 6% over previous year; ranking 14th	'Congo: Bringing Peace to North Kivu', *Africa Report*, 133 (31 October 2007)
Uganda: total population, 28.81 million	Latest IDP figure: 1,270,000 Number of refugees abroad: 21,752	Not in the top 40 asylum-producing countries for the EU	'Northern Uganda Peace Process: The Need to Maintain Momentum', *Africa Briefing*, 46 (14 September 2007)
Somalia: total population, 8.22 million	Latest IDP figure: 1,100,000 Number of refugees abroad: 455,357	Q1: 2,110; Q2: 1,992; increase: 20% over previous year; ranking: 5th	'Somalia: The Tough Part Is Ahead', *Africa Briefing*, 45 (26 January 2007) High concern
Afghanistan: total population: 32.74 million	Latest IDP figure: 132,000 Number of refugees abroad: 1,909,911	Q1: 1,992; Q2: 1,916; decrease: 5% over previous year; ranking: 6th	'Afghanistan: The Need for International Resolve', *Asia Report*, 145 (6 February 2008) High concern
Occupied Palestinian territories: total population, 3.70 million	Latest IDP figure: 24,500-115,000 Number of refugees abroad: 4,379,050 (UNRWA, 31 March 2006)	Q1: 143; Q2: 235; decrease: 9% over previous year; ranking 37th	'Inside Gaza: The Challenge of Clans and Families', *Middle East Report*, 71 (20 December 2007) High concern

Notes

[a] IDMC, *IDP News Alert*, July 2008.

[b] *UNHCR Asylum Levels and Trends in Industrialised Countries Second Quarter 2007 – applications lodged in the European Union.*

[c] From International Crisis Group, *February Trends CrisisWatch*, 55 (1 March 2008).

the data in this way is to provide an image of the relationship between armed conflict, displacement, the possibility of crossing an international border to seek protection, and the ability of people from the conflict-torn areas to seek protection in Europe, which represents, for these purposes, western liberal democracies which defend the international system of refugee protection.

Conclusions

The relationship between protection, security and persecution is governed by international law only in so far as the individual has been able to cross an international border. Where the individual is still within the territory of his or her state, national sovereignty applies foremost to the treatment which he or she will receive. Although international human rights law has been used as a basis for a set of guiding principles for the treatment of IDPs, the principles themselves are not law.

When the reason for the lack of security for the individual is related to natural disaster or other event, then the possibility of obtaining protection from the state increases. However, when the state is complicit or an actor in the conflict, the individual identified as an opponent or linked to an opposition group has little chance of gaining protection. The option of internal flight to another part of the territory may provide little help. Nonetheless, millions of individuals, fleeing their homes as a result of armed conflict, have no alternative but to seek protection, somewhere else within their state, from death, injury, torture or persecution. The exclusion of a group of people from the benefit of state protection may well result in the construction of alternative identities and groups which then fuel opposition to the authorities which have excluded them.

The countries which give rise to internally displaced persons also turn out to be those which give rise to very substantial numbers of refugees as a percentage of population across the world. The countries where there are the largest percentages of the population displaced and refugees fleeing the state altogether are all among the states of most concern regarding the presence of armed conflict. Thus, while the Geneva Convention is not an instrument to do with armed conflict, a matrix of armed conflict, flight and persecution is apparent. In the chapter which follows I will return to the struggles of the individuals caught in situations where they are at risk of persecution or torture.

5

Migration, torture and the complicit state

In the previous chapter I outlined the relationship between armed conflict, movement of persons and refugees. In this chapter I will develop this theme further, examining the role of the individual as an actor searching for protection within the international community. Protection generally comes from the state – strong states are often better placed to provide effective protection to the individual. However, that does not always mean they are willing to do so – the assessment of collective security needs can result in reluctance to protect the individual. The objective of this chapter is to understand how the claims of liberal democracies to be champions of human rights can be undermined by their perception not only of their own security needs but of those of their allies. I will examine how the suspected terrorist, in respect of whom the state is unwilling to provide any concrete evidence or allegation, escapes the label of 'terrorist' and becomes a refugee with a right to protection. The framing of the security issue as one of a balance, between the duty of the state to ensure public and national security and the right of the individual to protection against return to a country where he or she fears torture, leads away from the protection needs of the individual. The argument always privileges the state position as it is inherently state-centred: the state's duty to its people by definition excludes the refugee seeking protection. As the purpose of the state is to serve its people, the refugee is constructed as the outsider whose claims can be sacrificed in the name of the collective.

Nonetheless, the individual does not disappear simply because a state chooses to exclude him or her. The individual can challenge the state's assessment within the state, but also beyond the state, before international institutions where the state's authority, if it is found in breach of its human rights obligations, will be diminished. Where the state acts against the refugee at the prompting of its allies in accordance with their security claims, the cost can be very high indeed. A reconsideration of state interests in security can be the result. The failure of a state to protect the individual does not necessarily come cheaply. However, cooperation between states in a global counterterrorist regime does not necessarily lead to the protection of the individual. Indeed, as the cases show, the sharing of interests among states can lead to horrific outcomes for the individual. While I will begin this chapter by tying it into a subject matter I discussed in chapter 2, the forced migration of migrants to the US base in Guantánamo Bay, I approach it from a very different angle in this chapter. Rather than the question of citizen versus foreigner, here the issue is protection or application of torture. The heart of this chapter moves to the individualization of protection claims by a series of individuals in international dispute resolution mechanisms. By constructing the individual beyond the security-risk claim of the state, the politics of torture are revealed.

Torture, much to the surprise of many politicians, NGOs, lawyers and international organizations, rose to the top of the international agenda from 2001 onwards in respect of states where it had been generally accepted that all institutions were committed to the abolition of torture and the judicial pursuit of those who engaged in it. Philippe Sands, in his book *Torture Team* (Sands 2008), makes a convincing argument that key leaders in the US administration over the period 2002 to 2008 have been engaged in sanctioning torture. Clive Stafford Smith, Andy Worthington and Philip Gourevitch in their books describe how torture has become institutionalized in US practices in the detention centre at Guantánamo Bay and in other detention centres, such as Abu Ghraib in Iraq, run by US forces (Stafford Smith 2007; Worthington 2007; Gourevitch & Morris 2008). The Council of Europe's Special Representative, Dick Marty, has documented the complicity of many European states in torture (Marty 2006). From the perspective of the individuals who claim to have been subjected to torture, Moazzam Begg and Murat Kurnaz have written books on their experiences in US detention, which indicate the use of torture (Begg 2006; Kurnaz 2007). Sales and Sheppard published compelling books on the experiences of other detainees – the Australian, David Hicks, in respect of Sales, and the Canadian child Omar Khadr in respect of Sheppard (Sales 2007; Sheppard 2008). This impressive series of publications indicates a profound disquiet in academic and civil society about the issue. In respect of all these books, the people being tortured (or alleged to have been tortured) are foreigners in relation to the persons who are detaining them and inflicting the treatment on them.

In order to understand the issues at the centre of this debate, I will examine the international obligations in respect of the prohibition on torture and the duty to provide protection against torture. Instead of returning to the USA and Guantánamo Bay example, I will take as examples European states which, as Members of the Council of Europe, highly value their reputations as states which comply with international law. First, I will look at a case which involves France: the transformation of a dual French–Tunisian national into exclusively a Tunisian by the French government's decision to deprive him of French citizenship and then to expel him to Tunisia on the basis that he was a threat to national security in France. Second, I will look at the expulsion of a Turkish woman from Azberbaijan to her home state, which raised international concern about the treatment she would receive on return. Finally, I will turn to the case of Sweden, where the failure to provide protection to foreigners seeking refuge against a serious risk of torture in their country of origin has been the subject of deep social and political concern. The foreigners were sent with the complicity of the Swedish authorities to the country where they feared torture on the basis that that country had given assurances that it would protect the individuals against torture. But also, in this case, pressure from US authorities on the Swedish government to act in this way and thereby fail to respect its (Sweden's) international obligations is central. The subsequent consequences for Sweden within its own institutions (in particular the report of its Parliamentary Ombudsman regarding sovereignty) and international institutions (in particular the UN Committee against Torture) have rocked the reputation of this country, which has long prided itself on its compliance with international law.

Where does the prohibition on torture come from?

Among the most established of internationally recognized human rights norms is the prohibition on torture. Not only does it appear in the starting place of post-Second World War international human rights instruments, the Universal Declaration on Human Rights 1948, but it merits its own Convention, the UN Convention against Torture, Inhuman and Degrading Treatment 1984 (Convention against Torture). The Universal Declaration states simply at art. 5: 'No one shall be subjected to torture or to cruel, inhuman or degrading treatment or punishment.' There is no further elaboration and no exception (I have discussed this in chapter 4).

The Convention against Torture consists of thirty-three articles, of which sixteen are substantive. It has been ratified by 145 countries (including all the European countries, the USA and all other developed countries including China). It includes a dispute resolution mechanism – the Convention against Torture Committee (Committee against Torture). So long as the signatory state has expressly accepted the mechanism, the

Committee against Torture has the power to receive and adjudicate on complaints by individuals that a state has not respected its obligations under the Convention against Torture. There are 63 states which have recognized the jurisdiction of the Committee against Torture, and by June 2008 there had been 343 complaints received by the Committee.[1] I will examine some of these complaints in respect of foreigners below. But many countries do not recognize the Committee's jurisdiction – such as the UK and the USA – which means that the Committee cannot consider complaints made by individuals against these states. However, the Convention also includes a reporting procedure under which every four years, all signatory states are required to report to the Committee against Torture on the implementation of the Convention within their jurisdiction (art. 19). Under the reporting requirements, state officials are requested to appear before the Committee to explain their government's actions in respect of the Convention. The Committee also receives information from civil-society sources on the state of the implementation of the Convention in states, which it may use in the reporting procedures.

Not only does the Convention prohibit torture, it also defines it in art. 1. Article 2 requires all states signatories to take effective legislative, administrative, judicial or other measures to prevent acts of torture anywhere under its jurisdiction (which for the USA would include its base at Guantánamo Bay). Further, there is no exception to the prohibition on torture in any circumstance whatsoever: as the article states, 'whether a state of war or a threat of war, internal political instability or any other public emergency'. Simply put, in international law there is just no exception to the prohibition on torture. The ticking-bomb scenario, so often used to create doubt about the prohibition on torture,[2] just does not even make it to first base. This is not the result of oversight on the part of the drafters of the Convention against Torture, but express – the legitimacy, let alone the efficiency, of torture was intended once and for all to be denied.

The Convention against Torture also prohibits states from returning a person to a country where there are substantial grounds for believing that he or she would be subject to torture (art. 3). The Convention continues: 'For the purpose of determining whether there are such grounds, the competent authorities shall take into account all relevant considerations including, where applicable, the existence in the State concerned of a consistent pattern of gross, flagrant or mass violations of human rights.' It is through this state obligation not to send individuals to countries where there is a substantial risk that they will be tortured that the relationship between security, migration and torture is structured.

An individual can only be expelled from a state if he or she is not a national of that state.[3] Thus, individuals to whom the prohibition on return to torture applies are by definition foreigners (the prohibition on torture itself protects both the citizen and the foreigner). States expel migrants (and other foreigners) either on account of the irregularity of their stay on the territory or because they are a security risk even though their stay is regular. In the second case, the most common reason for expelling the foreigner is on account of his or her criminal activity (see chapter 2). However, cases do arise, and increasingly so, where the state argues that the expulsion of the individual is necessary for reasons of national security. If the state to which the individual is to be expelled is one where there is a substantial risk that he or she will suffer torture, the Convention against Torture comes into play. The expelling state cannot take the action without breaching its international obligation not to return a person to torture.

The prohibition on torture is also found in the UN's International Covenant on Civil and Political Rights 1966 (ICCPR) ('No one shall be subjected to torture or to cruel, inhuman or degrading treatment or punishment. In particular, no one shall be subjected without his free consent to medical or scientific experimentation': art. 7). Again there is no possible exception or derogation from this absolute prohibition. Here the prohibition includes inhuman and degrading treatment as well as torture, though no more detail is provided. The ICCPR includes a wide range of civil and political rights, forming one of the two early pillars of the International Bill of Human Rights (see chapter 2). By April 2008 there were 161 parties to the ICCPR. The dispute resolution mechanism of the ICCPR is the Human Rights Committee, which, like the Committee against Torture, may receive complaints from individuals who claim a state has breached its obligation under the ICCPR. As with the Committee against Torture, states are only bound to accept the Human Rights Committee's power to examine an individual case if they have ratified the optional Protocol. In April 2008 there were 111 parties to the optional Protocol – that is to say, countries which accept the jurisdiction of the Human Rights Committee to receive complaints regarding the application of the ICCPR.

The international arena – torture and the prohibition on return to torture

The relationship between the international human rights prohibition on torture (Sands 2008) and migration has developed in two security-related fields, both of which have substantial impacts on international relations. The first scenario is where an individual seeks international protection against his or her return to the country of origin because he or she is perceived as a security threat in the country of origin and claims that the country of origin will torture him or her on account of this. In respect of this category, I will look at two decisions of the Committee against Torture (CAT Committee), *Tedourski* v. *France* (Communication No. 300/2006 decided on 11 May 2007) and *Pelit* v. *Azerbaijan* (Communication No. 281/2005 decided on 29 May 2007).

The second category has developed more recently but is equally challenging to the international community. Here the host state seeks to expel an individual on the grounds that he or she is a threat not just to the national security of the host state but also to a close ally of the host state. In this case, the individuals had no link of citizenship or previous residence on the territory of the ally state. There was no issue of the individuals being sent to the territory of the ally. The ally state's security claim was that its security required that the foreigner be sent from the territory where he had sought protection to the territory of his nationality, where he feared torture. The host state's response to the individual's fear of torture in his or her home state was to obtain diplomatic assurances from the state of origin that it would not torture the individual, if he or she were sent back. The state where the individual sought protection relied on international relations undertakings by another state to deal with the individual whom the host state considered a threat to national security. The ally state, which provided material support for the expulsion, made no undertaking regarding the security of the individual. I will examine this situation as it has arisen in the CAT Committee case *Agiza* v. *Sweden* (Communication No. 233/2003 decided on 20 May 2005) and UN Human Rights Committee case *Alzery* v. *Sweden* (Communication No. 1416/2005 decided on 10 November 2006).

I will look at the two categories from the perspective of the individual who claims that his or her expulsion will result in torture. I have chosen judicial and quasi-judicial determinations to examine the issue as the question only arises before the courts, and indeed the international courts, when the conflict between the state and the individual has become intractable. Thus, in the determinations, each party puts forward the best arguments for its actions. The decisions provide an insight into how the issue of the risk of torture is developed and the international relations consequences of the individual's fear of torture.

Two other considerations are important. First, as regards the determinations of the UN Committees, here the struggle between the individual and the state has escaped the scope of national sovereignty, in so far as the final decision on whether the return of the individual to a country amounts to return to torture is no longer within the power of the national courts to determine. It has become an issue of international judicial decision. Thus, even through its judicial mechanisms, the state no longer controls the outcome of the conflict. Second, as regards the state's claim that expulsion is necessary in the interests of national security, the underlying presumption is that moving an individual to the other side of an international border will increase security within the territory. This argument has a number of flaws – not least the point that, when an individual is outside the territory, if he or she is free to carry on his or her activities against the state, there will be no institutions of the state which can follow and intervene to ensure the protection of national security. In these days of the internet and other mechanisms of globalization, it may be somewhat questionable whether national security is best served by moving individuals beyond the reach of national security agencies.

Prohibiting return to torture on national security grounds

Mr Tebourski was a dual French-Tunisian national. He had acquired French citizenship in 2000 on the basis of his marriage to a French national in 1995. In May 2005 he was convicted by the Paris Criminal Court of criminal conspiracy in connection with a terrorist enterprise. He was accused of having organized the departure of volunteer fighters for Pakistan and Afghanistan, including Abdessatar Dahmane who, together with others, assassinated Ahmed Shah Massoud, the leader of the Northern Alliance forces in Afghanistan. He was sentenced to six years' imprisonment, and on 19 July 2006 he was stripped of his French citizenship and served with an expulsion order. The grounds for the expulsion were 'imperative requirements of State security and public safety'.

Mr Tebourski applied for international protection in France but his application was rejected, not least on grounds of national security, and he was expelled before his appeal was heard. His reasons for fearing torture on return to Tunisia included the fact that terrorism cases involving Tunisian nationals provoke a strong state reaction. He presented documentation of examples where individuals who had been convicted of terrorism abroad had been severely tortured after being expelled from a third country to Tunisia. He further presented evidence that many persons accused of engaging in activities relating to terrorism were often tortured by the Tunisian authorities. The French Appeals Board rejected his claim to protection but found that

> the fact that, after his deportation to Tunisia, he remained at liberty but had been placed under close police surveillance without being arrested must be regarded as evidence of a desire on the part of the Tunisian authorities to disguise their true intentions towards him, particularly in view of the attention which this case has attracted in the international media.

Having failed to get redress in the French courts and having been expelled to Tunisia, Mr Tebourski brought a complaint to the UN Committee against Torture, claiming that France had acted in breach of its duty under art. 3 of the Convention by sending him back to a country where there was a substantial risk that he would suffer torture. Before the UN Committee against Torture, the French authorities justified their actions on the grounds that Mr Tebourski was a person who had shown himself to be highly dangerous to public order because of his subversive activities. It was because of this manifest danger that the French authorities had expelled him to Tunisia. Further, the French authorities argued that there was a demonstrable absence of risk in the event of his return to Tunisia.

Mr Tebourski disagreed. He stated that he was in grave danger of torture. Since his return, he stated,

> he frequently has to call his counsel from a public telephone box. Although he was not arrested upon or after his arrival in Tunisia, he is under constant surveillance (wiretapping and being followed). His personal belongings are still being withheld. He still has no Tunisian identity papers, in spite of his many attempts to procure some. He has learned from a friend of his brother who works for the police that an internal message was sent out to all Tunisian police stations and officers when he arrived in Tunisia, giving instructions that he should not be arrested under any pretext in the weeks that followed, probably because of the media attention surrounding the case.

He feared that, as soon as European media attention moved on, he would be tortured.

The UN Committee stated that the prohibition on return to torture in art. 3 is absolute:

> the purpose of the Convention in article 3 is to prevent a person from being exposed to the *risk* of torture through refoulement, expulsion or extradition 'to another State where there are substantial grounds for believing that he would be in danger of being subjected to torture',

> *regardless of the character of the person, in particular the danger he poses to society* [emphasis added].

Effectively the UN Committee held that there is no national security exception to the absolute prohibition on sending a person to a country where there is a serious risk that he or she will suffer torture. The UN Committee continued:

> once this person alludes to a risk of torture under the conditions laid down in article 3, the State party can no longer cite domestic concerns as grounds for failing in its obligation under the Convention to guarantee protection to anyone in its jurisdiction who fears that he is in serious danger of being tortured if he is returned to another country.

Thus the UN Committee found France in breach of art. 3 by expelling Mr Tebourski to Tunisia. It ordered France to make reparations.

The second decision of the UN Committee relates to Ms Pelit, a Turkish national. Between 1993 and 1996 she was detained in Turkey on charges of subversive activity and terrorism related to the PKK (Communist Party of Turkey). She was eventually released when the Istanbul State Security Court acquitted her on the grounds of insufficient evidence. She fled to Germany in 1998 where she was recognized as a refugee. She began working as a journalist for a pro-Kurdish news agency and went to northern Iraq to cover the war. While she was there her travel documents were stolen during an attack on the news agency in Mosul, so she travelled to Azerbaijan on 2 November 2004 to contact the German authorities to obtain new documents. She was arrested by the Azeri authorities for illegal entry. On 2 December 2004, she was sentenced in absentia to ten years' imprisonment by a court in Istanbul, Turkey, for subversive activities for the PKK, and an extradition request was issued to the Azeri authorities on 6 December 2004 to send her to Turkey to serve her sentence. The Azeri authorities accepted the extradition request and detained her, pending sending her back. She appealed (unsuccessfully) and eventually made a complaint to the UN Committee against Torture.

Ms Pelit argued that, if sent to Turkey, she would be tortured and forced to confess guilt; she would be taken into custody by the Department for the Fight against Terrorism as had happened to other Turkish nationals involved with the PKK whom the Azeri authorities had expelled to Turkey. The Azeri authorities rejected Ms Pelit's claim, stating that there was no real, foreseeable and personal risk that she would be tortured. Further, they confirmed they had received diplomatic assurances from Turkey that, if extradited, Ms Pelit would not face any criminal prosecution for a crime committed prior to her transfer other than the offence for which she was being extradited. The timing of the various events is not particularly convincing. Ms Pelit had been out of Turkey since 1998 yet a Turkish court only convicted her in absentia a month after she had arrived in Azerbaijan, at which point the Azeri authorities agreed to extradite her to Turkey. The whiff of collusion is strong in the facts of the case.

The UN Committee against Torture was in no doubt that the extradition of Ms Pelit to Turkey was a breach of art. 3. In finding so, it relied on the facts that she had been recognized as a refugee in Germany and that, under the UNHCR Executive Committee's interpretation of the UN Convention on the Status of Refugees 1951 (see previous chapter), refugee status determination should be recognized by other parties. Ms Pelit's past experiences, in the view of the Committee, indicated the strength of her claim to a real risk of torture in Turkey. It was not satisfied with the way in which the Azeri authorities had dealt with the diplomatic assurances given by the Turkish authorities. I will return to this question of diplomatic assurances shortly.

The relationship of the security of the state with the security of the individual disrupts the status quo of inter-state relations. Where the individual is considered a security risk by the state in which he or she is present, his or her expulsion to the state of nationality (origin) may be hindered by the state's obligations in international human rights law. The state's compliance with its international obligations may further disrupt its relationship with a foreign state. The temptation of the state to act in disregard of its international obligations is high – as with both France and Azerbaijan in the two cases considered above. However, the cost in terms of legitimacy of a negative decision of the UN Committee against Torture should not be underestimated either. The choice of the state to accept the jurisdiction of the Committee was made on the basis that the state considered that its actions should be the subject of supranational judicial scrutiny. The objectives of national security in themselves are insufficient, according to the international jurisdiction, to justify returning a person to a country where there is a real risk that he or she will suffer torture.

Return and diplomatic assurances

Where a state seeks to return an individual to the country of origin – expulsion or extradition – the question of the treatment that country will apply is central. As discussed above, such a forced return will only be in accordance with the state's international human rights obligations if there is no substantial risk that the individual will be tortured or subjected to inhuman or degrading treatment in the country of origin. The argument of national security can never trump the duty of states to protect individuals from torture. Thus, states which are concerned about their human rights obligations have increasingly turned to another possibility available in international relations – to seek diplomatic assurances from the receiving state that it will not torture the individual. These assurances create problems of their own: first, states may be offended at being requested to provide such an assurance or consider it an insult to their sovereignty; second, the reliability of such assurances is a matter of substantial concern, an aspect which has been much considered, in particular by non-governmental organizations (Jones 2006).

Whose security? Whose decision?

How are the international relations of the state disturbed by the individual and his or her rights in international law? At issue here is the question: whose collective security is the justification for the deprivation of the human being's individual security. To examine this issue, I will take the cases of Mr Agiza and Mr Alzery, whose treatment by the Swedish authorities became the focus of profound questions about the nature of security and sovereignty, for institutions both within Sweden – here I will examine the report of the Swedish Parliamentary Ombudsman – and beyond Sweden – here I will look at the determinations of the UN Committee against Torture in May 2005 in respect of the complaint of Mr Agiza, and those of the UN Human Rights Committee in November 2006 regarding Mr Alzery. These men are two of the many unexpected victims of 11 September 2001 (Guild 2003).

Mr Agiza is an Egyptian national born in 1962. Throughout the 1980s he alleged that he was subject to persecution and torture in Egypt on account of his activities at university in the Islamic movement. He fled Egypt in early 1991, first to Saudi Arabia, then Pakistan and, finally, after a failed attempt to get to Europe, Iran. In 1998, he was convicted in absentia in Egypt of terrorist activity against the state in a collective trial before the Superior Court Martial, along with over 100 other accused. As relations between Iran and Egypt improved in 2000, Agiza, together with his family, managed to get to Sweden where they applied for asylum.[4]

Mr Alzery, also an Egyptian national, was a chemistry and physics teacher who was active in an organization involved in Islamic opposition to the Egyptian government. His involvement included, according to the

UN Human Rights Committee, distributing flyers, participating in meetings and lectures, and reading the Koran to children in his village.[5] After harassment, then arrest, by the Egyptian authorities, he decided to leave in 1991. First he fled Egypt for Saudi Arabia, whence he departed for Syria in 1994. In 1999 he fled Syria after a number of Egyptians were extradited back to Egypt. Travelling on a false Danish passport, he arrived in Sweden in August 1999 where he applied for asylum (in his own name and identity). His claim was based on the substantial risk that he would suffer torture if returned to Egypt (the only country where he has a right of entry). At this point the cases of the two men converge.

The men's asylum applications took over a year to be considered. The Swedish Security Police advised the Swedish migration authorities that Agiza held a leading position in a terrorist organization and had responsibility for actions of the organization. Agiza denied the allegations, noting that one of the organizations the Security Police suggested was a terrorist organization to which he belonged was, in fact, an Arab-language publication. The claims to protection of both Agiza and his wife were rejected. According to the UN Human Rights Committee, the Swedish Security Police also submitted a report to the migration board on Mr Alzery, recommending that his application be rejected on security grounds.

The Swedish government entered into discussions with their Egyptian counterparts in early December 2001 to explore whether the men could be returned to Egypt without violating Sweden's international obligations (including the obligation not to return a person to a country where there is a substantial risk that he will suffer persecution torture, inhuman or degrading treatment or punishment by the Egyptian authorities). The Egyptian authorities responded: 'We herewith assert our full understanding to all items of this memoire, concerning the way of treatment upon repatriate from your government, with full respect to their personal and human rights. This will be done according to what the Egyptian constitution and law stipulates.'

The two men's asylum applications were rejected on 18 December 2001. According to the Human Rights Committee's review of the facts, the Swedish authorities assessed the risk of persecution, sentence of death, torture or severe ill treatment if they were returned to Egypt (all of which would constitute an absolute bar on Sweden's expulsion of the men). The authorities decided, however, that the assurances provided by the Egyptian authorities were sufficient to comply with Sweden's non-refoulement obligation. On the same day as the refusal of their asylum applications, they were arrested by Swedish Security Police and escorted to Bromma airport.

There they were handed over to ten foreign agents in civilian clothes and hoods. The Swedish Ombudsman's investigation subsequently disclosed that the ten men were US and Egyptian security agents.[6] Later that day they were expelled to Egypt on the plane which had brought the foreign agents to Sweden.

The treatment of the two men recorded in the review of the complaint by the Human Rights Committee (and repeated in the record of the UN Committee against Torture),[7] while they were still at the airport in Sweden, is remarkable:

> The author states that the hooded agents forced him into a small locker room where they exposed him to what was termed 'security search', although Swedish police had already carried out a less intrusive search. The hooded agents slit the author's clothes with a pair of scissors and examined each piece of cloth before placing it in a plastic bag. Another agent checked his hair, mouth and lips, while a third agent took photographs, according to Swedish officers who witnessed the searches. When his clothes were cut off his body, he was handcuffed and chained to his feet. He was then drugged per rectum with some form of tranquilliser and placed in diapers. He was then dressed in overalls and escorted to the plane, blindfolded, hooded and barefoot. Two representatives from the Embassy of the United States of America were also present during the apprehension and treatment of the applicant.[8]

It is worth remembering that in December it is very cold in Sweden.

Mr Agiza's wife went into hiding in Sweden. In January 2002 the Swedish Ambassador to Egypt met with Mr Agiza who was in prison but noted nothing untoward about his appearance. On the same day Mr Agiza's parents were allowed to see him for the first time. They alleged that he was in a shocking state, clearly having been the object of torture which he confirmed to them.[9] Various other people visited Mr Agiza in prison, including a journalist; he had visits regularly from his parents and once again from the Swedish Ambassador over the next twelve months. The Swedish Ambassador similarly met with Mr Alzery, though not in private, and when Mr Alzery complained of ill treatment in front of both the Ambassador and the Egyptian warden, the latter took notes. When the Ambassador asked for further information about the treatment of Mr Alzery, the Egyptian authorities rejected the claims, saying this was what could be expected of 'terrorists'. Mr Alzery was subsequently transferred to another prison where he was subject to very serious torture.[10]

The cases of the two men raise two distinct problems – first, did Sweden act in conformity with its international obligations in human rights law to protect the men from torture, inhuman or degrading treatment? Under this heading, two issues arise – their treatment in Sweden itself and, secondly, their treatment in Egypt. In respect of torture in Egypt, the issue was whether Sweden could reasonably rely on the assurances provided by the Egyptian authorities that they would not torture the men. Both these issues relate to the claims of collective security of Sweden, Egypt and the USA, and the degree of confidence their officials were willing to express in one another. The second problem is the sovereignty issue – to what extent was it legitimate or indeed lawful for the Swedish authorities to permit US and Egyptian agents to detain the two men and treat them in a degrading manner while still in Sweden? This second question is the subject of the Ombudsman's report which I will deal with below.

The allegations against Sweden arising from this case were expressed in two supranational venues: the UN Committee against Torture and the UN Human Rights Committee. First, the complaint of Mr Agiza was that Sweden had failed to comply with its duty to protect him from torture, including return to a country where there is a substantial risk he would be tortured, as required by art. 3 of the Convention against Torture. Mr Agiza's argument was that, in light of the information which the Swedish authorities had at the time they expelled him to Egypt, they should have known that he would be tortured, as indeed he was. His complaint was supported by international reports on the use of torture in Egypt and the high risk of torture for persons suspected of being Islamic fundamentalists. The Swedish authorities relied substantially on the diplomatic assurances which they had received from the Egyptian authorities before expelling him.

This complaint, made on 25 June 2003, was considered by the UN Committee against Torture, which published its decision on 24 May 2005. It found Sweden in breach of its duty to protect Mr Agiza from torture by sending him back to Egypt. It stated:

> The State party was also aware of the interest in the complainant [Mr Agiza] by the intelligence services of two other States: according to the facts submitted by the State party to the Committee, the first foreign State offered through its intelligence service an aircraft to transport the complainant to the second State, Egypt, where to the State party's knowledge, he had been sentenced in absentia and was wanted for alleged involvement in terrorist activities. In the Committee's view, the natural conclusion from these combined elements, that is, that the complainant was at a real risk of torture in Egypt in the event of expulsion, was confirmed when immediately preceding expulsion, the complainant

> was subject on the State party's territory to treatment in breach of, at least article 16 of the Convention[11] by foreign agents but with the acquiescence of the State party's police. It follows that the State party's expulsion of the complainant was in breach of article 3 of the Convention. The procurement of diplomatic assurances, which, moreover, provided no mechanism for their enforcement, did not suffice to protect against this manifest risk.[12]

Thus the international dispute resolution mechanism responsible for the Convention against Torture made three key findings:

- the evident interest in Mr Agiza (and possible collusion) of two foreign states' security services, one of which having a record of consistent and widespread use of torture against detainees, should have put the Swedish authorities on notice that sending Mr Agiza to one of them, Egypt, would place him at unacceptable risk of torture;
- the treatment of Mr Agiza in Sweden by the US and Egyptian agents constituted at least inhuman and degrading treatment if not torture and thus showed the Swedish authorities that he was at risk of further torture if removed to Egypt;
- the Egyptian diplomatic assurances were valueless, not least because there was no mechanism to protect Mr Agiza from their breach.

The second decision of an international complaint body was by the UN Human Rights Committee which considered a complaint made by Mr Alzery on 29 June 2005. It published its decision on 10 November 2006. The Committee considered the same facts as the Committee against Torture and came to very similar conclusions. Its key findings were:

- Sweden accepted, by its efforts to obtain diplomatic assurances from the Egyptian authorities, the fact that there was a real risk that Mr Alzery would be subject to torture or inhuman or degrading treatment if returned there;
- the diplomatic assurances given were inadequate not least as there was no mechanism for monitoring or enforcement and thus the expulsion was contrary to article 7 ICCPR;
- the acts of the US agents at the Swedish airport took place with the acquiescence of the Swedish authorities and therefore must be imputed to the Swedish authorities. The treatment which Mr Alzery suffered at the airport in Sweden (cutting off of his clothes, intimate body search, handcuffing, shackling, etc.) violated article 7 ICCPR not least as it was disproportionate to any law enforcement purpose.

The Committee made a number of other findings on breaches of the ICCPR (for instance, on the lack of a proper investigation of what happened on 18 December 2001 in Sweden) which are beyond the immediate scope of this chapter. However, one further finding of importance relates to the attempt by the state to frustrate any international supervision of its action. This took place in the form of the inaccurate information which the Swedish authorities provided to Mr Alzery's advisers regarding whether his asylum application had been rejected: the advisers were told that no decision had been taken, when the decision had already been made. As can be seen from the report of the Swedish Ombudsman, one of the reasons for this subterfuge appears to have been to make it impossible for the advisers to seek an injunction from one of the international courts to prevent Mr Alzery's expulsion from Sweden.[13] The Committee required two measures in respect of the breach: an effective remedy which includes compensation for Mr Alzery (in an amount unspecified); that Sweden take steps to ensure that there is no re-occurrence of such a breach. It welcomed the establishment of an independent immigration court with power to review expulsion decisions, including where a security aspect is present.

The interest of the UN bodies does not end with their two decisions. When Sweden was under examination as regards its compliance with the UN Convention against Torture in June 2008 under the general reporting requirements, the matter of Mr Agiza and Mr Alzery came back to haunt the Swedish authorities. *The UN CAT Consideration of Reports: Sweden*[14] regretted the lack of full implementation of the key elements of the two decisions and, in particular, the lack of an in-depth investigation and prosecution of those responsible.

The security claim of Sweden in respect of which the expulsion of the two men from Sweden became imperative is revealed as primarily based on cooperation with foreign states: the USA and, to some extent, Egypt. In order to help the collective security claims of these other countries, Sweden placed itself in the position of violating the individual security of two individuals, foreigners, on its territory. This violation took the form of permitting inhuman and degrading treatment of the men by foreign agents on Swedish soil (the treatment at the airport) and their expulsion to Egypt, a country where, as the Swedish authorities should have been aware, there was a risk that they would be subject to torture. The mechanism of state accountability to the international community has been through the UN's dispute resolution mechanisms where the two men took their claims.

The question in respect of whose security the two Egyptian men posed a threat was not only answered in the international context. The cooperation of states with one another for the purposes of achieving collective security objectives in the US-declared global war on terror led to the expulsion of the two Egyptians from Sweden. The condemnation of Sweden in UN fora, for its acquiescence and participation in privileging collective security claims which were never publicly justified in respect of the two men, was based on the rights of the individuals to personal safety. However, the question of security and the expulsion of the two men did not end there. The acts of parts of the Swedish state in the expulsion of the men led to an examination by other parts of the state regarding the impact of those acts on the security of the Swedish constitution. I will examine this next.

Whose security? Whose sovereignty?

The events surrounding the departure of Mr Agiza and Mr Alzery from Sweden for Egypt presented their own particular problems around the questions of sovereignty and security. Not only did they cause consternation in international venues but they also perturbed national settlements about the nature of Swedish sovereignty. These concerns found their clearest voice in the report of the Swedish Parliamentary Ombudsman on the matter.[15]

The facts regarding the case of the two men as revealed in the Ombudsman's report coincide with those found by the two UN bodies. However, as the remit of the Ombudsman's inquiry was different, further facts were revealed, which I will set out here before looking at the findings of the report. First, the Swedish Security Police had been investigating the two men since the spring of 2001, at the same time that the Swedish Migration Board was investigating their claims to asylum. In October 2001 the Swedish Security Police lodged objections to the two men's asylum applications. The Migration Board duly referred the applications to the Swedish government for a decision in November 2001. It appears that the Ministry of Foreign Affairs had the lead in this matter, while the Ministry of Justice appeared to be more and more marginalized as the events unfolded.

In the same month, the Security Police decided that expulsion could be required and began planning it. Although the advisers were told that a decision on the asylum claims would be made in January 2002, the Security Police file revealed that the Swedish government planned to take the decision on 13 December 2001, with expulsion following on 15 December. However, at a time unspecified, but well before any decision was taken, the Swedish Security Police received an offer from the American Central Intelligence Agency (CIA) of the use of a plane for the expulsion, with a guarantee that the plane could fly over Europe without having to touch down, thus avoiding the need to negotiate with any other state (though, according to the report, one official at least recalled some discussion that the problem of airspace would be resolved with US help, or help from 'colleagues in the West').

The timing changed again, this time with the Ministry of Foreign Affairs advising, on 5 December 2001, that a decision on the asylum applications would not be made until 20 December. However, there is a journal entry in the Security Police file of 14 December stating that the decision on the applications would be taken on 18 December and that a plane for their expulsion had been booked for 19 December. It is clear from the report that the decision, in the end, to use the CIA plane and to expel the men on 18 December was made at the highest levels in the Foreign Affairs Ministry and after substantial discussion and consultation with the Security Police and Migration Board.

The events of 18 December 2001 in Stockholm relating to Mr Agiza and Mr Alzery fall into two distinct periods. First, the two men were arrested quietly by Swedish police and without any use of force or resistance. They were notified that their asylum applications had been rejected, that they were about to be expelled to Egypt and that they were subject to a body search. They were then taken to the airport. At this point the second stage begins when the two men were handed over to the US agents. The CIA plane landed just before 9 p.m. and contained, in addition to its crew, a security team of seven or eight persons, including two Egyptian officials and a doctor. All were wearing hoods. Curiously, by this time there were no longer any senior Swedish Security Police officers present and, of those junior officers who were present, no one had been assigned operational command at the airport. None considered that he or she was ultimately responsible for the expulsion. Instead it was the US and Egyptian agents who carried out the cutting-off of clothing, intimate body searches, handcuffing and shackling, hooding and administration of sedatives anally (an act which none of the Swedish officers present accepted that they saw, each with a separate excuse for the lapse of attention or presence at that critical moment).

An individual reported the events of 18 December 2001 to the Swedish Public Prosecutor for consideration of whether any crime had been committed in connection with the enforcement of the expulsion order. The then Acting Director of Public Prosecution decided there were no grounds for assuming that any offence subject to public prosecution had been committed.

Following a television documentary on the events of 18 December, which was broadcast on 25 May 2004, the Swedish Ombudsman opened an inquiry on his own initiative. The central issue was two-fold: the actions of the Swedish Security Police and the use of public authority by foreign officials on Swedish territory. Sovereignty and its exercise is the stake in the competing claims of security which revolve around the expulsion of the Egyptians. The UN Human Rights Committee, as noted above, found that Sweden is responsible in international human rights law for the acts which take place on its territory and with which it has acquiesced. The Ombudsman examined the nature of Swedish sovereignty and to what extent the events of 18 December 2001 were compatible with it.

The Swedish constitution is set out in the Instrument of Government. It is the expression of Swedish sovereignty and sets out in the form of law what that sovereignty means and how it must be exercised. The Swedish constitution, like those of other liberal democracies, is founded on the assumption that judicial and administrative measures which take place on the territory are the concern of the Swedish authorities. According to the Ombudsman, only Swedish police officers are empowered to use force or coercive measures, including against individuals, or to exercise their authority in any other form on Swedish territory. There is no exception in respect of expulsion. He then examined Swedish criminal law to determine the legality of the events of 18 December and their consistency with the Swedish constitution. National criminal law controls on the use of body searches are the first target: as one of the most coercive measures permitted to the state, they can only be carried out by state actors – in this case, the police. While the Ombudsman recognized the importance of contact between Swedish and foreign security agencies, where this cooperation moved beyond the exchange of information to permitting foreign police officers or security agents to take an active part in police operations and to exercise public authority in Sweden a completely different, and unacceptable, state of affairs had been reached.

Among the key reasons why the action of foreign security agents in Sweden was contrary to Swedish sovereignty, according to the Ombudsman, is that because the national rules on the conduct of the police, and on liability for misuse of office in the event of transgression by the police, only apply to national police. Thus, the individual who is the object of these protections no longer is able to access them if the principle of sovereignty is not respected. He stated: 'In my opinion, it would be unacceptable to have a system which enabled foreign officials to exercise public authority in Sweden without being subject to the liability laid down in the Criminal Code for misuse of office.'

The Swedish constitution, in common with those of other liberal democracies, does not limit protection against unlawful police action to citizens. It applies to all persons who encounter unlawful action. As the Ombudsman states, 'it is self evident that in a democratic state, subject to the rule of law, police officers must treat all those who become the object of police actions in a humane and dignified manner. This means that nobody may be subject to degrading or humiliating treatment in the course of a police operation.' He found that the body searches and hooding constitute such treatment. Further (and perhaps in explanation of the failure of any of the Swedish officers to observe the administration of tranquillizers to the two men), he noted that coercive medication is one of the kinds of coercive physical measures specifically prohibited in the constitution and thus requires the support of law to be permitted.

The Ombudsman held the mirror of Swedish sovereignty as expressed in its constitution, to the actions taken by the Swedish authorities to permit their allies to carry out their security objectives in Sweden, and found that the principle of sovereignty itself had been compromised. The interests of Swedish sovereign security are offended by acts carried out in the name of collective security, including that of Sweden, the USA and Egypt, and allowed to take place on Swedish territory. As a result of concern regarding the events of 18 December 2001, the Swedish Security Police have been re-organized to enable better strategic planning and to enhance, substantially, direction and monitoring of its operations. Thus, one of the costs of the subordination of Swedish security to that of its allies has been the reining-in of the Swedish agency held most responsible for the event, and its subjection to greater democratic scrutiny.

Conclusions

In this chapter I have examined a number of competing security claims by individuals and states, and the ways in which these claims are challenged within the international state system and within states. The examples examined have been the international prohibition on torture, the claims of individuals to the right to protection against torture, and the claims of states to the right to expel foreigners whom they consider to be a threat to collective security, even where the state to which the individual will be expelled is one where there is a real risk of torture. The claim of the individual to security against return to torture is expressed against the claim of the state that collective security justifies the individual's expulsion. The international courts, including the Committee against Torture and the

Human Rights Committee, have expressly rejected the collective security argument as a justification, in any circumstances, for the expulsion of a person to a country where there is a risk of torture. There is no balancing of the individual and collective security where the risk of torture is at stake. The individual's protection is always paramount.

In the cases discussed, France first excluded the individual from its political community by depriving him of his French nationality, then expelled him to Tunisia on the basis of a collective security claim, notwithstanding his claim of a substantial risk of torture there. In the second case, Azerbaijan expelled a Turkish national to her home country, notwithstanding her claim to protection. The argument of the Azeri authorities was based on the claim for collective security of its neighbour, Turkey, against the risk the woman constituted as a convicted PKK supporter. The third case – the expulsion of the Egyptians from Sweden – provides the clearest example of competing security claims. Here, the collective security claim of a foreign state, the USA, becomes the grounds on which its ally, Sweden, permits foreign security agents to act on its territory to effect the expulsion of individuals who have claimed a right to protection against expulsion on the basis of the risk of torture in Egypt. This ceding of sovereignty, not only in the failure to protect the men from expulsion to torture but also as regards the Swedish territory, resulted in two decisions of UN dispute resolution bodies condemning Sweden for its failure to protect the human rights of the Egyptians, and also its condemnation within the state by the Ombudsman, for failure to protect Sweden's sovereignty.

In this chapter I have examined state violence against the individual, specifically in the form of the handing over of an individual to a state where there is a substantial risk that the authorities will torture him or her. The way in which the interests of states are constructed around international relations so as to privilege some coercive actors within the state to the detriment of the individual is not without cost. Both within the state and in supranational institutions, the aggrieved individual, even though he or she is a foreigner in a very weak position in relation to the state, is able to resist and to mobilize support through mechanisms of rule of law, both national and international, which can have the effect of diminishing the support upon which certain political actors depend for the legitimacy of their actions against migrants.

6

Migration and data: documenting the non-national

In the previous two chapters I focused on the individual foreigner and the risk which state violence constitutes for him or her. My premise has been that individuals are not simply passive victims of state violence, either in their state of origin or in the state where they seek protection. They struggle against the state violence, whether that is in the form of inhuman and degrading treatment on the territory of liberal democracies or their expulsion to countries where there is a substantial risk they will be tortured. In the process of those struggles, political and legal actors both within the state and in supranational institutions have become engaged in the migrant's resistance. The legitimacy of the state actors seeking to exercise coercion on the migrant is undermined.

In this chapter I will examine the insecurity continuum as the mechanism by which political entrepreneurs justify the need to have power over the foreigner through immediately available and accessible knowledge about him or her, through databases and technological means. Here it is the construction of the foreigner as a potential security threat greater than the citizen, because of the state's lack of information about him or her, which is central. The assignment of ignorance about the personal details of an individual as an important contributing factor to state insecurity is the first step which must be made. Only once this political move has been successfully achieved can political actors move to the next step: remedying the source of insecurity by collecting, storing, manipulating, exchanging and mining massive amounts of personal data about individual foreigners. The political justification of the foreigner as a 'real' potential security threat is central to the very substantial interference with the human right of privacy which then takes place as regards the foreigner. First I will examine the credibility of the claim that foreigners are a security threat, on the basis of publicly available statistics on political violence and criminality. Then I will look at the databases of information about individual foreigners which have been created in Europe and the USA (in relation to Europe).

State authorities have a strong interest in knowing who is on their territory. This interest is expressed in the claim to a sovereign right to control borders and the movement of persons across those borders (Salter 2003; Torpey 2000). The justifications for controlling frontiers, and in particular the movement of non-nationals across them, are couched in the language of security in a variety of ways, including the following:

- Military security: protection of the state against invasion by a foreign army; the infiltrating fifth column present on the territory is the object of concern here. The state must have knowledge of who is on the territory in order to be able to identify which individuals are likely to be spies, or sympathizers with the enemy. The state institutional actors as regards this intelligence are usually related to the armed forces and subject to substantial restrictions on the extent of activities which they are entitled to undertake within the state itself (Born & Caparini 2007; Guittet 2008);
- National security: protection of the state against foreigners who seek to harm national interests (for instance those seeking to commit acts of political violence); here the problem of political violence – terrorism – raises problems regarding its association with foreigners. The image of the home-grown terrorist presents serious problems for social cohesion (Bonelli 2008). The institutional actors here are usually related to the police;
- Public security: protection of the state against foreigners who commit crimes. This security concern is the heartland of policing – the differentiation of public security from national security is often particularly delicate (Edwards & Bloomer 2008). The possibility of expelling foreigners, in addition to any sentence of imprisonment or fine, creates different options in this regard (see chapter 3);
- Identity security: protecting the integrity of the people against influences brought about by the presence of foreigners on the territory of the state. This is a highly problematic category as it is based on characteristics of inclusion and exclusion which are highly suspect. Race, ethnicity, religion and membership of a social group (e.g. homosexuals) are all standard targets of claims made by political actors around identity security of states, although they are often couched in euphemism (Madood 2007). The institutions around identity security are multiple, starting with state schools. In respect of migrants, the creation of integration tests which they must pass at various stages of residence before obtaining security of residence through a permanent permit has proven a particularly popular mechanism of policing identity security in Denmark, France, Germany, the Netherlands and the UK (Carrera 2008).

Interest in the relationship between security and foreigners has intensified in the post-11 September 2001 period, not least as the USA created a new Department of Homeland Security which placed significant emphasis on the difference between foreigners and citizens as sources of threat to the state (Kanstroom 2007). The idea of the foreigner as a key source of insecurity has been rapidly incorporated into, or intensified in, policies in many liberal democracies, thus justifying ever more draconian measures in terms of surveillance and expulsion of foreigners from the state. In this chapter I will examine how this concern about security finds expression in relation to the identity of foreigners, and how it is preserved and documented.

The purpose of this chapter is to test the accuracy of a series of claims made by political actors in liberal democracies, particularly in Europe, about the nexus of migration and security, against the data control mechanism established around foreigners. While the claims about security risks – in particular around terrorist threats – and the need to 'de-radicalize' immigrant communities and give more powers to police are frequently expressed, not just by political actors but also in serious academic circles (Coolsaet 2008), the statistical information available about the relationship of political violence with migrants receives little attention. This is surprising as the sources of the statistical information are often the same political actors whose credibility regarding the seriousness of threats is undermined by it. The political calls for more detailed information about migrants and foreigners, the establishment of ever more powerful and complete databases, full of the personal details of individual migrants and foreigners, with wide access for all coercive institutions, are based on security claims. The security of the state requires information on foreigners, even before they leave their country of origin (i.e. when they apply for visas), including biometric data (fingerprints are taken and stored indefinitely for every individual applying for a visa to come to the UK and soon to the EU). The justification is that foreigners are a danger to security. So I will examine what we know about the danger which foreigners pose to the security of liberal democracies, taking the EU as the focus of my investigation.

Foreigners and terrorism

In the European context, the link between foreigners and political violence has been a matter of much uncertainty. Of the post-11 September 2001 terrorist attacks in Europe, two stand out as related to extreme Islamic movements – the bombing of the Madrid train station on 11 March 2004 and the London Underground bombings of 7 and 21 July 2005 (UK Intelligence and Security Committee, *Report into the London Terrorist Attacks on 7 July 2005*, Cm 6785, 11 May 2006). While the criminal convictions which followed the Madrid bombing have been primarily of foreigners, the London bombings were the work, primarily, of British citizens. Nonetheless, the image of extreme Islamic violence, somewhat removed from the category of political violence but not subsumed completely into the category of political religious violence, remains tied to the foreigner in the popular imagination (Guild & Baldaccini 2006).

The European Union's police agency, EUROPOL, is responsible for producing annual reports on EU political violence. The reports, which have been published since 2007 – the first was entitled *Report on Situation and Trend TE-SAT*[1] – classify the European political violence threat into four categories, defined by EUROPOL as follows:

- Islamist terrorism:[2] groups motivated by an extreme interpretation of Islam, including violence as a duty or sacramental act;
- ethno-nationalist and separatist terrorism: groups which seek international recognition and political self-determination, often motivated by nationalism, ethnicity and religion;
- left-wing and anarchist terrorism: groups which seek to change the entire political, social and economic system to an extreme left-wing model, or revolutionary, anti-capitalist and anti-authoritarian violence;
- right-wing terrorism: groups which seek to change the entire political, social and economic system to an extreme right-wing model (often traceable back to National Socialism).

The 2008 report adds a new category – single issue terrorism: 'violence committed with the desire to change a specific policy or practice within a target society. The term is generally used to describe animal rights and environmental terrorist groups.'

The underlying assumption of the report is that political violence (which is described as terrorism) is a tactic or a method for attaining political goals.[3] The 2006 report covers the preceding 12-month period as well as the period October–December 2005 for twenty-five European countries (all EU states, with the exclusion of Bulgaria and Romania which only joined the EU on 1 January 2007), though the amount and quality of data varies substantially from Member State to Member State. In the 2008 report, the period covered was the year 2007.

The data which were collected for the report were based on Member States' differing definitions of terrorism offences, which must be borne in mind when seeking to make sense of the statistics. Two types of offences of political violence are recognized: international, where there is an international or transnational character to the activity, and domestic political violence, where the activity is confined to the borders of one state. The 2006 data reveal 549 attacks, 128 acts of political violence, 810 arrested suspects and 303 trials in the EU. In 2007, there were 583 attacks (defined as 'failed', 'foiled' or 'successful'). The vast majority were arson, and only two persons were killed, both in Basque separatist attacks. There were 1,044 people arrested, the largest increases taking place in Spain and the UK. There were 418 people who stood trial in 143 criminal proceedings on charges relating to political violence.

In 2006, only eleven of twenty-five Member States were the target of attacks related to political violence. By far the largest number of attacks was carried out in France – 294, of which 283 were separatist-related and 11 were unspecified. The second-largest number of attacks took place in Spain – 145 – of which 136 were separatist-related, 8 left-wing and 1 unspecified. After those two outstanding examples comes Greece with 25 attacks, all left-wing. Germany is next in the list with 13 attacks, including 1 attempted extreme Islamic (the only one of its kind in 2006 across Europe), followed by 12 left-wing attacks. In total, there were 1 extreme Islamic attack, 424 separatist attacks, 55 left-wing attacks, 1 right-wing attack (in Poland) and 17 unspecified attacks. The unspecified attacks took place in countries which are already listed; only 2 unspecified attacks took place in countries which were not already centres for attacks of a specified nature, those 2 being in Austria and Belgium.

In 2007, only nine Member States were targeted. The largest number of attacks took place in Spain – 279, of which all but 7 were separatist – followed by France – with 253, where all but 14 were separatist. The remaining 14 in France and 7 in Spain were not specified. Germany comes next on the list with 20 attacks, of which 15 were separatist, 4 left-wing and 1 'Islamist'. The UK also notified that it had 2 'Islamist' attacks, and Denmark had 1. The only notified right-wing attack took place in Portugal in 2007, which also had the only single issue attack. Greece, which was third on the list in 2006, had only 2 attacks in 2007, both left-wing. In total, in 2007, there were 4 'Islamist' attacks (no casualties), 532 separatist attacks resulting in two casualties, 21 left-wing attacks, 1 each of right-wing and single issue attacks and 24 unspecified attacks.

Quite a different picture emerges when the figures on arrests of individuals for offences of political violence are considered for 2006 in fourteen Member States.[4] Here there were a total of 706 arrests, of which 257 related to extreme Islamic political violence. By far the largest number of such arrests took place in France (139) followed by Spain (51), then Germany with 11. As regards separatist violence, again France arrested the largest number of persons (188), followed by Spain (28), then Germany and Ireland tied at 4. For left-wing violence, Italy tops the list with 25 arrests, followed by France with 15, and 6 in Spain. Finally, right-wing violence resulted in only 15 arrests over the period, of which 12 took place in Belgium and the other 3 in Poland. Of the persons arrested, 32 per cent were suspected of preparation of or involvement in a politically motivated attack, while 41 per cent were suspected of being members of an organization promoting political violence. However, of this second group, only half of them were linked to a specific organization and only five of these organizations were on the EU list of 'terrorist' organizations, according to the report (regarding the lists, see Guild 2008). This raises questions about the effectiveness of the list of proscribed terrorist organizations in the management of political violence.

The figures of 2007 show a different trend. There were 1,044 arrests, of which 548 were separatist-related, 201 'Islamist', 48 left-wing and 44 right-wing. By far the largest number of people arrested were in France (409), followed by Spain (261), then the UK with 203 (the UK figures are not broken down by category of political violence). Once again, Italy topped the list for arrests on the basis of left-wing violence (31), followed by Spain (17). As regards right-wing violence, 31 people were arrested in Portugal and 10 in the Netherlands. In 2007, the numbers of people arrested for separatist offences increased seven-fold in Spain, which accounts for most of the increase in the number of persons arrested. In France, the number of arrests increased by 68 per cent. As regards the 'Islamist' category, there was a 35 per cent decrease in arrests in France alone, which accounts for the main drop generally. There was a 30 per cent increase in arrests in the UK and, although no breakdown is given by category, the authorities indicate that the vast majority are in the 'Islamist' category. Of those arrested in relation with this category, 45 per cent were charged with membership of a proscribed organization.

In 2006, just under half of the persons arrested were citizens of the Union – this means nationals of at least one Member State, though the report does not clarify whether these persons were arrested in their state of nationality or in another Member State. Further, this means that just over half the persons arrested in respect of terrorism offences were foreigners – persons from outside the EU. As regards gender, among women arrested, 71 per cent were EU nationals and 16 per cent non-EU (the nationality of the rest was unknown). For men, 51 per cent were EU nationals, 35 per cent non-EU nationals, and 17 per cent of unknown nationality. In 2007, the vast majority of suspects were EU citizens: 69 per cent – most having the citizenship of the country in which they were arrested; 22 per cent were not EU nationals and the nationality of the remaining 9 per cent was unknown. Women accounted for 10 per cent of suspects arrested.

Moving then to trial and conviction, 303 persons stood trial for offences related to political violence in 2005 and 2006, though the relationship between when the crime was committed and the date of the trial is not specified. Over that extended period, 205 persons stood trial in Spain, 24 persons in Belgium, 21 each in France and the Netherlands and 16 in Germany. The UK accounts for the final 4 persons who stood trial over that period. So, while by far the largest number of arrests in respect of terrorism took place in France (342) and over the shorter twelve-month period, Spain topped the list on the number of persons brought to trial. As regards the outcomes of trials, 257 persons were convicted and 46 acquitted, the later mainly in Spain (33 acquittals), Belgium and the Netherlands (both with 6). There is substantial variation among the Member States in respect of sentences, which is the result of the very different types of charges which were brought against individuals. For instance in Spain 33 convictions for murder or collateral fatalities were published, resulting in a seventeen-year average detention period there, while the average in Italy was three years.

In 2007, 418 persons stood trial on charges of political violence in a total of 143 proceedings. Among these, 34 were women. The largest number stood trial in Spain (231), followed by France (54), then Italy with 47. Of the trials, 54 per cent were related to separatism and 38 per cent to 'Islamist' political violence. There were a total of 449 verdicts – though in Spain 231 suspects received 255 verdicts. Of these, 331 were convictions which indicates an acquittal rate of 26 per cent (an increase from 15 per cent in 2006). The highest acquittal rates were in trials of persons accused of 'Islamist' political violence: 31 per cent overall. The largest number of persons convicted (181) was in Spain, with a 29 per cent acquittal rate. Least successful of the prosecutors were those in Denmark, who managed to obtain 5 convictions but 11 people were acquitted (69 per cent acquittal rate), followed by the Netherlands where there were 3 convictions and 5 acquittals (63 per cent acquittal rate). As regards verdicts, generally the convicted got longer sentences than in 2006. In Greece, the maximum, twenty-five years, was handed down, while in the Netherlands the convicted got a two-year sentence. In Spain, the average sentence has dropped since 2006. In the UK, 12 individual received forty-year sentences.

Trying to make sense of these statistics as regards the threat which foreigners pose to the EU in respect of political violence is complex. While more foreign nationals than EU citizens were arrested in 2006, the reverse is the case in 2007, and the report does not provide information on the nationality of those persons who are then brought to trial, let alone convicted. There is a very substantial difference between the numbers of persons arrested and those brought to trial for both 2006 and 2007 – so it may be unwise to extrapolate that the percentages of foreigners convicted are equivalent to those arrested. Also, as the vast majority of attacks involving political violence in the EU are separatist-inspired arising in only two Member States – France and Spain – the involvement of foreigners seems somewhat less likely than that of EU nationals; this is true for both 2006 and 2007. While the separatist organizations in Spain have a clear transnational element – covering the whole of the Basque country in both Spain and France – the main source of French separatist activity is in Corsica, where there is a less obvious cross-border dimension. Nonetheless, in its 2006 conclusions, the EUROPOL report states that 'terrorism in the EU is essentially a transnational phenomenon'. As EUROPOL depends on cross-border criminal activity to fulfil its mandate to investigate such transnational criminal activity, perhaps the emphasis on this aspect is understandable. In 2007, EUROPOL is somewhat more circumspect in its conclusions; it notes that the number of terrorist attacks in the EU is increasing, as is the number of persons arrested for political violence. Worryingly, EUROPOL notes that activities by the right-wing and extremists are increasing.

Foreigners and crime

The relationship between foreigners, i.e. non-EU nationals, and crime is a source of substantial anxiety in many EU countries. The image of the foreigner as a security threat because of his or her propensity to commit criminal offences is often seen in the press in many EU countries.[5] Of course, for crimes which only foreigners can commit – such as illegal entry into the state or remaining on the territory of the state after being notified to leave, both of which have been made criminal offences in a number of EU countries such as the UK – the conviction rate will reveal 100 per cent foreigners (Guild & Minderhoud 2006). However, in the more general crime statistics, the question of the role of foreigners in serious crime remains unclear. Nonetheless, for six serious crimes, the EU's statistical agency, EUROSTAT, now provides comparative figures across the EU.

The six crimes for which there are comparative figures are: homicide, violent crime, robbery, domestic burglary, theft of a motor vehicle and drug trafficking. For the crime of homicide, the statistics reveal the average rate per 100,000 population per year from 2004 to 2006, both by country and by capital city.[6] The countries and cities with the highest and lowest averages do not correspond to those where there are the highest and lowest numbers of foreigners. As a country, Lithuania tops the homicide table with 10.33 homicides per 100,000 population. This is followed by Estonia at 7.30 (there are no figures available for Latvia). The figure for Turkey is also included, which is 6.02, after which the figure drops dramatically to 2.66 for Bulgaria and 2.35 for Finland. The lowest rate of homicide in the EU is in Austria at 0.70, followed by Malta at 0.91, then Germany at 0.95. The relationship of the capitals to the countries in respect of homicide also reveals substantial variations. While Lithuania is top as a country, its capital Vilnius has 7.95 homicides per 100,000 population, which is substantially below that of Tallinn in Estonia, where the rate is 9.75. Valletta, the capital of Malta, had no homicides over the period, while Vienna in Austria had 1.12 per 100,000 population.

According to the UN,[7] in 2006 the foreign population (defined as migrant stock) in Lithuania accounted for 4.8 per cent, while in Estonia it stood at 15.2 per cent.[8] In Turkey, only 1.8 per cent of the population is foreign, while in Bulgaria the figure is 1.3 per cent. Foreigners account for 3 per cent of Finland's population but 15.1 per cent of Austria's. Malta's foreign population stands at 2.7 per cent and Germany's at 12.3 per cent. Statistics hide many things, but nonetheless they do also give indicators about population and comparative numbers of foreigners to citizens. While it may be the case that in some countries there is a higher rate of criminal convictions among the foreign population than among citizens, in view of the very substantial differences in percentages of foreign populations and rates of homicide – as an example of one of the most serious crimes – in various European countries, substantial doubts are raised about the possibility of making cross-border correlations which are coherent.

Foreigners and identity

The identity of foreigners and maintaining control over that identity have moved up the political scale, in Europe and elsewhere, as the technological capacities to attach identities to individuals through the use of biometric data have grown. In Europe, since 2000, there has been increased emphasis on controlling identity – expressed through concerns about fraudulent identity documents and identity theft – which has led to an explosion of state databases containing information about individuals and increasing focus on document security, with the inclusion of ever more biometric elements in passports, identity documents and other papers (Brouwer 2008). Foreigners have been a group which has been particularly targeted in this move. They have been the first group to be the subject of EU databases containing biometric information about them and it is in respect of them that further databases are being established. The resistance which citizens may have to their data being collected and stored by their state appears to be more muted when the object of the exercise is the foreigner. One of the driving arguments in the political discussions around databases and foreigners is the involvement of foreigners in political violence and serious criminality.

The relationship between foreigners and identity touches a number of very sensitive issues relating to security. The extent to which a foreigner has the possibility to participate in a community depends on the definition of the citizen and the foreigner (see chapter 2; Noiriel 2001); the way in which rights are shared between citizens and foreigners; the way in which the foreigner ceases to be foreign and becomes a member of the community. These considerations have an important sociological dimension – who is entitled to enact citizenship (Isin & Neilson 2008) – which is to some extent captured in legal norms, though not always adequately.

In the relationship of the individual to the state, however, the starting place is the state's capacity to allocate an identity to the individual. In respect of persons born on the state's territory, the UN's International Covenant on Civil and Political Rights 1966 provides that every child has the right to be registered immediately after birth and to have a name (art. 24). The provision is not limited to children who are born citizens of the state and, indeed, it is specifically stated that the right to identity is to be enjoyed without discrimination as to race, colour, sex, language, religion, national or social origin, property or birth. Most commentary on this provision focuses on the status of the child,[9] but for my purposes it is the right of the individual to identity which is of particular interest.

The state which is obliged or entitled to register a child is that on whose territory it is born. Normally, this will also be the state whose nationality the child acquires, by virtue either of its parents' citizenship or birth on the territory or both. The starting place for official recognition of identity is this registration. The subsequent acts of obtaining identity documents, passports, etc., flow from the first recognition by a state of the existence of a child as a human being. Occasionally issues will arise as to the nationality of the child – for instance in the case of a child born into the Russian ethnic minority in Estonia. The child may well be born stateless, though it will still have an entitlement to be registered and to have its existence acknowledged formally. While, frequently, concern is expressed at the excessive interest of states in the identity of persons on their territory, and I will return to this shortly, the right to have an identity at all is a critical point of departure for the individual (Brouwer 2008). Where individuals are not registered, which happens in some liberal democracies as regards persons irregularly present on the territory, the unregistered individual has no starting place from which to claim rights dependent on existence. For instance, even the possibility of attending school is usually dependent on the ability to produce some identity document for the child.

The identity of the individual, traditionally, is a matter which straddles the private domain and the public one. In Europe, one of the venues of struggle about identity and the state has been the right of an individual to have changed the gender on his or her identity documents following gender reassignment. Here the European Court of Human Rights held that it was contrary to the right of private life for a state to refuse to adjust official documents.[10] However, in this case the individual and the state are in disagreement about the on-going status of state-controlled identity documents and their reflection of the individual's reality. When the relationship of identity and the individual moves from one with the state of origin to one with a host state – a place where the individual is a foreigner – the issues change quite substantially.

First, the identity of the individual is one of negotiation with his or her state of origin/nationality, as in the above case. Second, the state of nationality negotiates on behalf of its citizens for the recognition of its travel documents by other states, thereby enabling its citizens to cross borders. In this second field, the issue of relations between states is key, but increasingly in western liberal democracies the role of the state of origin is questioned. The uncertainty around recognition of Palestinian travel documents in EU countries creates many tensions for Palestinians seeking to cross borders. The travel document is issued by the state of origin and it is within the inter-state system that the recognition of an entity as capable of issuing a valid travel document to its nationals is regulated.

Third, a step away from this classic inter-state relationship is taken when the state to which an individual seeks to travel determines that the individual must obtain a visa before he or she can travel there. The visa is a document issued in the country of origin (or residence) of the individual by the authorities of the state to which he or she wishes to go. So, for the first time, the state of destination comes into contact with the individual who has been documented by his or her state of origin. By creating a visa requirement for some countries but not others, states of destination provide themselves with the opportunity to examine each individual potential visitor before he or she leaves home. Rather than the use of relations between states in the state system, a different dynamic is deployed – between the state of destination and the potential traveller (Bigo & Guild 2003).

In Europe, among the most important criteria for deciding whether a country will be placed on the mandatory visa list are the perceived migratory propensities of its nationals, as well as security.[11] For example, on 10 July 2008 the UK authorities announced that a tough new visa regime would be instituted for eleven countries[12] unless these countries could significantly reduce the risk their nationals pose to the UK in terms of illegal immigration, crime and security.[13] The UK authorities announced that the criteria on the basis of which the states would be assessed as regards their citizens were:

- passport security and integrity;
- degree of cooperation (with the UK) over deportation or removal of a country's nationals from the UK;
- levels of illegal working in the UK and other immigration abuse;
- levels of crime and terrorism risk posed to the UK;
- the extent to which a country's authorities were addressing these threats.

In this move, the state of potential destination of an individual used the wish of citizens of another state to travel to the destination state as a tool in inter-state negotiations in a wide range of security-related fields, ranging from the home state's approach to its own citizens who are being expelled to its policies on political violence. While the politics remain inter-state, the potential destination state seeks to reach into the state of origin of the potential traveller and, by creating a threat of compulsory immobility which will affect primarily middle-class citizens, mobilize support among people within the second state for that state to take action against its own citizens. The recent negotiations between some EU countries and the USA over the US visa waiver scheme and its application reveal a similar pattern of inter-state negotiations in which one state reaches behind the state negotiations to the citizens of the other state to seek to limit the options of the partner state.[14]

In terms of identity, it is upon the identity of individuals that inter-state negotiations are played out. 'Bad' foreigners need to be disciplined by their state of nationality in order that the other citizens of the state continue to enjoy visa-free access to the destination state. The destination state claims the right to determine who are good and bad citizens of another state and, having done so, then requires the state of origin to behave differently towards some of its nationals than towards others on the basis of the interest of the potential destination state. The negotiation of identity is no longer between the individual and his or her state or nationality. The allocation of security risks follows the individual from the potential destination state back to his or her state of nationality.

Another important change also takes place with the changing role of mandatory visa regimes: the potential destination state claims an entitlement to identify individuals and to provide them with an indelible identity which only it retains. This takes place through the creation of a file (now a data file) on each individual visa applicant and, to ensure that the individual cannot escape the file, biometric identifiers are collected from the individual and held on the file. Thus, the individual's identity is secured by the potential destination state in a form which is no longer dependent on the travel and identity documents issued by the state of origin. In the same press release from the UK authorities of 10 July 2008, a good example of this move is apparent: 'Everyone applying for a UK visa now has their finger prints checked before their identity is fixed. So far more than two million sets of finger prints have been collected flagging up almost 3,000 attempted identity swaps.'

The individual's identity is fixed not by his or her country of origin in a negotiation about citizenship but by the potential destination state where the individual plans to go for a short stay of less than six months. In order to effect that short stay, the individual must surrender to the foreign state his or her fingerprints and, on the basis of those fingerprints, a new identity, determined by the potential destination state, is allocated. This new status is then the basis on which the potential destination state allocates negative epithets such as attempted identity swaps, etc., to the individual. The potential destination state holds the one 'true' identity of the individual, captured in his or her fingerprints and allocated to a name, gender, date of birth, address, nationality, etc. Any deviation from this identity reality which the potential destination state has determined is by definition fraudulent and abusive. As the UK Minister Liam Byrne is quoted as saying in the press release: 'Our tougher checks abroad are working even better than expected. We've now checked two million fingerprints of foreign nationals applying for visas and stopped 3,000 people trying to hide their real identity.'

Many problems are posed by this change. Taking simply the decision of the European Court of Human Rights regarding the entitlement of individuals to have their identity documents changed once they have undergone gender realignment, the capacity of a state to comply with this entitlement of the individual can only apply between the individual and his or her state of nationality – the state which purports to negotiate the 'true' identity of the individual and to provide the documentary evidence of that identity. When the state's documents are no longer the decisive evidence of identity but rather the individual's identity is stored in the databases of, possibly, numerous other countries where the individual had travelled or sought to travel, the individual no longer has any security of identity. Any changes to identity may be captured in one set of documents but not in another database. The individual no longer has any security over his or her identity, nor can he or she rely on his or her state of nationality to provide such security, even on its own territory (see above the requirement of the UK authorities that eleven countries change their policies, even within their territory, vis-à-vis their nationals, in order to retain visa-free travel to the UK for their nationals).

Data security and the individual

Ascertaining the correct identity of the individual, and in particular the foreigner, is increasingly accepted as a security issue. Behind this political acceptance is concern about identity fraud, the use of false documents and other means by which the individual ceases to be visible in the identity assigned to him or her by the state. The rising concern in Europe and elsewhere about document fraud is focused around the individual. Are passports and identity documents sufficiently secure so that individuals cannot tamper with them or falsify them easily? Are the mechanisms for confirming identity sufficiently robust to prevent the individual from circumventing them and becoming someone else? To address these insecurities, databases containing substantial amounts of data information about individuals as an important security tool have become widely accepted in many liberal democracies (Brouwer 2008). The EU Member States have all joined in the creation and use of many databases containing information about individuals (Geyer 2008). The most developed databases containing such information are those which relate to foreigners. Three deserve further comment – these are the Schengen Information System (SIS: I and II), the EURODAC database and the Visa Information System (VIS; not yet active). Additionally, the US Department of Homeland Security agreement with the European Union on the collection of passenger name records provides a further insight into the issue of security and identity and the foreigner.

The SIS

The Schengen Information System became operational on 26 March 1995. When it started it applied to seven states: Belgium, the Netherlands, Luxembourg, France, Spain, Portugal and Germany. By 2008 it included all EU Member States except Ireland and the UK. Bulgaria and Romania were waiting to join, while Iceland, Norway and Switzerland participated. Originally the creation of a treaty among five European states (the Schengen Implementing Agreement 1990 (CISA)), it became part of the European Union in 1999 (Brouwer 2008). The SIS (and its intended successor, SIS II) is a data system which permits the participating states to signal individuals and objects for a variety of reasons related to public security, criminal justice or aliens law. As regards individuals, the participating states may also enter onto the SIS the names of persons to be refused admission to the EU by any of the Member States. The reasons for entering an individual's name on the SIS are contained in art. 96 CISA and may be based on the decision of the state that the presence of the foreigner on the territory of the EU would be a threat to public policy or public security or to national security. Much discretion is left to the Member States as to how they interpret this requirement. As Brouwer has shown, notwithstanding the fact that the SIS can contain information on persons and objects of interest to the criminal justice system, in fact it is overwhelmingly used as a register of foreigners to be excluded. On the basis of data she collected between 1999 and 2006, the percentage of data on the SIS which related to foreigners never dropped below 85 per cent of the total entries on the system. While the system originally did not provide for biometric identifiers to be included, the revised system which is under construction will permit the inclusion of numeric photos and fingerprints, thus fixing the identity of foreigners according to the data system (Brouwer 2008).

The SIS is a system designed to operate via the internet in consulates of the Member States abroad, providing them with information on foreigners who should not be issued visas. It also operates at all the external borders of the Member States (leaving aside Ireland and the UK), where border officials consult the SIS in order to refuse entry to any foreigner who is listed on it. The details of any foreigner seeking a visa or entry to the EU may be checked against the SIS and if the person has been entered on the system he or she is refused the visa or entry. According to the published statistics, a match between a data file and an individual on the SIS under art. 96 (which is called a 'hit') occurred in respect of 2.8 per cent of files in 2004 and in 2005 (Brouwer 2008). This accounted for approximately 21,000 persons.

EURODAC

This is a database, operated by the European Commission, which contains the fingerprints of all persons who have applied for asylum in any European Union Member State or who have been apprehended irregularly crossing an external frontier into the EU. It began operating on 1 March 2003. It consists of a Central Unit, established within the European Commission, and a computerized central database in which data are processed for the purpose of comparing the fingerprint data of applicants for asylum and others with fingerprint data sent by Member States which seek to find out whether an individual who has turned up in their country has ever applied for asylum anywhere else in the EU. In EU law, an asylum seeker has only one chance to have his or her asylum application considered, and it is according to EU rules (not the individual's wish) where that one consideration of the application will take place. Thus, the database serves two main functions: it provides a way to find out whether an individual has already applied for asylum in another Member State, and to allocate the state responsible for taking care of and considering the application.

The data which are recorded in respect of an asylum applicant are limited to:

(a) Member State of origin, place and date of application for asylum;
(b) fingerprint data;
(c) sex;
(d) reference number used by the Member State of origin;
(e) date on which the fingerprints were taken;
(f) date on which the data were transmitted to the Central Unit;
(g) date on which the data were entered into the central database;
(h) details in respect of the recipient(s) of the data transmitted and the date(s) of transmission(s).

Thus, for EURODAC, the individual becomes no more or less than his or her fingerprints. Of course the exclusion of information on the individual's name and nationality is a protection for the asylum applicant against any possible misuse of the database. The data is stored for ten years, after which time it is automatically erased from the central database. Member States may send to EURODAC fingerprint data of any third-country national found illegally present on its territory, for the purpose of checking whether the individual has applied for asylum in another Member State. These data can only be used for the purpose of a comparison and not stored. Nor can such data be compared against the database of those apprehended in connection with irregularly crossing the external frontier. From its inception until the end of 2005, approximately 6,570,000 fingerprints were sent to EURODAC.[15] For 2005, the number of fingerprints sent to the database which resulted in a 'hit', i.e. corresponded to a set of fingerprints already in the database, was 16 per cent for asylum seekers. However, the transfer of responsibility for asylum seekers for Germany in 2005 resulted in 2,716 individuals being sent to Germany for their applications to be processed and 2,748 individuals being sent out of Germany to other countries to have their applications processed.

The German Presidency (first half of 2007) proposed that all EU information systems, including EURODAC, be made available to relevant police and security authorities as needed to fulfil their duties.[16] It argued for 'access to EURODAC by Member States' police and law enforcement authorities for the purposes of preventing, detecting or investigating criminal offences, in particular terrorist offences'.[17] This, of course, presupposes that asylum seekers (the vast majority of the persons whose fingerprints are contained in EURODAC) or persons apprehended irregularly crossing the border (the minority of fingerprints, but mainly consisting of those apprehended, for instance, arriving in the Canary Islands in small boats) constitute an important criminal and political violence risk. By 2008 the proposal had still not been adopted, though it continued to be on the table.

Leaving aside the problem of use of the data, simply getting the administrations to apply the system correctly has proved difficult. In 2005 the matter of a Sudanese asylum seeker came before the High Court in the UK.[18] The UK authorities sent the fingerprints of an asylum seeker to EURODAC and received back a report that there was a hit: the man's fingerprints had already been registered in the database by Italy. The UK authorities advised their Italian counterparts of the hit and that they would be sending the man to Italy. In due course, Mr Ali was put on a plane to Italy, notwithstanding his strenuous contention that he had never been there before. When he arrived in Italy, the Italian authorities took his fingerprints and found that he was not the same person for whom they had accepted responsibility but someone else, who was registered in the EURODAC database as having applied for asylum in the UK. As he was registered already in the database as an asylum seeker, under Italian law any application for asylum which he might try to make in Italy was inadmissible. As he could not make an asylum application, he was not entitled to any social benefits, food, housing, etc. Further, he was irregularly present in Italy.

The Italian authorities notified the UK authorities of the error but no action was taken to bring Mr Ali back to the UK. Mr Ali had no resources or family in Italy and was excluded from all entitlements to support. He found his way to the Italian Refugee Council which, as a matter of charity, gave him some food and notified the Italian authorities that he should be returned to the UK. Nothing happened, not least as the UK authorities failed to respond to communications from their Italian counterparts. Finally, the Italian Refugee Council contacted its British counterpart which brought legal proceedings against the UK authorities for their action in sending Mr Ali to Italy and failing to bring him back. After many months of delay and a number of hearings before a judge in the UK, the UK authorities conceded liability and arranged for Mr Ali's return there.

VIS

In 2004 the European Commission proposed the creation of a Visa Information System which will contain the fingerprints and other data (including digitalized photos) of all persons who apply for visas to come to any EU Member State (with the exception of Ireland and the UK, which do not participate in the system). It is planned to become operational in 2012. The purpose of the VIS according to the Commission is to:

- prevent threats to internal security in the Member States;
- ensure asylum seekers are dealt with in the state allocated;
- facilitate the fight against documentary fraud;
- facilitate checks at external border checkpoints;
- assist in the return of irregular migrants.

While the proposal was still under negotiation, a further proposal was tabled to make the information in the VIS available to national authorities responsible for internal security and to EUROPOL (Brouwer 2008). Thus, the fact of having made a visa application, whether successful or not, to go to the EU means that an individual's biometric data (including fingerprints) will be held on a database available to all EU Member States (with two exceptions). The national authorities responsible for internal security – which includes the police, *gendarmes* in those countries where they exist, but also intelligence services – are planned to have access to VIS information, including the fingerprints. This move fits in with a wider trend in Europe to grant law enforcement agencies access to EU databases and other large-scale information systems.

The European Data Protection Supervisor (EDPS), an independent body established by the EU to advise on data protection issues, published an opinion on the issue of access by internal security services to VIS data in 2006.[19] The opinion is largely critical of the proposal on the grounds that it is far too wide and does not circumscribe sufficiently the conditions which should apply to access to the VIS.

Protecting identity in Europe

The relationship between the state and individual data in Europe has had a troubled history in the twentieth and twenty-first centuries. The persecution of Jews by the Nazi regime in Germany from the 1930s onwards depended heavily on the collection and use of personal data to identify the individuals, objects of persecution. The use of surveillance and personal data files by security police in the former Soviet Block, in particular after 1945, gave rise to anger, expressed in 1989 and after, in many Central and Eastern European countries which had been under communist rule. The case of the burning of the security files in Romania is only one very immediate example (Deletant [1995] 2006).

Thus the development of rules on data protection and their insertion into national law, EU law and European regional treaties occurs within a framework of social concern about state access to and use of personal data. At the European regional level, there are two main sources of rules on personal data – a Council of Europe Convention for the Protection of Individuals with regard to Automatic Processing of Personal Data 1981, and a right to privacy in the ECHR (art. 8). In the EU, a separate set of data protection rules were established, mainly through Directive 95/46. There are two main rationales for data protection: the first is the right of the individual to privacy, which, by extension, limits the right of the state to collect and retain data about the individual unless this is justified. Second, the duty of the state to comply with rules of good administration means that it is not entitled to intrude into the private life of individuals without justification. Individual data may be the subject of a number of steps: collection, storage, use, transfer, modification and destruction. All of these steps are the subject of control.

The main principles of data protection in Europe from the above sources are as follows:

- the purpose of data collection must be explicit, legitimate and exclude aimless data collection with a view to possible future use;
- the individual must give his or her consent to the collection and use of the data;
- the use of data must be limited to the purpose for which they were collected;
- data cannot be transmitted to third parties without the consent of the data subject and transfers must be consistent with the general purposes for which they were collected;
- data must not be retained for any longer period than is necessary and consistent with the reason why they were collected;
- sensitive data must be subject to extra protection (for instance data on health, sexual preference, etc.), and separated depending on the degree of accuracy;
- the data subject has a right to know what data are being held in respect of him or her and the reason; he or she is also entitled to access to the data and to have them corrected if inaccurate;
- data which are held in automated databases must not be used for automated decision making;
- all data must be held in a secure form which excludes unauthorized access to it;
- the entity which holds the data is responsible for damage caused by illegal or inaccurate processing. (Brouwer 2008)

All collection and use of data is subject to a duty not to discriminate on prohibited grounds such as race, sex, ethnicity, religion, etc. The rules on data protection may be subject to limitations by the state on grounds of general interest or national security. Thus, the rules are not absolute but allow states to argue for the use of data outside those rules, but any such argument must be justified on one of these two grounds.

All of the data protection principles set out above are much easier for a citizen to access than for a foreigner. Further, when the foreigner is in a vulnerable position – for instance seeking a visa, seeking entry into the state – even if he or she is aware of his or her data rights, it is highly unlikely that he or she will seek to exercise them. The lack of complaint in respect of the collection of biometric data in the form of fingerprints in the US Visit programme (where all foreign visitors to the USA are required to provide two fingerprints before being admitted to the state) is often used to justify data collection at the border. However, the inequality of the power relation between the state and the individual as a foreigner in that situation raises questions about the legitimacy of the apparent consent which the individual gives to the collection and retention of his or her data.

Our citizen, your foreigner: the EU–US Passenger Name Record debate

The citizen of one state is the foreigner of another state. The decision by one state to collect, retain and use personal data of foreigners means that it is doing so in respect of the citizens of another country. In the European context, states have a duty in data protection law to ensure that their citizens' data are handled in accordance with the rules set out above. The principle which guides database use in the USA is that there is a property right in data which belongs to the person who collected it. The difference of perspective has given rise to substantial friction between the EU and the USA, most publicly in the matter of the transmission of personal name records. This dispute did not engage biometric data, but rather information which airlines collect on their passengers for commercial purposes.

The background to the trouble was the US legislation passed in November 2001 which requires air carriers operating flights to or from the USA (or across it) to give electronic access to data stored in their reservation and departure systems (Passenger Name Records: PNR) to US customs authorities. The rationale for this legislation was the risk foreigners constitute to the USA in respect of political violence (Cole 2005). The European Commission notified the US authorities in 2002 that this requirement could be in conflict with EU data protection rules. The US authorities went ahead and imposed the requirement on airlines (subject to fines for failure to comply). A flurry of activity in Europe resulted in the US authorities providing certain undertakings regarding the use of personal data, the European Commission accepting those undertakings as adequate and signing an agreement on EU–US PNR. The European Parliament challenged the adequacy of the data protection undertakings and took the EU Council to court. The European Court of Justice found that, although the data were collected for commercial purposes (itself problematic as such data tend to be subject to lower accuracy thresholds than data collected by the state for law enforcement purposes), it was being transmitted and used for purposes of preventing and combating terrorism and related crimes, and other serious crimes, including organized crime, and flight from warrants or custody for those crimes.[20] As a result, the objective of the EU–US Agreement was beyond challenge by the European Parliament (for a variety of rather arcane reasons relating to the powers of the Parliament), but the EU–US PNR agreement was void because it had been adopted on the wrong ground.

The Commission and the US authorities proceeded to adopt a new agreement in 2006 and a further one in 2007. Each time, the agreement provided less robust data protection provisions.[21] The 2007 agreement includes a letter from the US Secretary of Homeland Security setting out the US undertakings. In comparison with EU data protection rules, they are rather weak.

First, as regards the right of the US authorities to enter the databases of airlines to obtain information, notwithstanding criticism of this system which makes it very difficult to control what data are being obtained, the so-called 'pull system' remained in the new agreement. Second, while in the previous agreements the US authorities had only seventy-two hours before the flight to obtain information, in the 2007 agreement that time limit was no longer definitive. Third, while the purpose limitation of the data was already very relaxed, permitting use of personal data for a wide variety of reasons, in the 2007 agreement the purpose limitation was even more elastic. Fourth, the agreement permits even wider sharing of personal data across US authorities and fewer constraints on the reasons for doing this. Fifth, the number and nature of data were reduced from thirty-four items to nineteen but the nineteen categories are wide enough to include not only the contents of the previous thirty-four but possibly more. Sixth, as regards retention of data, they are retained in an active form for 7 years (as opposed to 3½ years in the first agreement), after which they may be held in a dormant form for a further 8 years, but there is no clear commitment to their destruction at the end of that period. Seventh, the US authorities undertook to extend their national legislation, the Privacy Act, to PNR data, regardless of the country of residence of the data subject. But the US Privacy Act is not an equivalent to EU data protection obligations. Eighth, the legal position of EU citizens as regards their data is covered by the US Freedom of Information Act which permits access only in accordance with US law and on request to the US authorities, though under the agreement the US authorities may deny or postpone access to PNR information under the Act. Ninth, the agreement deals with the issue of reciprocity: the US authorities are entitled to act as they wish, notwithstanding the higher data protection standards applicable in Europe (where the data are collected). Tenth, provision is made for a periodic review of the agreement and undertakings, but no specific time periods are foreseen (Guild 2007b).

The grave concern expressed by various bodies in Europe, the European Parliament, the EDPS, national parliaments, civil society and others, regarding the use by the USA of personal data of European nationals, took place at the same time as the adoption of EU measures to collect and retain personal data of foreigners. It is easy to level the charge of hypocrisy against the Europeans in this regard. Central, though, to the issue is the understanding of the relationship of the state and the individual: protections which are considered normal for the citizen are considered luxuries for foreigners. The security justification for the collection of data about the foreigner is more easily accepted or is the subject of less critical evaluation than when the issue touches the citizen, irrespective of the relative risk the foreigner constitutes as regards political violence or serious crime. The pressure from civil society in Europe, in particular via the European Parliament, indicates the level of concern which individuals have about the collection, retention, manipulation and transmission of their personal data by foreign governments.

Conclusions

In this chapter I have examined how the states' security concerns find expression as regards the foreigner. The linking of the foreigner with terrorism, while tenuous at best in the EU situation, nonetheless becomes the rationale for obtaining and retaining large amounts of data on foreigners under circumstances which raise questions as to the legitimacy of the objective. Fears about the engagement of foreigners in political violence and criminal activity – although this is statistically unclear in Europe – are primary grounds on the basis of which foreigners must be the subject of special measures to fix their identity and to enable destination states to hold data on them.

The relationship of the individual to his or her state of nationality has been the core element in the establishment of the individual's identity. It is in this arena that struggles about identity have been played out. However, with the linking of the foreigner with political violence and crime, destination states in liberal democracies increasingly claim a right to provide a specific and immutable identity to foreigners, which permits them to identify them not only when they are on the territory of the state but wherever they are in the world. The mechanisms which are used to establish this identity are applied through immigration and border controls – visas, border controls and, in the case of the USA, the databases of airlines which are carrying foreigners to the territory or over it. The ability of the state of nationality to protect its citizens and their identities is weakened as a result. The wish to travel renders their citizens less theirs, through the creation of new identities controlled by foreign states and beyond the reach of constitutionally settled rules on identity and personal data. In the name of security, the individual acquires an increasing number of identities over which he or she has less and less control, but the existence of which may have dramatic consequences for his or her life.[22]

I have examined how immigrants, although each an individual within his or her own trajectory, are homogenized into a single category. As a category, the immigrant is accepted as a threat to national security as a potential terrorist, to public security as a potential criminal, and to identity as a challenge to the homogeneity which is presupposed to exist within the state. Although available statistical evidence in Europe indicates that both the category and the threat are inaccurate – at best, partial – nonetheless they provide the justification for the creation of databases with large amounts of personal details about foreigners, including biometric data. The principles of data protection in Europe are generally disapplied when it comes to foreigners. Their identity is constructed by states other than that of their nationality on the basis of the individual's interest in travelling. The identity of the foreigner is not treated with the same respect as that of the citizen. Because the foreigner and immigrant are inherently suspicious categories, sacrificing their security of identity and movement on the basis (unproven and doubtful at best) of reinforcing national and public security within the state is an easy choice. Sacrificing someone else's liberty for one's own perceived security is not such a difficult choice. Or is it? Does the degradation of the foreigner's right to privacy not also impact on the citizen's right of privacy? I follow the example of the EU's negotiations with the USA regarding collection and use of personal data about EU nationals to make the comparison. The inability of the EU negotiators to obtain greater protection for EU citizens' data, which was in their mandate, also results from a consensus among political actors in the field of homeland security, whether in the USA or in the EU, that it is legitimate to collect and use personal data about foreigners. When the foreigners whom one state's negotiators are discussing are the citizens of the other party, the same arguments which that party made to disregard the privacy interests of the general category of foreigners come back to haunt it.

7

Economy and migration

In the previous chapter I looked at how foreigners are homogenized into categories, notwithstanding their differences, and how those categories become associated with threats to national security and public security, notwithstanding the dearth of supporting evidence. The construction of the foreigner as a potential threat then justifies the state collecting, using and sharing, not only among government departments but with foreign states, substantial amounts of personal data about individuals, defining their identities and disregarding basic principles of privacy. When faced with other states behaving in the same manner towards their nationals, states which have already begun down this path have a diminished capacity to object. I started the last chapter examining the relevant data available regarding the security threat which foreigners pose in Europe. Surprisingly, it is in spite of the data, and contrary to the indications of the data, that the argument of the immigrant as security threat is made. The continuum of insecurity easily attaches to the foreigner. The construction of the foreigner as inherently risky permits the extension of the argument that the unknown is potentially threatening. Thus is it legitimate to collect more, and more invasive, information about the foreigner than about the citizen (though in the longer term the citizen may well be in sight).

In this chapter I will move to another aspect of the insecurity continuum: economic migration. Among the more common complaints which are heard in Europe about asylum seekers is that they are 'bogus' because, in fact, they are economic migrants. The structure of this argument presupposes that economic migrants are somehow worse or less deserving than asylum seekers, as even 'bogus' asylum seekers prefer to pretend to be 'real' asylum seekers than to present themselves as 'real' economic migrants. This shard of apparent common sense, prevalent across Europe, rests on another assumption, which is that would-be economic migrants are not needed, unskilled, desperate and likely to undermine wages and working conditions in the host country. This prejudice leads then to the concern that economic migrants are unable to provide for themselves, and become a burden on the social assistance system of the state. The foreigner is constructed as a potential threat to collective security expressed in the economic wellbeing of the state. The foreigner is homogenized into one category and that category is allocated negative characteristics. It is for the foreigner to extract him- or herself from the category and thus escape the negative normative allocation. In the next chapter I will examine the struggles of another set of actors – transnational companies – to insulate the field of economic migration against national political entrepreneurs seeking to privilege the insecurity continuum which stigmatizes the foreigner in the labour market.

The issue of economic migration is thus cast as one which affects security of the state, the jobs of the economically weak, and the wellbeing of the state in the form of social assistance and social solidarity. These opinions are often bundled up together and presented under the heading 'absorption capacity' of the state. To sweeten the argument, which is susceptible to charges of anti-immigrant rhetoric, one often finds protection of vulnerable immigrant victims of organized crime thrown in as an argument in favour of restrictive policies on economic migration. The European Pact on Immigration and Asylum 2008 manages to combine all these elements in one paragraph:

> The European Union, however, does not have the resources to decently receive all the migrants hoping to find a better life here. Poorly managed immigration may disrupt the social cohesion of the countries of destination. The organisation of immigration must consequently take account of Europe's reception capacity in terms of its labour market, housing, and health, education and social services, and protect migrants against possible exploitation by criminal networks.

Consistent with the approach that I used in the preceding chapter, I will start with the information we have about economic migration and highlight the inconsistencies between the discourse which is promoted by various political actors and the statistics. Then I will take an example of the complete liberalization of labour migration among a substantial number of countries – the realization of free movement of workers in the twenty-seven countries which make up the European Union. With specific reference to the big jump in 2004 when ten states joined the EU, I will examine what we know about economic migration from poor to rich countries, and the opposite, once immigration controls are abandoned, looking both at nationals of the EU Member States and at third-country nationals living in the EU. Finally, I will address some of the issues around social benefits and foreigners.

Many arguments are made for and against economic migration, though in general there is agreement that some forms of economic migration are beneficial to developed and developing economies. However, there is much disagreement on what kinds of economic migration are good for which countries. In developed economies, there is general agreement that highly skilled / highly qualified migration is beneficial for growth and innovation.[1] There is much less of a consensus regarding semi-skilled, low-skilled and unskilled migration. Nonetheless, most developed economies attract semi- and low-skilled migrants, particularly in sectors where, notwithstanding national levels of unemployment, jobs are difficult to fill because of wage levels or social status attached to them. Agriculture, construction and low-end service sectors figure largely in this discussion (Martin, Abella & Kuptsch 2006).

In some developing countries there is a very different approach. The argument of brain drain – that is, the effects of the loss of highly skilled / highly qualified citizens of countries with developing economies to countries with developed economies – arises. The argument goes that the facilitation of highly skilled migration from developing countries to developed ones results in a loss of skills and capacity in the developing economy. The result is to create an obstacle to development. Instead, developing countries often seek agreements with developed economies to facilitate the migration of their semi- and unskilled workers who are unemployed in their country of origin.

Into the mix of conflicting interests, a number of other issues arise. First, there is the question of remittances. To what extent do remittances from migrant workers from developing countries working in developed countries contribute to the welfare of their home states (Pozo 2007)? Second, the education and vocational training possibilities in developed countries for citizens of developing countries becomes woven into debates about economic migration, particularly promoting the perspective of temporary labour migration in order to encourage skills acquisition and export.[2] Much less public discussion takes place around the migration of workers from developed economies to developing ones, though this accounts for a not insignificant number of persons. It includes not only workers in multinational companies who are moved around the world, often in economic activities related to resource extraction, but also aid workers and other workers in social fields (Smith & Favell 2006).

The question of security in relation to economic migration arises in a number of other ways as well. These are primarily based around economic security – the relationship of the state, economy and workers in promoting the economic wellbeing of states and, as part of that, the wellbeing of workers. Some of the key issues are:

- The impact of migrant workers on the labour market: this has two facets. First, in buoyant economies, do migrant workers depress wages? Second, in depressed economies, do migrant workers take jobs which would otherwise go to nationals?
- Migrant workers and access to social benefits: are migrant workers a threat to social security systems which are founded on the principle of social solidarity?
- The impact of foreign investment (and the arrival of investors) on the state's ability to plan economic growth.
- Labour migration as a mechanism to assist development through permitting migrant workers to acquire skills not available in their countries of origin and through the sending of remittances to the country of origin.

In order to examine these issues, I will first consider what we know about migrant workers and their participation in labour markets. Then I will look at the policy issues around migrant workers in Europe. Europe is a particularly interesting example as it reveals most distinctly many of the inconsistencies in discussions about security and labour migration. On the one hand, the European Commission spends very substantial amounts of money encouraging labour migration within the EU. Described as free movement of workers, labour migration from one Member State to another, according to EU law, is characterized as follows: 'mobility of labour within the Community must be one of the means by which the worker is guaranteed the possibility of improving his living and working conditions and promoting his social advancement, while helping to satisfy the requirements of the economies of the Member States'.[3] On the other hand, labour migration from outside the EU is framed in a very different way: as the Council stated in 2006, the objective of EU labour migration policy from outside the EU is 'to develop as far as legal migration is concerned, well-managed migration policies, fully respecting national competencies, to assist Member States to meet existing and future labour needs'.[4] The focus is on a state-centred approach in which states manage migration. The objectives of individuals to move or not to move, as expressed in EU free movement of workers, is most noticeable by its complete absence.

Migration and employment: who is working where?

In 2008 the Organization for Economic Co-operation and Development (OECD)[5] published the most comprehensive profile of immigrant populations currently available (OECD 2008). The report makes twelve general findings and provides a wealth of information about labour migration in OECD countries. I will start with the twelve principal findings and then look at some of the specific data in respect of Mexico and the USA.

The first finding of the study is that, by 2000, on average 7.5% of the total population in OECD countries was foreign-born (rising to 9% for those persons over fifteen). Some caution must be exercised in understanding this figure as it relates to foreign-born, not persons who are foreign nationals, as the report recognizes this is particularly an issue for countries with large repatriate or expatriate populations, such as France or Portugal in the first category and the UK or Germany in the second. For the OECD, the category 'immigrant' includes people covered by national definitions which depend on national rules on permanent residence, as well as foreigners with limited residence permits or registered on the population register and intending to stay in the host country longer than a specific number of months.

The second finding is that migration to OECD countries is gender balanced – indeed 51 per cent of migrants are women. There has been an increase in the migration of women is response to two main factors: family reunification (presupposing that at an early period there were more men migrating) and service sector labour migration. Third, immigrants are primarily aged between twenty-four and sixty-four, though there are substantial variations. This appears to indicate that most immigrants arrive when they are already well into their working life, and leave at the end of their working life. Fourth, in the OECD area, immigrants are more highly qualified than nationals of the state. While among immigrant populations, 23.6% have tertiary education, in national populations the percentage with such education is only 19.1%. Similarly, among the population with no qualifications, immigrants exceed national norms. Fifth, the average employment rate of citizens in OECD countries is 66%, while that of immigrants is 62.3%, though the difference between the two groups is lower for women.

Sixth, unemployment is higher among highly skilled immigrants than it is among nationals. The gap gets greater, the higher the skills level. Additionally, immigrants are more likely to be working at jobs beneath their qualification level than are nationals. Seventh, generally, immigrants are distributed widely across economic sectors, though there are substantial differences in comparison with nationals in a variety of fields: 33% of nationals and 28.2% of immigrants work in agriculture and industry; 10.6% of nationals and 12.4% of immigrants work in producer services; in distributive services, the figures are 21% compared to 20%, while in personal and social services the comparison is between 35.4% of nationals and 39.3% of immigrants.

Eighth, four out of every ten OECD immigrants aged fifteen and over live in the USA, consistuting 6.6% of the population (though 12.3% of the US population is foreign-born, indicating both high rates of naturalization and high rates of citizens born abroad). Leaving aside two small states with very high migrant populations, Luxembourg and Switzerland, Germany comes next with 12.1% of its population foreign-born (though no figures are available on how many of those persons are German nationals). Austria and Belgium have 8.8% and 8.2% immigrants, as a percentage of their populations, followed by Australia and Greece at 7.4% and 7.0%, respectively.

Ninth, Mexico is the most important country of origin of immigrants in OECD countries with 8.4 million nationals abroad, followed by the UK and Germany with 3 million and 2.4 million emigrants elsewhere in the OECD, respectively. China and India rank seventh and eighth at 2 million emigrants each. Tenth, while the 57 million non-OECD-born living in OECD countries in 2000 represent 5% of the OECD population, they constitute no more than 1.1% of the populations of their countries of origin. Indeed, they account for less than 0.5% of their home populations for India, China, Indonesia, Russia, Nigeria or Brazil. These figures are quite different though for some small island states, and even for some small European states – for instance immigrants in the OECD account for 20% of the Albanian population.

Eleventh, the OECD has found no evidence of a generalized brain drain from developing countries to the OECD. As regards most large countries such as Brazil, Indonesia, Bangladesh, India or China, emigration of citizens with tertiary degrees stands at less than a few percentage points. However, some small countries, and in particular some Caribbean (and other) islands, have more than 40% of their highly skilled population resident abroad. Twelfth, women with tertiary degrees are more likely to emigrate to OECD countries than their male counterparts. Teriary degrees are held by 17.6% of women migrants and 13.1% of male migrants.

There is a wealth of additional information in the report which confounds a number of expectations about migration. Just a few further examples are worth adding here: for instance, the USA is host to a positive inflow of highly skilled immigrants from the EU of about 1 million, while Australia and Canada also benefit from an inflow of highly skilled Europeans in excess of their outflows. While the USA is also the main destination country of Latin American emigration, the other main destination countries are Brazil, Jamaica, Ecuador and Colombia. In comparing Latin American migration to the USA with that to Spain, gender proves to be an important aspect. While 43.9% of these immigrants to the USA are women, 54.8% who go to Spain are female.

When considering the main ocupations of foreign-born populations by the country of origin, the outcomes are not always self-evident. For example, in Spain, while 19.3% of the total population is engaged in professional activities, for the Moroccan immigrant population the percentage is 9.0, and for Colombian immigrants, 7.6%. In Australia 25.7% of the population is engaged in the category of technicians. However, 27.0% of the UK immigrants are engaged in this sector and 18.3% of Vietnamese; 15.9% of immigrants from the former Yugoslavia are engaged in this category, while 68.1% of them are working in the lowest category: operators. In Canada, the lowest occupational category by skills level, operators, accounts for 45% of the population. Immigrants from India and the Philippines are each represented in this category at rates of 54.1 and 54.4%, well above the national average, while Chinese immigrants are almost exactly at the national average in this category.

As regards the USA, Mexican immigrants represent 3.4% of the population, 43.6% are engaged in agriculture and industry and 37.4% in personal and social services. The corresponding figures for Chinese immigrants in the USA are 21.7% in agriculture and industry and 46.1% in personal and social services. Of the German immigrants in the USA, 19.7% are in agriculture and industry and 45.9% are engaged in personal and social services. One might conclude that the statistics on occupation by country of residence and origin provide a fairly clear picture which only partially corresponds to national images of social inclusion and exclusion.

The information available on emigrants and their education rates raises interesting questions about some assumptions about certain groups. For instance, among US emigrants, 20.7% have primary education and 48.5% have tertiary education. This indicates that, by and large, it is well-educated Americans who emigrate to other OECD countries. However, it is perhaps less well known that, among Sudanese emigrants, 24.3% have primary education while 41.4% have tertiary education, a rate not far from that of Americans. Further, among Nigerian emigrants, 16.0% have primary education and 54.7% have tertiary education – surpassing, as a percentage US emigrants in qualifications. Malaysian emigrants are also, as a group, more likely to have tertiary education than are American emigrants at 50.2%, while 47.1% of Iranian emigrants have tertiary education. Only 34.7% of British emigrants have tertiary education while 26.9% have primary education, indicating that British emigrants are less likely to be well qualified than their Nigerian counterparts. Mexican emigrants stand out, however, as regards their relatively low levels of education – only 5.7% have tertiary education though 69.6% have primary level.

Remittances in 2005 exceed official development aid by a factor of two to one according to the OECD. However, among the top thirty countries of origin, based on remittances as a percentage of GDP, the top nine countries where remittances account for a percentage in the double digits tend to have fairly small populations (with the exception of the Philippines). The first on the list is Honduras, where the percentage is 22% of GDP, followed by Lebanon at 22.2%. The Dominican Republic is tenth at 9.5%. For many of the countries with the largest numbers of citizens working abroad, remittances are not a significant part of GDP – for instance in both India[6] and Mexico[7] they account for only 2.8%. In Nigeria this drops to 2.3%.

Finally, as regards the management of economic growth, the OECD information, if one takes only the figures of inward direct investment flows, the UK, USA and France are the top three in terms of value of inflows in 2005 (in millions of US dollars, respectively, 164,499, 109,754 and 63,540), while China, Brazil and South Africa are behind at 79,127, 15,193 and 6,257. It is worth noting that employment in affiliates under foreign control as a percentage of total employment among OECD countries only shows that, for instance in manufacturing in the Czech Republic, 32.8% of employees work for companies under foreign control. In the UK the percentage in the same sector is 26.6%, while in Germany and Spain it is just over 15%.

What conclusions can we draw from these statistics as regards the five key issues I identified at the start of this chapter? First, as regards the effects of migrant workers on wages, it appears that, the better educated they are, the more likely it is that they will be excluded from the labour force (i.e. unemployed). This may mean that in developed economies there are well-developed mechanisms which privilege own nationals in highly skilled (and paid) employment. The statistics on underemployment support such a conclusion, as an important obstacle to highly skilled employment is recognition of qualifications. If the state or quasi-state regulatory bodies refuse to accord recognition of diplomas, then immigrants will be forced to take jobs for which they are overqualified.

As regards access to social benefits, the unemployment rates of immigrants are only marginally higher than than those of citizens – even where they have access to benefits paid in the event of unemployment, the difference will be marginal. Further, taking as an example the European Union, 39.9% of expenditure on social protection by the twenty-seven Member States goes to old age benefits.[8] As the majority of migrant workers in OECD countries are under sixty-five, they are less likely to be a charge to this part of the welfare budget.[9]

Flows of capital around the world in the form of direct inward investment seem to privilege developed economies to a greater extent than developing ones. Remittances – which may play an important part in the economies of some countries with small populations – for the large migration-sending countries, as a percentage of GDP, are not significant. Remittances may be very important as a mechanism to keep migrants involved in the family and social structures in their states of origin, but as regards their impact on the economy in general, the picture is more uncertain.

Economic migration, security and Europe

The European Union was built on the principle of labour migration. In the post-Second World War period, the shortage of labour in Europe was dramatic – a result of the destruction wreaked by war and the need to reconstruct whole economies. Many Western European countries faced with labour shortages, such as Germany, Belgium and the Netherlands, entered into bilateral agreements with countries with labour surpluses in the region, such as Italy, Turkey and Morocco, under which agreements workers were recruited (Castles & Miller 2003). It was the oil crisis of 1972–3 and the ensuing economic downturn across Western Europe which led to an end to labour migration and the decision in Germany and France to stop labour migration altogether (Zolberg & Benda 2001).

Confounding this intention to end European labour migration in 1972–3 was the European Union. In its then form of the European Economic Community (and two other Communities – Coal and Steel and Atomic Energy), the six original Member States – Belgium, France, Germany, Italy, Luxembourg and the Netherlands – had undertaken to permit free movement of persons, including workers, among themselves. The Treaty was signed in 1957 and the transitional period for the achievement of free movement of workers ended in 1968. Thus, while labour migration could be halted as regards workers from Turkey or Morocco, Italian workers (or workers from any other Member State) were still entitled to move freely to seek work in other Member States (Guild 2001). The right to move and to work only applied to nationals of the Member States who were economically active as workers, self-employed or service providers and recipients. The Member States were only allowed to restrict economic migration in this form on two grounds. First, if the state could establish that an individual was a threat to public policy, public security or public health – all of which concepts were carefully limited by the European Court of Justice (ECJ), the EU court with the final word on the meaning of EU law – it could expel him or her. Second, the right of free movement for workers did not apply to employment in the public sector (again narrowly defined by the ECJ). The exclusion of workers from other Member States on the basis of public policy or public security was specifically prohibited if the objective was to serve economic ends.[10]

The European Union has been surprisingly restless as an institution. Not only does it change its treaties increasingly frequently it also changes its membership, though for the moment only Greenland has ever withdrawn from it (Weiler 1985). While it started in its form of the European Economic Community in 1957 with six members, it welcomed Denmark, Ireland and the UK into its club in 1973. No restrictions were placed on free movement of workers, though in some of the press, particularly in France and the Netherlands, there were fears that their labour markets would be flooded by British workers, who had no history of minimum wages at that time (Bohning 1972). In 1981 Greece joined, and for the first time there was a delay in granting free movement rights to workers (though not to the self-employed or service providers and recipients). This was resolved in 1986 when Portugal and Spain joined the EU but their citizens were made subject to a delay in the exercise of the right to free movement of worker which ended in 1991. Austria, Finland and Sweden joined in 1995 but no restrictions were placed on the movement of their workers. In 2004, ten states joined the Union. Two, Cyprus and Malta, had no restrictions on free movement of workers. The other eight – the Czech Republic, Estonia, Hungary, Latvia, Lithuania, Poland, Slovakia and Slovenia – were subject to five-year transitional restrictions on free movement of workers, with the possibility of extending the delay a futher two years. In fact, by 1 May 2009, only Austria, Germany and the UK were still making use of the transitional restrictions on free movement of workers.

The EU grew again on 1 January 2007, to include Bulgaria and Romania. Again a transitional period, in which free movement of workers could be restricted, applied – first for a period of two years, which was extendable for a further three years, and finally extendable for an additional two years, but only if there were serious disturbances in the labour market. By 2008, ten Member States had opened their labour markets to workers from the two new states: Cyprus, the Czech Republic, Estonia, Finland, Latvia, Lithuania, Poland, Slovenia, Slovakia, Finland and Sweden (though three of them instituted registration requirements for statistical purposes).[11]

Thus, the area within which workers have a right to move and seek employment irrespective of their nationality has grown dramatically since 1968 when the first transitional restrictions on free movement of workers were lifted. Similarly, the number of persons entitled to move for the purpose of exercising economic activities in any other Member State has grown dramatically. The current population of the EU is approximately 498 million, of which the majority are entitled to move, reside, and look for and take work in any other part. The two most excluded Member States – Bulgaria and Romania (with populations of approximately 7.1 million and 21.7 million) do not count for a significant proportion of the EU population. Nonetheless, only in the region of 2 per cent of the EU population makes use of its right to move for labour purposes.[12]

From 1990, the right of free movement within the EU for economic purposes was augmented by a right to move for non-economic purposes, so as to include students, pensioners and the economically inactive in free movement rights. This was consolidated in 1993 into an immigration status described as 'citizenship of the Union' (art. 17 EC), but as the status does not include an absolute right of entry into the whole of the territory of the EU, nor does it completely prevent a citizen of the Union from being expelled from one Member State to that of his or her nationality, it is not clearly a nationality status (unless one assimilates expulsion from one Member State to another to an internal exclusion order within a state). The right of free movement for the economically inactive carries with it an obligation that the individual is able to support him- or herself financially and has sickness insurance (Bigo & Guild 2005).

The gradual opening-up of labour markets across the EU to workers from the new 2004 and 2007 Member States provides an interesting example of the relationship of job security and labour migration. When, in 2004, three Member States – Ireland, Sweden and the UK – were the first to open their labour markets to workers from the then new Member States, the discussion was dominated by projections that indicated that not many workers would move to seek work (Boswell 2000).[13] In fact the numbers far exceeded state expectations but buoyant economies, in particular in Ireland and the UK, meant that the substantially greater numbers of migrant workers who moved to those two countries found employment.[14] In the UK, in particular, the government commissioned a number of studies on the effects of the arrival of almost 800,000 workers from the newer Member States over the period 2004.[15] For the most part, in the face of political pressure regarding the arrival of not insignificant numbers of foreign workers, the government defended its decision not to take advantage of the possibility to limit access to the UK labour market. A number of studies indicate that workers from the then new Member States did not constitute a threat to the jobs of British workers and, further, that, except for very specific sectors, they had little influence on wage levels (see Pollard, Latorre & Sriskandarajah 2008).

While the UK authorities found themselves wedded to a policy whose ramifications they had not foreseen, they remained loyal to their decision and defended it against all suggestions that the arrival of migrant workers was having a negative impact on the conditions of British workers. However, they chose not to open their labour markets immediately to Bulgarian and Romanian workers in 2007.[16] The position in Ireland was broadly similar but Sweden chose a different approach altogether. Instead of implicitly indicating a change of heart regarding the decision to open its labour markets to the 2004 Member State workers by refusing to do so for the Bulgarians and Romanians, Sweden chose to maintain the same open labour market position for the 2007 Member State nationals. It is somewhat surprising, then, that in fact workers from Bulgaria and Romania went to Italy and Spain after 1 January 2007 (nationals of the two states increased by 200,000 in Spain and almost 300,000 in Italy) even though both countries continued to restrict access to the labour market. The numbers of Bulgarians and Romanians in Sweden in 2007 dropped from the previous year, from 3,000 to 2,000.[17] This information is not very helpful to those who argue in favour of state-controlled migration regimes.

Generally, in the EU, who moves? Polish nationals are the most likely to move to another Member State, accounting for 25% of intra-EU movement. Next come the Romanians at 19%. In third and fourth place, respectively, come the Germans (7%), and the British at 6%. All other nationals constitute smaller percentages of EU migrants. How long do these migrants stay? Here it appears that there are substantial variations. While 7.5% of Irish nationals and 7.8% of Portuguese nationals of working age (as a percentage of the working-age population of their countries of origin) have lived and worked elsewhere in the Union for more than four years, only 4.1% of Romanians fall into this category, along with 3.5% of

Cypriots and 2.8% of Greeks. The figure for Spanish nationals is 0.6%. The number of nationals of Member States who go to live and/or work in another Member State (as a percentage of the national labour force of the country of origin) never exceeds 3.1% (Latvia is the highest), and for fifteen Member States the figure does not even reach 1%. If one compares the mobility rates of EU nationals against the risk of poverty in the Member States, there is no clear correlation. The European Commission has designed a measure of risk of poverty which includes the percentage of the population for whom the equivalized income is below 60% of the median income of their country.[18] The risk of poverty for the overall population ranges from 10% to 12% in the Czech Republic, Denmark, the Netherlands, Slovenia, Slovakia and Sweden, but rises to 20–23% (i.e. doubles) in Italy, Greece, Latvia, Lithuania and Spain. Yet Italy's mobility rate is 1.6% of the working population, Greece's 3.3%, Latvia's 1.9%, Lithuania's 4.4% and Spain's 0.7%. On the other hand, the Netherlands' mobility rate is 1.9%, higher than Italy's, or Spain's and the same as Latvia's. The Commission also calculates that the income of the poor people in the three richest EU Member States – Austria, the UK and Luxembourg – is nearly four times higher than that of poor people in the three poorest states, Latvia, Poland and Lithuania.

What do these statistics mean? They indicate that there is no clear correlation between poverty, either absolute or comparative, and movement of workers. When one takes out of the equation the effectiveness or otherwise of immigration controls, as is the case in the EU where there is free movement of persons for economic purposes, the risk of poverty and absolute levels of poverty in countries does not correspond to the levels of movement of workers. People do not move in statistically significant numbers because of poverty. The relationship of poverty and migration is at least in part anecdotal in the EU. This raises serious questions as to whether it is siginificant as regards migration elsewhere in the world.

EU migrant workers do send remittances back to their countries of origin. The amounts vary dramatically as a share of GDP.[19] In 2006, remittances from Romanian workers (who were not yet EU nationals, as Romania only joined the EU in 2007) accounted for over 6.5 per cent of the GDP of their home country. For Bulgaria the amount was only marginally less. Those two states are quite exceptional in the EU context: after them, the next highest remittances as a percentage of GDP, were to Luxembourg at 3 per cent, whereafter the figures drop to below 2.5 per cent, and for sixteen Member States remittances account for less than 1 per cent of GDP.

Another aspect of the perceived security threat of migrants which is evident in the EU enlargements of 2004 and 2007 is the approach which some Member States took towards access to social benefits for workers from the newer Member States. According to EU law, workers from any Member State who move to and work in another Member State are entitled to equal treatment in all social and tax advantages.[20] This includes access to all non-contributory social benefits. The EU also has a very complex system of coordination of social security which ensures that workers who move from one country to another do not lose out on their social contributions, health benefits, pension rights, etc.[21] Between the two systems, in principle, workers from any Member State should be entitled to the same social security benefits as nationals of the host country. The UK was concerned, on the eve of the 2004 enlargement, that workers from the new Member States would come there and, after only minimal employment, seek to enjoy UK social benefits. As a result it restricted access to social benefits by creating a new test – the right to reside test – which/ at least nominally, applies to everyone – British citizens, nationals of all Member States, foreigners, etc. However, its application fell disproportionately on nationals of the 2004 Member States, as the legal construction of their right to reside in national law meant that, if they were out of employment, their right to reside ceased and thus their entitlement to benefits ended.[22]

Labour migration to the UK from the newer Member States was constructed as a benefit for the economy and the UK labour force, but the government considered that these workers should not be incorporated into the British system of social solidarity in the form of social security. Instead they should be left in a state of insecurity, excluded from social benefits. The level of insecurity was in fact quite substantial. A leading challenge to the UK government's exclusion of these labour migrants from social security was made by a Polish woman, who, having worked in Northern Ireland for some months, was joined first by her child and then by the child's father. As a result of domestic violence, she fled her job and home and took refuge in a women's hostel with her daughter. She applied for social benefits. These were refused on the basis that she did not have a right to reside. The issue is, directly, the security of the individual worker versus the scope of social security. Before the UK courts, the government argued that:

> The right to exclude workers from the labour market included the right to take steps short of exclusion but which themselves were designed to help protect the labour market and to avoid the need to pay public money in a form of benefits when there was no work necessarily

> available. The national measures were necessary and proportionate and struck a fair balance.[23]

In fact, according to UK statistics on the issuing of National Insurance numbers, very few migrant workers, whether they are nationals of EU Member States or others, claim out-of-work benefits within the first six months of arrival in the UK.[24]

In comparison with the UK's approach to workers from the newer Member States, Sweden adopted a somewhat different one not only in respect of access to the labour market but also in respect of social benefits. In a more even-handed approach, Sweden did not seek to exclude migrant workers from other Member States, or specifically the newer Member States, from its social security system. It only took measures to exclude those nationals of other Member States who had not engaged in any economic activity.[25] Thus, notwithstanding the fact that Sweden's expenditure on social protection as a percentage of GDP is 32.0 (while the UK spends 26.8 per cent), it was willing to extend social security to EU labour migrants, bringing into play the full range of social solidarity and social inclusion measures.[26]

The example of the European Union reveals a labour migration system where states give up the right to control the entry, residence and economic activities of migrant workers, with only very limited exceptions which, in each case the state must justify against the right of the individual to move and work. Two aspects are worth noting: first, the EU actively encourages workers to move from one Member State to another on the ground that this will help them to fulfil their potential. Second, in the context of enlargement when states join the EU, although on four occasions, as part of the accession processes, there has been a delay for nationals of the acceding Member States in the realization of the right to move to other Member States and work, the right is realized within a few years. Member State fears about the security of their labour markets is controlled, and concerns about maintaining social solidarity through the social security systems in the face of the arrival of migrant workers are kept in check. These are political choices made by the governments of the twenty-seven countries, not essential facts about labour markets or social solidarity.

While some Member States have taken action to reduce access to benefits for migrant workers, other Member States – indeed, even ones which, on account of their investment in social security, arguably have more to lose – have not done so. They have rather accepted the logic of the EU that the right to equality of treatment for migrant workers includes the right to social security. The purpose of this analysis is to question what is often presented as a self-evident relationship between exclusionary moves by states in respect of migrant workers and the security of the labour market and social security (Bommes & Geddes 2000). The example of the European Union does not support the logic that only by strict management of access to the labour market by migrant workers, and their exclusion from the systems of social security, can job security, labour standards and social solidarity be protected.

The EU, foreigners and migrant workers

Does the EU system, which is so generous to migrant workers, depend on its exclusivity? Is the rule of reciprocity an element central to a system which permits the individual to make the choice of where to work unimpeded by arguments of market security? In order to examine this part of the question I will look at how the EU deals with third-country-national migrant workers. 'Third-country national' is the term normally used in EU-speak to describe someone who is not a national of any of the EU Member States, which is not to suggest that all third-country nationals are the same.

One of the most striking aspects of the EU's relationship with third countries and their nationals has been its diversity. So while nationals of Iceland or Norway (neither of which are EU Member States) have rights which are virtually the same as EU citizens as a result of international agreements between their countries and the EU, nationals of other countries are excluded to increasing levels (Bigo & Guild 2003). Leaving aside here the agreements with numerous countries which provide for privileged treatment of third-country nationals in the EU, in this section I will concentrate on nationals of those states which do not benefit from such treatment. Similarly, I will not examine the position of third-country family members of EU citizens, as their rights are assimilated to those of their EU national principal (Guild 2004).

Until 1999, the EU did not have the power to make any binding law on the admission of third-country nationals generally. This position changed with the entry into force of the Amsterdam Treaty in that year. The EU was given power to adopt laws on asylum, borders and immigration, including family reunification and irregular migration (Verdun & Croci 2005; Vink 2005). For the purposes of this section I will look at what happened as regards labour migration, and at the extent to which the moves in this regard mirror, or differ from, the development of labour migration rights for EU nationals.

The only group which, by 2008, was the subject of EU rules on labour migration was third-country nationals who have already lived (regularly) for five years in any one Member State.[27] In 2003 the EU adopted a Directive on long-term-resident third-country nationals which provides a common set of rights for third-country nationals, whichever Member State they happen to be living in (Directive 2003/109).[28] While the Directive excludes a number of categories of third-country nationals, it is intended to cover the majority who reside for five years in the Union (students, however, must first acquire a secure residence status before they can qualify, and their years of residence only count for half of that of others – see chapter 3 regarding the protection this Directive gives third-country nationals in respect of expulsion).

In addition to the acquisition of rights on the territory of the Member States where the residence has been acquired, the Directive provides a right to move and exercise economic activities in any other Member State. However, a number of possible restrictions may be applied to the right so that Member States can protect their labour markets. The most important of these restrictions is that Member States are permitted to delay the exercise of the right for up to twelve months (art. 21). This means that, while the third-country national who has acquired long-term resident status has the right to move to any other Member State, the state can delay his or her access to the labour market for twelve months. This restriction does not apply to self-employment or service provision. Nonetheless, it does constitute a considerable obstacle as the individual would have to survive in the host state for a year without working. In theory at least, the individual could continue to work in his or her first EU state of residence after having set up home in the second Member State, but this creates all sorts of problems of travel, distance, etc. It also means the individual could be classified as a frontier worker and therefore fall into another category (Groenendijk 2007).

Another obstacle which Member States may place in the way of third-country nationals with long-term residence status who wish to work in their countries is that they are entitled to examine the situation of their labour markets and apply their national procedures regarding the requirements for filling vacancies or exercising self-employed activities. While there is a right to work for third-country nationals with the required status, the ambiguity around how far the host state is entitled to hinder access to the labour market through the application of its procedures has yet to be tested. Further, Member States are permitted to give priority to nationals of EU Member States, those third-country nationals who are privileged by EU law itself or third-country nationals who reside legally and receive unemployment benefits in the Member State concerned. While this may appear to be a problematic requirement, in practice it usually is not so onerous as, administratively, this preference is very difficult to apply.

Member States are also permitted to take into consideration national quota provisions which applied at the time the Directive was adopted (art. 14). This provision applies only to those Member States which had quotas at that time. The Member State with the most impressive quota system is Austria, which is also the Member State which was most keen on this provision being included in the Directive (Boelart-Suominen 2005).

In addition to these rather overt obstacles, the Directive permits Member States to assess the economic capacity of a third-country national who seeks to move to another Member State on the basis of his or her long-term residence status. While for EU nationals who are not economically active, the economic test is firmly fixed at the level sufficient to avoid becoming a burden on the social security system of the destination Member State, for third-country nationals the test is quite different as it is not tied to social solidarity. The state is allowed to assess whether the third-country national who fulfils the residence requirement has stable and regular resources which are sufficient to maintain himself/herself and the members of his/her family, without recourse to the social assistance system of the Member State. Further, the state is entitled to evaluate these resources by reference to their nature and regularity and may take into account the level of minimum wages and pensions (Minderhoud 2006b).

This means that, while the reference point at which the third-country national is not considered a risk to the economic wellbeing of the state – above the social security threshold or minimum level of pensions – must be achieved by the third-country national who seeks the stable status, the state is not required to apply only this lower level. It can require a higher level of resources for a third-country national and, indeed, with the qualification that the nature and stability of the resources can be taken into account, the third-country national can be refused the status on the basis that his or her employment contract is temporary or limited. At least in theory, this permits Member States to apply much higher economic sufficiency tests for third-country nationals than for citizens of the Union – in fact the Netherlands has done this and requires third country nationals to show they earn 120 per cent of the minimum wage before permitting them access to a secure residence status (Groenendijk, Srtik & van Oers 2007).

The main argument against a wide flexibility among the Member States as regards the income levels which third-country nationals must have before they acquire a secure residence right under EU law is that this would permit too much variation in the way third-country nationals are treated in different Member States. The European Court of Justice used this argument in its decision in *Metock* regarding third-country national family members of migrant citizens of the Union, rejecting variations in national legislation on the grounds that this:

> would vary from one Member State to another, according to the provisions of national law concerning immigration, with some Member States permitting entry and residence of family members of a Union citizen and other Member States refusing them. That would not be compatible with the objective set out in Article 3(1)(c) EC of an internal market characterised by the abolition, as between Member States, of obstacles to the free movement of persons. Establishing an internal market implies that the conditions of entry and residence of a Union citizen in a Member State whose nationality he does not possess are the same in all the Member States. Freedom of movement for Union citizens must therefore be interpreted as the right to leave any Member State, in particular the Member State whose nationality the Union citizen possesses, in order to become established under the same conditions in any Member State other than the Member State whose nationality the Union citizen possesses.[29]

This reasoning applies also to third-country nationals who fulfil the conditions of the Directive, though the European Court of Justice has not (yet) been asked to apply it to them.

A further difference which exists between EU-national migrant workers and third-country national migrant workers with EU long-term residents' permits relates to social security. Third-country nationals acquire the right to equal treatment with nationals as regards social security, social assistance and social protection but, exceptionally, Member States are permitted to restrict this equal treatment to what are described as core benefits (art. 11(4)), defined in the Preamble of the Directive as including at least 'income support, assistance in case of illness, pregnancy, parental assistance and long term care'. Key benefits which are excluded from this core group relate to unemployment and old age.

Another possible difference relates to sickness insurance. The individual seeking to move from one Member State to another will have to show that he or she has sickness insurance covering all risks in the second Member State which are normally covered for its own nationals in that state (art. 15(2)(b)). The very complicated EU system of coordination of social security means that EU-national migrant workers are normally able to take with them their benefits entitlements (Regulation 1408/71). This system has been extended to third-country nationals lawfully residing in the EU (Regulation 859/2003), which should be sufficient to cover the sickness insurance problem as long as the individual is not moving from a state with a very limited sickness insurance system, in terms of its coverage, to one where the standard is very high. Through these obstacles, EU states construct the third-country national as a potential risk to economic security (Minderhoud 2006).

Another obstacle, which is not directly economically related but rather related to a social construction of identity within the state, is the integration test. In general, integration tests, as a mechanism for testing which foreigners should have secure immigration statuses, swept through European policy discussions like a dose of salts in the late 1990s and early 2000s. In a number of Member States they were perceived as the solution to a whole series of social problems – social exclusion, petty criminality, alienation, etc. The argument began that foreigners need to integrate into European societies better. From this being perceived as a two-way process entered into by the state and the foreigner, it rapidly became a matter of testing – the state applying a test to foreigners to see whether they have sufficiently integrated (Carrera 2008).

The testing then became tied to immigration status, whereby if the foreigner failed to pass the test he or she would be refused a desired immigration status. At first the policy was oriented towards the acquisition of a secure residence status (which gives access to social benefits) but then, as it took root, some Member States, such as the Netherlands, followed by Denmark and Germany, commenced a programme of making integration tests part of the procedures for first admission, in particular for family members (Groenendijk, Guild & Carrera 2009). In this way a new ground for exclusion of foreigners came into European immigration law, based on the security risk of failure to integrate.

The content of integration tests became the next field of contestation. To what extent should conviction for minor criminal offences be evidence of a failure of integration? Here the French government implemented a programme of contracts between new immigrants and the state, whereby their residence status depended on their acceptance of a contractual obligation (as opposed to a state criminal law obligation) not to commit criminal offences (Carrera 2008). As Ryan points out in his examination of the UK experience, those most likely to fail the test and therefore to remain without a strong immigration status which permits them access to social benefits are exactly those migrants who have the greatest need – the ones who are in socially marginal positions and are struggling (Ryan 2009).

Long-term resident third-country nationals in the EU can be required to comply with integration conditions according to national law (art. 5(2)). The exact scope of these integration conditions is not specified. If the third-country national has to comply with them in the first state which grants him or her the status of long-term resident, then when he or she moves to another Member State, integration conditions cannot be applied a second time. But if the individual did not have to fulfil the conditions the first time round, then the second Member State can apply an integration conditions requirement.

These provisions in respect of delaying and complicating access to the labour market, assessing economic capacity, requiring sickness insurance and applying integration conditions are included in the Directive. This means that the possibility for the state to change these rules in accordance with national law is not possible. If a Member State wants to come up with a new obstacle to labour market access for a long-term resident third-country national and that obstacle does not come within the list (for instance a Member State which does not have a quota wants to introduce one), it is prohibited from doing so by EU law. Further, the principle of proportionality in EU law means that a measure must not be excessive in relation to the objective which it is designed to achieve. As yet it is not evident exactly how this constraint may be applied in respect of third-country nationals and economic requirements applied as a condition for the acquisition of a secure residence status. However, it is apparent that, just as in respect of the state's power to expel a third-country national on the basis that he or she is a threat to public policy or public security, so too the capacity of the state to act in the interests of economic security are diminished when this is a question of third-country nationals who have completed five years' residence in another Member State.

The experience of implementing the Directive in the national laws of the Member States has shown a substantial resistance in some to acknowledge fully the extent of the right of third-country nationals, who objectively fulfil the conditions, to enjoy the protection of the Directive. For example, the Cyprus government refused an EU long-term resident permit to a Filipino domestic servant who had lived and worked continuously in Cyprus for six years, on residence permits which were each of limited duration and marked 'not renewable' though each time they were renewed by the authorities without difficulty.[30] The Cyprus Supreme Court agreed with the state that the woman was not entitled to the status relying on the provision in the Directive which permits the exclusion of persons 'who reside solely on temporary grounds such as au pair or seasonal worker' (art. 3(2) (e)). Eventually, the problem of just how far Member States can apply obstacles to third-country nationals with the required status, to exclude them from their labour markets, will be decided by the European Court of Justice. To this extent, the Member States no longer have control over the measures which they consider necessary to protect their labour markets from third-country nationals holding the correct status.

Conclusions

The relationship between migration and economic security is characterized by very substantial inconsistencies between public discourse, particularly in developed countries, and the practices. While there is substantial noise in many developed countries about the negative economic impacts of immigrants on their countries, statistically, labour migration is generally insignificant as regards the working populations of both host countries and those of origin. The very few exceptions relate to small states, most commonly islands. The profile of labour migrants in developed countries provides a picture of a population more qualified than the host population but working below the level of their qualifications and marginally more at risk of unemployment than citizens of the state.

The inconsistencies between the realities of economic migration and security discussions are compounded when one examines one part of the developed world – the European Union. Here, at the moment when governments in France, Germany and elsewhere moved against labour migration on the basis of their duty to protect jobs for their own nationals, in 1972–3, there was already in place hard law providing a right of labour migration for many of the countries which have been sources of migration to north-western Europe (most importantly Italy, soon to be joined by Greece, Portugal, Spain and then, in 2004, by the Central and Eastern European countries). Not only did the system of free movement for workers survive the end of labour migration declared in north-western European countries, but the EU expanded to include many countries which have traditionally sent labour migrants to those same north-western states.

Examining then, in slightly greater detail, the fear of economic migration as a threat to economic security, and the treatment of workers from the states which joined the EU in 2004 and 2007 from Central and Eastern Europe and the Balkans, the political discussion and the reality of the threat diverge. While, in the UK, substantial political energy was put into excluding migrant workers from the 2004 Member States from social benefits, the same was not the case in Sweden, also a state which permitted immediate access to its labour market for the newcomers. The outcomes in the two countries, in both political and social terms, also diverged. After three years of political discussion and various changes to the rules to exclude from social benefits migrant workers from Central and Eastern Europe, in 2007 the UK chose to exclude from its labour market, for as long as possible, migrant workers coming from the two states which joined the EU in 2007. Sweden, on the other hand, after a much less hectic political debate, took no measures to exclude migrant workers from the 2004 Member States from their social benefits system (which accounts for significantly more of GDP expenditure than the UK system does). Further, it immediately welcomed labour migrants from the 2007 Member States.

The construction of the migrant as a threat to economic welfare does not disappear from the EU political landscape. It reappears in the context of non-EU nationals – those persons who do not hold the citizenship of any Member State. In respect of this group, where the EU has legislated, specifically in regard to third-country nationals who have lived for more than five years in any Member State, substantial emphasis can be seen on their presence as a potential threat to economic security. Not only is their access to the labour market in the context of a right of free movement subject to obstacles, but their access to a secure residence status at all is subject to them providing evidence that they are self-supporting beyond any minimum threshold applicable to the state's own nationals. The rules reveal the political position of the governments that foreigners are a greater threat to economic security than citizens and thus they must prove to a higher level their economic capacities. Further, even after acquisition of a secure residence status, Member States are still permitted to limit the migrant's access to social benefits to so-called 'core' benefits. The relationship of foreignness with economic threat is both revealed and reinforced through the rules which are adopted. Notwithstanding evidence that the correlation is insignificant, the insistence on its centrality by political actors, which is shown through the rules and their application to individuals, indicates that political goals unrelated to economic security are at stake in the discussion.

8

Foreigners, trafficking and globalization

Migrant workers are only one part of the economic migration equation. Employers are equally interested in ensuring that they are able to employ the workers they want in the places where they are carrying out their activities. The insecurity continuum eases the passage of security concerns from one aspect of the presence of foreigners on the territory of a state to another, taking as its organizing principle the construction of foreignness as an inherent risk. Thus political actors are able to reformulate the 'bogus' asylum seeker as a threat into the 'bogus' economic migrant as a threat through the prism of lack of state control over the individual and his or her relationship with a border.

The insecurity continuum as it embraces migrant workers, however, comes up against an increasing organized group of economic actors for whom this presents obstacles to their economic objectives. Transnational companies depend on being able to do business in a number of different countries with a minimum of problems surrounding the crossing of borders. The OECD has signalled that the growth of international trade in services has become increasingly important for the developed world. For OECD countries, the value of international trade in services rose from US$ 82.1 billion in 1997 to US$ 140.4 billion in 2005.[1] In 2004, employment in manufacturing and services in affiliates under foreign control among OECD countries ranged from a low of 6 per cent in Turkey to 46 per cent in services and 22 per cent in manufacturing in Ireland. In Hungary the rate in services was about 43 per cent while in the USA it was 11 per cent.

When companies invest in countries other than that where they are based, generally they also send workers from headquarters to the subsidiary to carry out activities such as technology transfer, management, etc. The larger the company, the greater the need for international integration, so workers from subsidiaries and related companies around the world need to move to gain knowledge by working in different parts of the company in different countries. For these increasingly important transnational economic actors, state obstacles to the movement of workers are problematic.

The capacity of national political actors to mobilize national anti-foreigner sentiment on security grounds which spill over into the labour market constitutes a problem not only for foreign workers but for companies which depend on being able to move workers around the world. In this way, economic migration becomes a concern of the entrepreneurs of globalization in their effort to avoid the stigmatization of migration, which may constitute an obstacle to their ability to do business. There is another side of this coin: those transnational actors whose activities are categorized as trafficking in human beings. States in the international community have entered into a UN agreement to criminalize this kind of globalization, which is just as dependent on movement of persons for economic purposes, under the control of an economic actor. In this chapter I will examine how actors engage with the migration–security construction to achieve their objectives.

'Globalization' is a term which is much used, both as a signal of the transformation of sovereignty in the face of the pursuit of corporate profit across state borders and as a pole around which to mobilize resistance to certain moves in the development of western capitalism. Most fundamentally, it expresses a principle which places the interest in movement in search of economic gain above that of the nation state to exercise controls across and within its borders. Companies whose activities are based in many different countries use their economic power to ensure the best possible conditions for those activities, irrespective of national borders. Border controls which offend against the interests of the beneficiaries of globalization may be the subject of attack by them or of negotiation to accommodate their interests. However, behind the simplicity of this formulation lurk the complex processes through which, as Beck puts it, sovereign national states are criss-crossed and undermined by transnational actors with varying prospects of power, orientations, identities and networks (Beck 2000).

Susan Strange sets out three premises as vital to understanding the modern world: first, the position of politics – the exercise of politics is not a monopoly of the state but is equally exercised by non-state actors; second, power over outcomes is exercised impersonally by markets; and third, authority in society and over economic transactions is legitimately exercised by agents other than states (Strange 1996). Friction among these actors presupposes the successful expropriation by the state, from individuals and private entities, of the legitimate means of movement across international borders (Torpey 2000). The regulation of economic migration between states requires the identification of foreigners, whose access is controlled through state regulation. Nationals of a state are entitled, by international law norms, to enter their state of origin. They do not then qualify for regulation as economic migrants. The state's ability to identify persons outside its borders is determinant of the status of those persons on crossing the border.

Strange's modern state is characterized by a changing relationship among four factors of power: (1) the possibility to offer security; (2) the capacity to grant or withhold credit; (3) the ability to control access to knowledge (which includes the power to define the nature of knowledge); and (4) the mechanisms to control production. The struggle over all four of these fields is at the heart of globalization. The four fields all determine how and where economic activities are exercised, and by whom. For instance, obtaining credit or not is frequently subject to rules on residence within the state, the ability to produce masses of documentation regarding assets within the state which provide security for credit, etc. The ability of companies lawfully to secure the services of foreigners they consider to be highly skilled, and thus to obtain the knowledge they want where they want it, depends on the rules on immigration and work permits in the host state. If that state does not accept that the skills of the individual meet the criteria which the state has determined are decisive for the issue of a work permit, the company will not be able to hire the person in the country where it wishes, thus the state both controls the definition of knowledge and access by private-sector actors to it (Ruhs & Martin 2008).

The control of production is a particularly contested area as regards state and private actors. Where production takes places is a highly political decision, but one which is taken first and foremost by private actors (Underhill 1998). The movement of production facilities from Western European countries to Eastern European ones or beyond, on the grounds of lower labour costs, has been highly controversial throughout Europe, though it is a decision taken for the most part by private actors. From the migration perspective, this is often viewed somewhat differently: should people cross borders to go to jobs or should jobs cross borders to go to people? In this formulation, outsourcing across borders, the moving of production facilities abroad, etc., changes from an issue of security of domestic jobs to one tied to the possible influx of foreign workers. By shifting the discussion to the territory of foreigners, the constituency of interests in many liberal democracies changes.

I will be examining in this chapter the struggle around globalization and the offer of security in the context of migration. Suffice it here to note that security reveals a number of different facets in the context of globalization:

- the security of domestic markets for domestic economic actors, which entails the power to exclude foreign competition – this aspect is central to globalization which is premised on free markets across borders, thereby diminishing state capacity to exercise exclusionary practices vis-à-vis foreign companies;
- the security of borders as a mechanism by which states differentiate between citizens and foreigners and their respective access to the economy;
- the security of market access and equal treatment – issues which engage the interests of companies and individuals moving across borders for economic activities and which find their place in the tools of globalization;
- the security of the individual against exploitation in the exercise of economic activities, coupled with the security of economic actors that their market position is not undermined by other actors whose exploitative labour practices provide a competitive advantage.

The changing relationship of the state and economic actors has profound consequences regarding the capacity to regulate movement across borders. The intersection of globalization with security, revealing many of its different facets, is the place where the changing relationship is most clearly evident. The state's claim to control security, in a number of the forms set out above, while apparently abandoning other facets of security, finds expression in the mechanisms of globalization around the movement of persons.

Elsewhere I have examined how migration exemplifies the struggles which Strange outlines (Bigo & Guild 2005). Here it is Strange's first and final principles, the claims to control over security and to the means of production, which I will examine. The aim of states to control security has been the subject of much debate and discussion, in particular since the attacks in the USA on 11 September 2001. However, it is the way in which the negotiation of states (in particular western liberal democracies) with markets works, as regards movement of persons for economic interests, which I will tease out in this chapter.

My premise is that Strange's insight into the operation of states and markets is central to understanding the way in which globalization has worked with regard to economic migration. On the one hand, faithful participation in the system of global trade is gradually, but apparently inexorably, moving towards obliging states to withdraw, or limit substantially, their activities regarding the control of movement of persons for economic purposes across their borders. On the other hand, the loss of control over movement of persons across borders is closely tied to security and presents particularly difficult political issues for liberal democracies (Lund Petersen 2008). The categorization of issues as security-related often insulates them from political arguments in favour of globalization. Once a politically difficult issue is re-categorized, from a policy field in which governments have invested much effort to present the benefits (such as the advantages of free markets and the limitation of obstacles to global trade) to one where other political concerns arise (such as the exploitation of foreign labour not so much by local economic actors as by unscrupulous parts of the international trade system – traffickers in human beings), the security issue fixes political concern at a legitimate target – unscrupulous traffickers of human beings – but the measures proposed to address this target are likely to be inimical to having borders open for movement of persons. Just as the norms of globalization are found in international instruments which have consequences for sovereignty as regards borders and the control of movement of persons, so, too, what has become the international movement against trafficking in human beings has been expressed in international instruments which require border control measures, which are difficult to reconcile with the instruments of globalization.

What is the home of globalization?

The pursuit of corporate profit across borders has been both reified and vilified (Stiglitz 2002). There has certainly been an intensification of cross-border economic activity since the end of bipolarity when the Soviet Union and its sphere of influence dissolved, thereby permitting the extension of the principles of market economies to a substantial number of countries (WTO 2007). However, officially approved forms of international activity sooner or later need rule books so that states can justify their actions on the basis of the rules or argue about whether there is a level playing field. For globalization this set of rules are found in the World Trade Organization (WTO). The objective of the WTO is to ensure that international trade is as fair as possible and as free as practical. The first of the agreements which over time have become the WTO was signed in 1947, though the WTO itself did not come into existence until 1995. It is the only organization which deals with the rules of trade between nations (and it is not part of the UN system). Its goal is to help producers of goods and services, exporters and importers conduct their business.[2] Only states can be members of the WTO – 151 had signed up as at 15 October 2007 (according to the WTO website, a further 30 were negotiating membership).[3] The WTO rule book on international trade is comprised of over 30,000 pages and 30 agreements, according to the organization. It focuses on six main activities:

- administration of trade agreements;
- a forum for trade negotiations (an area in which it has been particularly active and successful with 30 agreements signed);
- a dispute settlement mechanism for international trade disputes (the Dispute Settlement Body);
- a policing mechanism in respect of national trade policies (the Trade Policy Review Body);
- providing a venue for technical assistance to developing countries;
- participating in the system of international organizations.

Approximately 97 per cent of the world's trade takes place among states which are parties to the WTO agreements. The decision-making bodies of the WTO include a Ministerial Conference, including delegates from all the Members, which meets every two years. There is then a General Council, which is made up of ambassadors and heads of delegation, based in Geneva, which meets several times a year. This body also sits as the Trade Policy Review Body and the Dispute Settlement Body. Under these bodies, one finds the three sector-specific venues: the Goods Council, Services Council and the Intellectual Property Council, all of which report to the General Council.

The international community opens borders?

Of particular interest to the issue of individuals is the Services Council. Among the many agreements which constitute the WTO, the General Agreement on Trade in Services (GATS) is the one which touches the individual most directly. A late-comer to the WTO system, it was only in 1995 that services acquired their own agreement. While many services can be provided without the movement of persons, such as telecommunications, many others cannot. This is particularly the case for services which are created and consumed simultaneously, for instance most kinds of installation or repair work where the service cannot be provided if a person is not able to be physically on the site where it is provided to do so. In GATS-speak, this is called 'Mode 4' service provision. As the whole system is designed to regulate cross-border economic activities and as the decision was taken to extend the system to services, including those which can only be carried out if a foreigner is permitted entry to the state, a clash between the security interests of the state and the international system was inevitable. The first manifestation of this struggle between the international rule book and state sensitivities about movement of persons is that, on the GATS website, the second paragraph on Mode 4 is consecrated to immigration worries: 'Movement of "natural persons" refers to the entry and temporary stay of persons for the purpose of providing a service. It does not relate to persons seeking citizenship, permanent employment or permanent residence in a country.'[4]

The transformation of 'migration' into a term designed around temporality – temporary versus permanent – is clearly a mechanism designed to deal with the sovereignty problem. In order to frustrate an insecurity continuum move by some political actors, service provision movement of persons is defined out of migration – it becomes something else. Unlike other agreements in the WTO system, for instance on goods, the GATS works backwards in that, instead of all sectors being covered by the agreement unless they are specifically excluded, all sectors are excluded unless specifically included.

Within the GATS framework, service provision can encompass three types of movement of persons: first, where the consumer moves to the service provider. This is the most common as it is what tourists do – cross borders to consume goods and services such as hotel rooms, restaurant meals, etc., in other countries. The second type of service provision in the GATS is the equivalent of the right of establishment in the EU: the establishment of a commercial presence on the territory of another GATS member country. Thirdly, service provision includes the movement of persons from one country to another to carry out service provision which does not involve the establishment of a commercial presence. The GATS system is based on a number of basic principles in respect of which member countries are entitled either to retain exceptions listed in the annexes or to sign up in accordance with sectoral annexes. There are two key principles which have a direct impact on state control over migration:

- The general obligations – (a) member countries will provide to one another most favoured nation (MFN) treatment for access to the market, i.e., the territory (art. II GATS). For included sectors, the best treatment which one member provides to another country must be extended to all GATS member countries. Exceptions and exemptions to the MFN treatment were permitted, but had to be tabled at the time of adoption and could not be added to subsequently. This principle applies to the three

types of movement of persons within the GATS framework: access by persons seeking to use services, to set up a commercial presence or to provide services on a one-off basis. Where states wished to preserve special treatment for nationals of certain countries, these exceptions had to be listed in a schedule (Jackson 1997).
(b) transparency: there must be published rules available to all economic actors on the limitations which have been placed on market access (if any).

- The specific commitment – (a) market access – this is negotiated sector by sector to determine which markets are opened to economic actors from other members and under which conditions, and which remain closed.
(b) treatment 'no less favourable than that [the country] accords to its own like services and service suppliers' (GATS art. XVII) – the equal treatment provision covers both direct and indirect discrimination. Formally different treatment is permitted only so long as it does not modify the conditions of competition in favour of the services of service providers of the host country. Exceptions and limitations to this equal treatment provision are permitted but must be made public through inclusion in the schedule of specific commitments. Again these are submitted for each state individually.

Leaving aside the exceptions, exemptions and limitations contained in the annexes (which restrict the impact of the GATS), what are the consequences of two principles? First, if economic actors have a right to market access, then they need to be able to cross borders to enjoy this. Economic actors may be either individuals who, as self-employed persons, are carrying out contracts they have won on the territory of another state, or companies which seek to move their employees to carry out contracts elsewhere (from the fields which have been the subject of greatest liberalization, one can see that it is transnational companies which are favoured in the system). In either case, in Mode 4, people will need to cross borders in order that the promises of the GATS are fulfilled. The GATS mechanism for achieving this is to permit members to maintain their systems of immigration control, but whatever regime applies to the most favoured country must apply to all GATS members' economic actors. This is a sort of lockstep arrangement – whatever is agreed for the closest trading partner must be extended to all.

The second principle is also challenging in the migration context. If equality with domestic actors is guaranteed, then, when the foreign economic actor has access to the market, obstacles to the exercise of economic activities should also be abolished. In principle, this should include restrictions on the immigration status of the individual who is carrying out the economic activity which would operate as a constraint on the completion of the service provision. These come in the form of time restrictions on lawful presence on the territory and on the type of activity which can be carried out. Equal treatment also raises the question of recognition of professional qualifications and compliance with national rules on consumer protection. Additionally, equal treatment with national economic actors engages the issue of working conditions, wages and social protection – to what extent are service providers, in the form of either individuals who are providing services themselves or of companies which are service providers and provide the services through their employees, obliged to comply with national rules?

The GATS expressly permits states to contravene their obligations if this is necessary to protect public morals or maintain public order; to protect human or plant life or health; or to secure compliance with law or regulations not inconsistent with the GATS, in particular those necessary to prevent deceptive or fraudulent practices.

The GATS framework of economic migration is based on the principle that private enterprises are the determiners – if they are self-employed, they move to where the work is; if they are corporate entities, they select, recruit and move workers depending on the demands of the market, as determined by themselves. The provisions of the GATS are designed to promote market access for service providers – in other words, to restrict the power of states to impede access to their territory by foreign competitors in the services field through the use of restrictive economic migration laws. The provisions are written in terms of the rights of service providers based in one of the GATS signatories.

Migrants and GATS

The question of market access for natural persons has been a matter of substantial negotiation within the GATS. As mentioned above, the principle of the GATS – access to the territory on the same basis as the most privileged of foreigners and equal access to the market once within the state – enters immediately into conflict with the principle of national immigration control. Immigration control is based on the principle that sovereignty gives states the right to discriminate against foreigners in comparison with their own nationals (this is the reason why it is possible to have border controls on persons). This right to control the entry of foreigners onto the territory is not tempered by any obligation to treat all foreigners the same way (otherwise it would not be possible to submit the nationals of some countries to mandatory visa requirements while exempting nationals of others). Thus, immigration control is based on the right of state officials, in the exercise of sovereign powers, to discriminate against foreigners and among different groups of foreigners. It remains an open question to what extent the exercise of sovereign powers is subject even to a duty to provide reasons for the decision of the immigration official, be it at the consulate on a visa application or at the border.[5]

Equal treatment with nationals as regards market access within the state is also complicated from the perspective of immigration controls. Immigration controls in liberal democracies are based on limiting two main aspects of the individual's presence: (a) the length of time which the individual can spend on the territory (for instance tourists and visitors are limited to three months out of every six in the EU); and (b) the economic activities which the individual can enter into (in the EU tourists and visitors are prohibited from engaging in economic activities except in very limited ways). Both of these principles of immigration control are in conflict with the GATS principle of equal treatment with own nationals.

In order to resolve, at least in part, these conflicts, there is an Annex to the GATS on movement of people supplying services.[6] It applies both to individuals who provide services themselves and the employees of companies which are providing services via them. The Annex specifies that the GATS does not apply to measures:

- affecting natural persons seeking access to the employment market;
- citizenship, residence or employment on a permanent basis.

There are a number of points of difficulty in these exclusions. The first, which has arisen in the context of the EU, is whether the employees of service providers who arrive to carry out work in a state are seeking access to the employment market. The European Court of Justice has answered this question with a decisive 'no'.[7] However, the EU is only one collection of members of the GATS, and its decision is not decisive for the meaning of GATS commitments. The second relates to residence or employment on a permanent basis. While the exclusion of citizenship does not raise any particularly problems, the exclusion of residence and employment does. Clearly, if an individual does not have access to residence on the territory, he or she is unlikely to be able to provide services which require personal presence. Thus, the meaning of 'residence' needs to be modified so that it does not mean temporary residence for the purpose of the service contract but something else. In this way, for the GATS, 'residence' becomes assimilated to an independent right of residence disconnected from service provision. The residence which is necessary for the service provision is defined out. 'Employment' as a term also undergoes a similar change. 'Employment' is not only divorced from access to the labour market but is divided into two kinds – temporary and permanent. Thus, temporality is the key which permits differentiation of labour into the GATS-permitted kind – temporary employment on the territory – and the GATS-excluded kind, which is associated with right of individuals regarding long-term residence on the territory, independent of the economic activity undertaken.

Further, the Annex specifies that members are free to negotiate specific commitments which apply to all categories of people providing services under the agreement, and the provision of the commitment then applies in respect of the activity. This provision of the Annex permits the inclusion in the schedules relating to different sectors of limitations such as professional qualifications, etc. Finally, the third provision of the Annex states that the agreement does not prevent members from applying their own measures to regulate the entry, or temporary stay, of natural persons. Members are also entitled to retain measures which 'ensure the orderly movement of natural persons across its borders provided that such measures are not applied in such a manner as to nullify or impair the benefits accruing to any Member under the terms of a specific commitment'.

This provision, more than any other, evidences the incoherence between the objective of the agreement and the sovereignty claims of the members regarding border controls. It recognizes the sovereign power of members to apply immigration measures, while at the same time it seeks to limit those powers by reference to the GATS obligations of market access and equality within the market. Thus, national sovereign powers are only consistent with the GATS commitments so long as they do not interfere too substantially with (i.e. nullify or impair) the benefits which other members are entitled to under the agreement. These benefits are, of course, the possibilities for nationals of the member, or companies based in the member, to have access to the territory and market of other members. It is difficult to argue that immigration controls do not impair access by individuals to the territory. Indeed, the purpose of immigration controls is to do exactly that – to make it more difficult for some people, rather than others, to have access to the territory of a state. It is, then, interesting to return to the formulation of the GATS Annex – the right of the state to apply immigration controls ends at the place where the GATS commitment to other states starts. But there is no clarity as to where the rights of individuals who claim a benefit to their state under the GATS start, in comparison with where the sovereignty of a state ends in respect of immigration controls. Nonetheless, the principle is one of access against which obstacles must be weighted.

Exploitation and the foreigner – closing the borders again

As I have discussed above, the GATS can be read as a tool which is inimical to border controls and thus requires numerous exceptions to be inserted into it to permit states to continue immigration controls and thereby limit access by foreigners to the market. The GATS system is dynamic; the 1995 agreement included an obligation that a new round of negotiations aimed at further development of the system had to begin within five years.[8] Concerns about the impact of liberalization of service provision on working conditions were increasingly expressed by trade unions – particularly after the entry of China into the WTO system.[9] Free trade became increasingly linked with the degradation of working conditions.

The field of immigration was not left out of this discussion on free trade and working conditions. Indeed, the GATS principle of access to the territory and market for companies and service providers encouraged questions regarding the treatment of migrant workers in the GATS context. While the 1996 Ministerial Conference made specific reference to labour conditions, acknowledging that the venue for setting them internationally was in the International Labour Office (ILO),[10] even the WTO itself acknowledges that the issue of free trade and labour standards has not gone away.[11] In the migration arena, the issue has circled around the possibility of companies engaging workers in a low-wage state at local wages, then moving them to a high-wage state to carry out service provision while maintaining their wage levels at that of their country of origin. Two kinds of question arise: first, does this constitute an abuse of competition rules, as the playing field in which the companies compete is not level? And second, does this constitute exploitation of the workers? It is to the second set of questions that I will now turn.

Since the end of bipolarity, the international community has been reticent about entering into international agreements about border controls or migration. While the ILO obtained fairly wide acceptance of its 1949 Convention on Migration for Labour, at the height of the post-

Second World War labour shortages in north-western Europe, even that Convention deals primarily with the conditions under which migrant workers are received and treated rather than the conditions around their entry. The UN Convention on the Protection of the Rights of All Migrant Workers and their Families 1990 also does not deal with issues of border controls or the conditions under which an individual may migrate, but rather with the rights of migrants and their families once they are on the territory of a state. It has been ratified mainly by countries of origin of substantial numbers of migrants, rather than receiving countries. Neither agreement places substantive obstacles in the way of states' choices regarding admission or expulsion of migrants.

The international community rethinks border controls

In 2000 the UN opened for signature a Convention against transnational organized crime which includes three Protocols. The first is the Protocol to Prevent, Suppress and Punish Trafficking in Persons, Especially Women and Children; the second is the Protocol against the Smuggling of Migrants by Land, Air and Sea; and the third is on a completely different topic – the Illicit Manufacturing and Trafficking of Firearms, Their Parts and Components and Ammunition. Clearly this was a Convention which was subject to pressure from a number of interest groups, which managed to insert, as Protocols to it, international rules on a rather heterogeneous selection of issues (Kyle & Koslowski 2001). Of interest here is the Protocol on trafficking in persons as it is the international community's statement on what exploitation is, in the context of migration, and on what states which have signed up to the protocol are required to do about it. In this regard, it deals with questions of borders, how they should be crossed and who should be able to cross them for economic purposes. While the title of the protocol focuses on women and children, in fact the content is more gender-neutral. The academic and NGO concern regarding the exploitation of women and children undoubtedly contributed to the success of the Protocol (Radin 1996; Ehrenreich & Hochschild 2002).

The Protocol entered into force in 2003 and so far has 117 states party to it, which include most western liberal democracies.[12]

According to the Preamble and Statement of Purpose, the Protocol's objective is to achieve a comprehensive international approach, across borders, to prevent and combat trafficking in persons (especially women and children) in four ways:

- by preventing trafficking of persons (this requires action in states where the journey starts, so before any cross-border migration has taken place);
- by punishing traffickers (this requires the engagement of legal systems);
- by protecting victims of such trafficking (which requires mechanisms by which to identify who victims are);
- by promoting cooperation among states to meet the objectives.

One of the key difficulties regarding trafficking is its legal definition. This question is dealt with in art. 3 of the Protocol which provides a rather detailed and unwieldy definition:

> *(a)* 'Trafficking in persons' shall mean the recruitment, transportation, transfer, harbouring or receipt of persons, by means of the threat or use of force or other forms of coercion, of abduction, of fraud, of deception, of the abuse of power or of a position of vulnerability or of the giving or receiving of payments or benefits to achieve the consent of a person having control over another person, for the purpose of exploitation. Exploitation shall include, at a minimum, the exploitation of the prostitution of others or other forms of sexual exploitation, forced labour or services, slavery or practices similar to slavery, servitude or the removal of organs;
> *(b)* The consent of a victim of trafficking in persons to the intended exploitation set forth in subparagraph *(a)* of this article shall be irrelevant where any of the means set forth in subparagraph *(a)* have been used;
> *(c)* The recruitment, transportation, transfer, harbouring or receipt of a child for the purpose of exploitation shall be considered 'trafficking in persons' even if this does not involve any of the means set forth in subparagraph *(a)* of this article;
> *(d)* 'Child' shall mean any person under eighteen years of age.

This definition is the subject of substantial explanation in the agreed notes for the *travaux préparatoires*. The definition only covers situations where the offences 'are transnational in nature and involve an organized criminal group, as well as to the protection of victims of such offences'. Thus, the potential offences relate to activities which involve an organized criminal group and the crossing of international borders. This raises two issues: the definition of an organized criminal group, and the relationship with the international border.

As regards the first issue, there is a degree of controversy which exists around the concept of an organized criminal group (Mitsilegas 2001). One of the problems is to differentiate between the perpetrators of trafficking and the victims, so as to avoid the possibility that victims, even when they have ostensibly consented to be trafficked, are the objects of criminal charges. As regards the second aspect, where activities are wholly internal to one state or do not involve an organized criminal group, the Protocol is not applicable. The UN legislative guide for the implementation of the Protocol, prepared by the United Nations Centre for International Crime (Draft 3 Vienna, March 2003), suggests that 'the degree to which such involvement must be established is then set by the specific Articles, but is generally not very high' regarding the difficulties. The international law duty to create new criminal offences at the national level engages rather complex and sensitive issues. Constitutionally, criminal law is the means by which a state may lawfully punish individuals for unacceptable activity on behalf of society. The integrity of the criminal justice system is an important concern in all states which respect the rule of law. Measures of civil law – recognizing and protecting rights of action between individuals – and administrative law – setting out the duties of state agents – are most frequently the subject of international obligations.

There are four main elements to the definition of trafficking contained in art. 3(a):

- it must involve: 'recruitment, transportation, transfer, harbouring or receipt of persons'; these are framed as alternatives, thus only one is sufficient for the purposes of the Protocol;
- the means must include: 'threat or use of force or other forms of coercion, of abduction, of fraud, of deception, of the abuse of power or of a position of vulnerability or of other giving or receiving of payments or benefits to achieve the consent of a person having control over another person'; again the means are stated as alternatives;
- this activity must be for the purpose of exploitation;
- exploitation is not finitely defined but must include as a minimum: 'exploitation of the prostitution of others or other forms of sexual exploitation, forced labour or services, slavery or practices similar to slavery, servitude or the removal of organs'.

To these elements, it is added in art. 3(b) that the consent of the victim shall be irrelevant where the means set out have been used; and in 3(c), where the victim is a child (defined as any person under eighteen years), the activity will still be trafficking even if the means set out are not used.

Trafficking or smuggling?

Article 4 of the Protocol specifies that the activity must be transnational – i.e. cross-border (unless otherwise stated). Thus, the definition of trafficking is tied to a cross-border activity. Even the UN draft legislative guide for implementation accepts that trafficking must be an intentional activity. The activity of the trafficker must be one which involves intentional exploitation. Here there is a difference between smuggling and trafficking. Smuggling does not involve the concept of exploitation. Its core principle is the way in which a foreign national crosses the border. The activities which the individual carries out after the crossing of the border are irrelevant to the smuggler. For the activity of assisting a person to cross a border irregularly to constitute trafficking there must be a direct relationship between the individual who is assisting the crossing of the border and the organized criminal group which is carrying out the exploitation of the individual crossing the border.

Smuggling involves only the irregular crossing of a border, i.e. a border crossing which the authorities of the destination state would not sanction if they were in possession of all of the facts of the situation and the capacity to control it. Trafficking may also involve the irregular crossing of the border, though the crossing of the border by the trafficked person may be or appear to be regular. The person may well be in possession of genuine travel documents which authorize entry onto the territory. For the activity to constitute trafficking, it is necessary that there is the intention of exploitation following the crossing of the border. The agreed notes for the *travaux préparatoires*, when providing guidance on art. 11 of the Protocol relating to the strengthening of border measures, note that

> victims of trafficking in persons may enter a State legally only to face subsequent exploitation, whereas in cases of smuggling of migrants, illegal means of entry are more generally used. This may make it more difficult for common carriers to apply preventive measures in trafficking cases than in smuggling cases and legislative or other measures [against carriers] taken in accordance with this paragraph should take this into account.

The definition of trafficking includes activities on two sides of a border (as well as in transit countries). 'Recruitment' involves activities in the country of origin. An individual who is part of an organized criminal group seeks to persuade an individual to cross the border with the intention of exploiting that person's labour in the second country. 'Transportation' may involve smugglers or it may be carried out by national airlines or other transport companies in good faith. The transport may or may not be lawful depending on how it is carried out, but whether it constitutes trafficking or not depends on whether the individual who carries out the transportation is part of the organized criminal group which is carrying out the trafficking.

'Transfer' includes the activities of individuals who may be facilitating trafficking in intermediate countries between the country of origin and the country of destination. 'Harbouring' of trafficked persons requires an individual to have knowledge of, and participate in, the organized criminal group. For instance, staying in a hotel or guesthouse may or may not involve the owner in trafficking, depending on the amount of knowledge which he or she has of the activities, whether he or she was in fact participating in the trafficking, or whether the owner was merely renting out rooms in the normal course of business. Finally, 'receipt' of persons is also an opaque concept. At one extreme, there is the contract of employment which an employer offers to a prospective employee without knowledge of the intention of a third party, the trafficker, to exploit the individual. Provided that the conditions of work do not constitute forced labour or servitude, the employer may not be involved in trafficking, irrespective of the relationship between the trafficker and the victim of trafficking. At the other end of the scale, the employer may be centrally involved in the trafficking as part of the organized criminal group.

To constitute trafficking, the activities must engage the threat or use of force, etc., as cited above. While force, coercion and abduction may be unproblematic, deception and abuse of power are trickier. For instance, if the victim was fully aware that he or she was agreeing to move across international borders for the purpose of prostitution, but instead of ending up in one country was intentionally taken to a neighbouring one, there will be deception. But was the change of country sufficiently important to the consent of the individual to transform the activity into trafficking? Abuse of power also gives rise to similar problems. The agreed notes for the *travaux préparatoires* provide some assistance with the difficulties attendant on the concept of a person in 'a position of vulnerability'. They state that this shall mean 'a situation where the individual has no real and acceptable alternative but to submit'. While this gives some clarification, it still leaves substantial questions – for instance, to what extent do conditions of economic hardship amount to a position of vulnerability?

Where the activities engage the 'giving or receiving of payments or benefits to achieve the consent of a person having control over another person' and this is for the purpose of exploitation, the Protocol also requires this to be criminalized. In effect, this part of the definition seeks to include the quasi-'sale' of an individual to someone else for the purpose of exploitation by the person who has first gained control over the individual. Here the difficulty is to differentiate this activity from lawful sub-contracting of labour across borders, an activity which GATS seeks to liberalize. The key to the illicit nature of the activity is the degree of force, coercion, deception, etc., which are used against the victim in order to carry out the transfer. Where children are involved, however, the means are irrelevant according to the Protocol. The offence shall be committed provided that there has been the 'recruitment, transportation, transfer, harbouring or receipt of a child for the purposes of exploitation'.

The objective of the means must be exploitation. At a minimum, it must include 'exploitation of the prostitution of others or other forms of sexual exploitation, forced labour or services, slavery or practices similar to slavery, servitude or the removal of organs'. The inclusion of 'exploitation of the prostitution of others' creates some separate difficulties. On the one hand, it recognizes that in many countries prostitution is a legal occupation. There is no duty under the Protocol to criminalize prostitution. However, the definition could include the individual who employs a prostitute, depending on whether the employment relationship is one which comes within the definition of exploitation. As regards the issue of consent of the victim, in order to protect victims, the agreed notes for the *travaux préparatoires* state that this provision should not be interpreted as imposing any restriction on the right of accused persons to a full defence and to the presumption of innocence.

The scope of the Protocol, according to art. 4, extends only to 'the prevention, investigation and prosecution of offences . . . where those offences are transnational in nature and involve an organised criminal group', as well as to the protection of victims. States are obliged to make three other activities related to trafficking in persons criminal offences:

- attempting to commit the offence of trafficking in persons;
- participating as an accomplice in the offence;
- organizing or directing other persons to commit the offence.

Thus there are four criminal offences which must be created: trafficking in persons; attempting to do so; participating as an accomplice in doing so; and organizing or directing other to do so. For the offence of trafficking, there is a fairly wide scope of activities which are included. For the other three, attempting, participating and organizing or directing trafficking in persons, the evidential burden on the state to prove the relationship with the principal offender to the standard of proof required by a criminal trial may be difficult.

As regards the protection of victims, the UN Protocol provides that states must ensure that their domestic and administrative systems contain provisions which provide victims with information on relevant court and administrative proceedings, and assistance for their views and concerns to be presented and considered at appropriate stages in criminal proceedings. They must also protect the privacy of victims, and consider implementing measures for their physical and other recovery, including housing, counselling, medical assistance, employment, and educational and training opportunities. While destination states are not under any obligation to permit victims of trafficking to reside on their territory, they must consider this possibility, taking into account humanitarian and compassionate factors. States of origin are under a duty to receive back their nationals or permanent residents who are victims of trafficking.

One of the difficulties of the UN Protocol is the elision of victims and workers. While a number of rights are set out for victims, the issue of workers' rights is not addressed. While the protection of victims / workers has consequences in the criminal law system, it is primarily an issue for civil and administrative law. There are three main concerns regarding victims / workers:

- compensation for their labour: can victims / workers receive retrospective wages at the levels required by minimum wage legislation and under collective agreements?
- compensation for non-contractual loss suffered by the victim / worker. Where the victim / worker has suffered harm, as in the case of an industrial injury or as a result of violence used against him or her, does he or she have a right to compensation?
- continued residence and work: this is the most sensitive issue around victim / worker protection in the context of trafficking. State concerns to safeguard the integrity of border controls have meant they have been reluctant to provide any residence-related 'incentives' for the victim / worker to cooperate in law enforcement. Traffickers may use the threat of denunciation to state authorities, thereby putting into motion state expulsion procedures against the individual, in order to extract forced labour from victims / workers. Where law enforcement agencies seek to prosecute traffickers but victims / workers are not protected against expulsion, very considerable difficulties in achieving convictions are encountered.

The alternative approach to protecting victims of trafficking lies in treating them as rights holders entitled to the protection of labour standards. The advantage of using labour standards as the mechanism to fight exploitation is that they apply equally to nationals and non-nationals in excluding employers' ability to exploit workers. The trafficking approach brings the immigration status of the victim to the centre of the debate on exploitation. By focusing on the foreignness of the victim, which is determined by the fact of the border crossing and the lack of a right of residence, the issue is moved from one about working conditions to one about immigration. The central issue about security within the labour force is exchanged for the issue of the security of border controls and foreigners.

Conclusions

In this chapter I have brought together two quite different international approaches to the relationship of international trade, migrants and security. The first, the free trade approach contained in the WTO agreements, presupposes the right of corporate entities to require employees or contractors to move across borders to carry out economic activities for them. The constraints, while numerous and very wide, are treated as exceptions to the rule which, in time and as the international trading system moves more centrally into the field of service provision, are intended to fall away. The second approach is that of the UN Protocol to prevent trafficking in human beings, which starts from the premise that all cross-border movement of foreigners is potentially a criminal offence related to exploitation, in particular of labour.

The two approaches are coherent at their extremes – for instance, where, on the one hand, the foreigner who is moving is a very highly paid financial consultant going from one high-income economy to another for a short period; on the other hand, the examples of trafficking in human beings as the equivalent of the selling of humans (and the most common examples used are of women in the international sex trade, which examples have the effect of both horrifying and titillating the public at the same time) clearly show serious exploitation. But the majority of cases lie somewhere between those two extremes. A useful example is found in the report on the treatment of Polish workers in other EU Member States commissioned by the Polish Bureau of the Commissioner for Civil Rights Protection (Carbey-Hall 2008). Here the workers in question, while foreigners, had a right of residence, so the crossing of the border, in itself, could not become a criminal offence. The research, nonetheless, reveals exploitation including intimidation, financial exploitation, hate crime and anti-social behaviour, bonded labour and silent exploitation where the workers chose to keep quiet for fear of the repercussions. Some exploitation is minor; other, serious. None, however, is easily addressed through immigration rules. All the problems were related to failure to comply with labour standards, civil law on contractual obligations and crime committed against migrant workers by members of the host population. To the extent that crimes are committed, these are on the part of the nationals of the host state engaged in economic activities, or anti-social crimes based on racism.

The relationship between globalization and the foreigner is framed as a security issue related to the successful cross-border exercise of service activities in the context of free trade, and as a security issue regarding the threat of traffickers to their victims, foreigners who are being exploited by them. Both frameworks engage the question of the border as the place at which obstacles to either trade or criminal activity take place. In the final chapter I will return to the border as regards the movement of people, and its transformation in response to security claims.

9

Sovereignty, security and borders

The border as a line which separates different territories of sovereignty is one of the most cherished fictions in international relations. So long as there is a border between states, then it is possible to think about migration – people belong on one side or the other of the border. If the international community is characterized by anarchy, then the border provides the line of resistance against that disorder. Within the state there is order surrounded by the border of sovereignty. What happens, though, when borders start to move or reconfigure themselves? If sovereignty is embedded in the capacity of a state to govern and be governed – to regulate activities within its area, be that coercive in respect of criminal law, or distributive as in respect of social security – the edges of authority are important.

In this chapter I will examine borders and their security. How do borders as sites where controls on persons take place become associated with the delivery of security, and how does this configuration change? To what extent does the nineteenth-century understanding of sovereignty, as invested in solidarity based on nationality circumscribed by borders and performed through the spectacle of border controls on persons, become less and less satisfactory as a mechanism for understanding the way politics, community and economy are constructed? While in the preceding chapters I have taken the state border as a given, in order to seek to understand the meaning and nature of inclusion and exclusion from state and community which is inherent in the citizen/immigrant divide, the subject of this chapter is even more problematic, as it is the border itself. When the border changes its nature as a result of the changing conceptions of sovereignty, the concept of migration itself is fundamentally changed. Without the border, there cannot be international migration. Instead of a state-centred view of movement of persons, the state disappears and the subject matter of migration studies must be adjusted. When the border remains for some purposes but not for others – for instance control of movement of persons – the illusion of migration studies remains but the practices are transformed. The capacity to include or reject moves away from its most brutal frame – at the edge of the territory – and, if it is to be exercised at all, it must find other venues.

Understanding sovereignty?

Statehood, according to western political theory, depends on three central elements: a people, a territory and a bureaucracy (Weber 1964). The territory is delineated by a border which holds in place the people, identified as citizens, and the bureaucracy whose actions are defined by those borders. A necessary condition of statehood is that the bureaucracy has established a credible claim to a monopoly over the legitimate use of violence within the territory. The term 'authority' is often used instead of 'violence' but the core concept of the state is its capacity to determine and enforce its order, which is otherwise called 'sovereignty'.

Inter-state relations revolve around the dilemmas which are posed within the context of these fixed characteristics of people, borders and order (Albert, Jacobson & Lapid 2001). The European Union, however, increasingly challenges this theoretical settlement. In this final chapter I will examine the deconstruction of border controls on persons in the EU. In doing so, I am looking at two things:

- what happens to the relationship of migration and security – where does it become vested, if no longer at sovereign borders?
- in so far as sovereignty is vested in border controls as the place where it is most emblematically delivered, where does it go when it migrates away from the border?

In the EU, people no longer belong exclusively to the sovereign states which form the European Union (twenty-seven at last count) but have acquired a status – citizenship of the Union – which renders them the subjects of a non-state actor. This actor, the EU, is capable of conferring on them rights which a state, either that of their nationality or that of their residence (i.e. a host state as regards a migrant), cannot (or, as in the case of family reunion, may not want to) confer (Baldaccini, Guild & Toner 2007). Most importantly, for my purposes, the classic symbol of state sovereignty, the border control on persons entering and leaving the state, which provides the mechanism for the state to evidence its sovereignty to its citizens and foreigners, is no longer possible for (almost all) EU Member States.

Where is the territory?

The territory over which the state exercises its jurisdiction is challenged by the European Union. While the European sovereign state remains the building block of the EU, the symbol of territory – the state border – is only visible in very specific places in most of the EU. This invisible border is commonly called 'the Schengen border', after the agreement signed in 1985 by five Member States, in which, in advance of EU law, they agreed to abolish inter-state border controls on the movement of goods and persons, and common controls on the admission of non-EU nationals arriving from outside the common space (Brouwer 2008). Gradually all the other Member States signed up to the agreement, with the exception of Ireland and the UK. The first agreement was supplemented by a second agreement in 1990 and the lifting of common border controls on the movement of persons took place only on 25 March 1995 (Belgium, France (with some delays because of Dutch drugs policy), Germany, Luxembourg, the Netherlands, Portugal and Spain lifted controls on that date, followed by Italy and Austria in 1997, Greece in 2000, Denmark, Sweden, Finland, Norway and Iceland in 2001(though the last two are not EU Member States; Peers 2006) and the Central European Member States – including Switzerland, another non-EU state – in 2008 (Faure-Atger 2008)). The result was the transformation of what had been borders subject to control on the movement of persons into internal borders without controls (for instance that between Poland and Germany) and the creation of new external borders for the common area for the purposes of controls on persons (for instance that between Poland and Russia; Potemkina 2003).

The control of persons at the borders common to twenty-four sovereign states is no longer permissible, as a result of EU law. It affects about 498 million citizens of the Union (Balzacq & Carrera 2006). The EU outsiders are Ireland and the UK, by choice; Bulgaria and Romania, as they have not yet been admitted; and Cyprus, which as an island with a disputed territory is not able to participate. Denmark participates through an intergovernmental agreement with the twenty-three. Iceland, Norway and Switzerland, which are not EU Member States, like Denmark also participate in the Schengen invisible border through agreements. Bulgaria, Cyprus and Romania are to enter the Schengen system as soon as their own systems are considered sufficiently secure.

As the EU has not finished enlarging, so too the Schengen area, which mimics but is not identical to it, is also likely to enlarge. While Ireland and the UK have been permitted to maintain their national border controls with the other EU Member States, all states which now join the EU are required to participate fully in the Schengen project. The current candidate states for the EU are Croatia, the Former Yugoslav Republic of Macedonia, and Turkey. The anticipated candidate countries are, according to the European Commission, Albania, Bosnia & Herzegovina, Montenegro, Serbia and Kosovo, under Security Council Resolution 1244.[1]

The way in which the movement of persons, whether EU citizens or third-country nationals, occurs across the national borders of the Schengen participating states is uncontrolled. The objective (and reality) is that it should approximate the movement of people inside the territory of a state.[2] The authority of sovereignty which is expressed in border controls is excluded in the internal Schengen regime. As regards immigration controls on persons seeking to enter the Schengen territory from outside its space, here a common set of controls apply as the sovereignty of all the participating states is inherent in the external control which takes place at the external border of any one of them. So long as the Schengen regime remained an intergovernmental one regulated by an international agreement, the fundamental nature of the control did not change – an expression of sovereignty. However, once the regime was transformed into EU law, its nature changed into one governed by the hierarchy which is central to EU law. The capacity of the state to enforce its order is changed and impaired in so far as that state is governed by the principle of rule of law.

Sovereignty, law and people at the borders

The exercise of the state's capacity to determine its order as regards its borders is found in its laws and regulations on immigration and border controls on the movement of persons. In this section I will examine the change in the law and law-making capacity of the state as a result of entering into the Schengen regime.

While the first Schengen Agreement dates from 1985 and sets out the common aim of abolition of border controls among the five states which signed it, it did not arrive in a vacuum. Indeed, it took shape as an agreement controlled by the partners just before the EU sought to dominate the field. In 1986 the EU (under its then name of 'the EEC') agreed the Single European Act, the first major amendment to the Treaty, which included the duty to abolish border controls on the movement of persons across inter-Member State borders by 31 December 1992, but included no mention of the external border (Guild 2001). This was part of the great 1992 project to complete the internal market of the EU undertaken by the then President of the Commission, Jacques Delors. The obvious overlap (to avoid calling it outright competition) between the Schengen Agreement and the Single European Act is hard to miss. Nonetheless, the EU institutions and Schengen states decided to proceed through two parallel universes as regards the abolition of border controls, rather than tackle the rather obvious incoherence (Elsen 1997). The reasons are multiple but two have a particular resonance: first, the UK, under Prime Minister Thatcher, was implacably opposed to the abolition of border controls between the Member States (she has been followed so far in this position by all subsequent British Prime Ministers); second, the possibility that border rules would become hard EU law rather than an exercise of state sovereignty, even though that sovereignty would be temporarily exercised to abolish their existence, was a step too far too fast (Gortazar 2001).

This arrangement was, of course, untenable in the longer term, and that longer term came fast enough. With the continuous enlargement of participation in the Schengen project, and the increasing detail which the Schengen system produced regarding how the inter-Member States borders were not to be controlled, how the extra-Member States were to be controlled, how visas were to be issued, what exceptions should exist and how they should be exercised, the administration and coherent application of the system became ever more fragile. No effective policing mechanism to make sure the participating states were actually doing what they were supposed to be doing existed. As a result, in the end, the Schengen states threw in the towel and handed the whole, by this time rather messy, arrangement over to the EU by virtue of a Protocol to the Amsterdam Treaty (which, as soon as it entered into force, transferred the Protocol to the EC and EU Treaties). All of this took place in 1999, but by 2008 the EU had still not yet managed to integrate fully the Schengen legacy.

Under the Schengen arrangements as transposed into EU law, a common set of rules apply, which the state no longer has the exclusive power to amend or change as an exercise of sovereignty regarding the movement of persons into and out of the state (Guild 2007a). Indeed, the administration which carries out the control of the territory is increasingly colonized by EU rules which the official must ensure are properly carried out, rather than the border laws of the sovereign state. In the event of a conflict between national law and EU law on borders, the official is obliged to apply EU law and disregard national law which is contrary. This principle is at the centre of the EU system and, as such, it applies equally to rules about movement of persons and to those on goods, services or capital (Tridimas 2007).

The Schengen Borders Code entered into force on 13 October 2006. It provides the common EU law on how the internal and external borders of the Union are managed for the purpose of movement of persons. As a Regulation (562/2006), the Code has direct effect in the Member States and is not the subject of transposition into national law. The abolition of the checks at the internal border is specified in the Regulation and thus no longer a matter for national law. Similarly, the duties of border guards to admit or refuse admission to third-country nationals (albeit mainly limited to those arriving for short stays) at the external border are now set out in the Code. Thus, the EU has acquired common internal and external border control law, although it is not a state.

Starting then with the intra-Schengen Member State borders, among the states which participate in the system, all persons, whether citizens of a Member State or third-country nationals, are entitled to move freely for up to three months across the whole of the territory (only those seeking international protection or irregularly present are excluded from the right). This is a very impressive example of removing security obstacles to the enjoyment of liberty – indeed that most basic of liberties, freedom of movement. Free movement of persons in the EU is one of the most immediately visible and highly valued of the rights of persons living there. It includes the right of individuals to move, for a wide variety of reasons, across the EU, and has gradually been widened to include third-country nationals. One must nonetheless acknowledge that there is all too often a gap between the rights of individuals and their exercise, first at the hands of the administrations of Member States other than that of their nationality, and second by actors in the economic and cultural sectors (Carbey-Hall 2008). Still, for many persons entitled to free movement, the most obvious personal reward of EU law has been the right not to encounter the public administration at all. The internal border is mainly characterized by its absence of controls on persons.

Member States, nonetheless, according to EU law, have the right to know who is on their territory. The right of free movement is not absolute. The interests of public policy, public security and public health are expressly recognized in EU law as the grounds on which the right of free movement of persons may be limited. However, in exercising their duties regarding public policy, security and health, the Member States must respect the priority of the right of free movement. The exceptions are exactly that. Their use must be justified by the Member States when seeking to rely on them, and the measures taken must be proportionate to the legitimate interest protected. As the European Court of Justice stated:

'[t]he requirement for legal certainty means that the legal situation resulting from national implementing measures must be sufficiently precise and clear to enable the individuals concerned to know the extent of their rights and obligations'.[3] Nonetheless, without the power to maintain officials at the inter-Member State borders in order to check persons, there is no way that the individual Member State can use the mechanism of borders for this purpose. The state's right to know who is on its territory is no longer related to the border but to the organization of the state – for instance population registers, etc.

Regarding the external EU borders – what kind of borders are these, according to the rules? The Code specifies that 'external borders' mean the Member States' land borders, including river and lake borders, sea borders and their airports, river, sea and lake ports, provided that they are not internal borders (art. 2(2)). Further those borders are ones which 'may be crossed only at border crossing points and during the fixed opening hours. The opening hours shall be clearly indicated at border crossing points which are not open 24 hours a day.' Thus the external border, for the purposes of individuals seeking to cross it, consists of a series of points defined in both space and time. According to the Commission, there are in the region of 300 million external border crossings per year. According to the Member States, there are nearly 900 million external border crossings. Both sets of figures include EU citizens and third-country nationals.[4] According to the Council, the external border is about 3.6 million kilometres long. It is unclear why there is such an important discrepancy between the Commission and the Member States regarding the number of external border crossings. However, the answer may be that, while the EU external border is a pixilated one, the external borders of the Member States are still perceived of as lines on the map.

The Member States were required to notify the European Commission of the location of the points which constitute the external border for the movement of persons. There are 1,792 designated external border crossing points with controls in the EU. Of these, 665 are air borders, 871 are sea borders and only 246 are land borders.[5] On the basis of this information, one would be forgiven for thinking that the EU is an island much like Australia, rather far from everywhere, thus encouraging sea and air travel. As any casual glance at a map will reveal, this is not entirely geographically correct, so the explanation must be elsewhere. Clearly there is a very strong preference among Member States to designate controlled external border crossing points at EU sea ports. This may well be because the infrastructure to carry out a control at sea ports is well developed. The second most popular place for controlled external border crossings is airports. For the purposes of control, airports are very convenient as they bring together many travellers at a time and funnel them through various controls in rapid succession. Least popular are land borders. Only 246 places have been designated controlled external land borders.[6] No doubt the length of the EU's land borders with its neighbours makes it difficult from the perspective of designated controlled border management.

The Code has changed the nature of the external border of the Member States as a matter of law. The act of an individual crossing an external border, which is intended to be captured in the Code, does not appear to correspond to a common understanding. The aggregate of individuals entering the EU, according to the Commission and according to the Member States, varies by a factor of 1:3. Perhaps this is the mathematical expression of sovereignty.

Sovereignty beyond the border?

The EU border divides the world's population into two main groups, though I will return to the divisions later. As set out above, there is the group of persons who are already inside the external border. This group can be fragmented into many subgroups – for instance EU nationals, third-country nationals with EU long-term resident status, refugees, persons irregularly present, etc. I will leave them, though, for the moment and consider that part of the world's population which is not inside the EU. This vast majority of people – according to the EU, for the purposes of its border management – can be subdivided into two main groups, both of which are subject to further fragmenting. The first key group is those who require visas to enter the EU for a three-month stay, and the second key group is those who do not.

The Visa Regulation (539/2001, as amended) sets out the lists of countries whose nationals require visas to enter the EU and those who do not (Meloni 2005). The countries whose nationals do not require a visa to enter the EU are able to arrive at the EU's external border and must be admitted or refused admission according to the Code. They can do so as the effect of their country not being on the Visa Regulation is that the EU's Directive on carrier sanctions (2001/51) will normally not result in a fine on any carrier which brings them to the EU. The countries which are not on the black-list number 44 (though 6 were to be added in 2008) and include North and most of South America with some exceptions, Australia, Japan and a small number of (fairly wealthy) countries in South-East Asia. There are over

120 countries and territories on the visa black-list. These countries include almost all of Africa, the Middle East (except Israel), non-EU Europe, Asia and the Indian sub-continent. The division of white- and black-list countries reflects the ethnicity, religions and GDP of the world (Bigo & Guild 2003). For nationals of black-listed countries, obtaining a visa is a necessary prerequisite to travelling to the EU. In 2006 over 12 million Schengen short-stay visas were issued. Under 1 million applications for visas were refused (under 10 per cent).[7] However, the rate per country varies dramatically. For instance, French authorities received 18,507 applications for Schengen (A, B or C) visas in Abidjan, Ivory Coast, in 2006. In response, 13,335 visas were issued and 5,172 refused, a refusal rate over 30 per cent. However, French authorities in Beijing, China, issued 96,001 visas and refused 8,163, less than 10 per cent (Beaudu 2007).

Once an individual holds a validly issued Schengen visa, he or she has a presumption of admission to the Schengen territory, irrespective of where he or she arrives first. So the Ivoirian who obtained a Schengen visa from the French authorities can expect to be admitted whether he or she arrives in Paris, Frankfurt or Stockholm – the carrier has no fear of a fine for bringing the individual to the EU and when he or she arrives, the Code applies. Article 5 of the Code requires the individual to produce a number of items, provide information and fulfil certain conditions to be admitted at the external border:

- to produce a valid travel document and visa (if required);
- to justify the purpose and conditions of the intended stay (but a list of supporting documents is included in an annex) and to show sufficient funds for subsistence, which are set as a fixed daily sum, though the amounts vary wildly among the Member States;
- not to be notified as a person to be excluded from the EU (i.e. on the Schengen Information System); and
- not to be a threat to public policy, internal security, public health or the international relations of any of the Member States.

While this may seem a rather substantial and vague list, in practice the immigration official at the port of entry, particularly if it is an airport, will normally have less than a minute to check the documents and identity before making the decision. Any longer period of time to consider the individual can result in major queues. Further, if the official refuses the individual admission, he or she is entitled to reasons in writing and a right of appeal, again notified in writing, against the refusal (art. 13). This takes even longer for the official to prepare.

Accordingly, the important control of the foreigner for the purposes of coming to the EU takes place first with the decision whether his or her country is on the visa black-list, which results in the main control being exercised outside the EU when the individual is still within his or her own state of nationality. The EU's functional border control is transferred to a site where it can take place over a long period of time and under conditions over which there is not yet a fully 'EU' law which applies. This extraterritorial check still takes place under the control of the Member States but far from their common or individual borders (Mitsilegas 2007).

Mutual recognition of sovereignty

There is an important exception in the Code to the principle that all black-list nationals require a visa to enter the common territory. The Code exempts nationals of countries on the black-list from the visa requirement if they have a valid residence permit issued by a Member State. Article 2(15) defines a valid residence permit as all permits issued by the Member States in the common format (dealt with by Regulation 1030/2002 which sets out the uniform format for residence permits) or other documents which Member States issue to authorize stay in and re-entry to their territory (barring asylum seekers awaiting a first decision).

On 13 October 2006, the Commission published the list of documents of which the Member States had notified it in relation to Article 2(15).[8] At the time of publication, a number of Member States had not yet included their lists – specifically, Bulgaria, Cyprus, Malta and Romania (the first and last not having been Member States at the relevant time). The number of different documents which a state issues indicates the number of different residence statuses which third-country nationals have within the territory. Thus, in principle, the more residence documents a Member State issues, the more finely it carves up the possible residence categories it has in its national law. The limitations on residence of third-country nationals fall into three main areas:

- length of time the individual can remain on the territory – this can range from indefinite to highly limited;
- the activities which the individual can undertake – for instance studies, work, work with a specified employer or within a skills category, etc.;
- the part of the national territory to which the individual must limit his or her residence.

So the numbers of different groups of third-country nationals increase with the number of different residence documents which the state issues. In any event, for the purposes of the Schengen external border-crossing, the Member States, altogether, notified 188 different types of residence documents which have the same validity as a visa. This means that a border guard at any of the 1,792 designated external border crossing points must be able to identify:

- nationals of which countries require a visa to enter the common territory;
- what Schengen visas look like and when they are valid;
- 188 different documents issued by the Member States which have the same legal effect as a visa for the purposes of entry.

This is a skilled job which depends on a high degree of confidence, among the border guards of the Member States, in one another's capability to get the law right. Where a border guard gets the law wrong, the Code provides a right of appeal to the individual refused admission.

Security and authority: the use of force

In 2004 the EU adopted a Regulation establishing the External Border Agency, FRONTEX. The functions of the agency are multiple, but among them is to coordinate operational activity among the Member States in the field of external border management (Mitsilegas 2007). Among the areas where there has been much concern regarding the management of the external border has been Spain, in particular the Canary Islands. FRONTEX was requested to coordinate Member State controls around the Canary Islands, which were designed to support Spanish border patrols in the area. These operations were given names, among the first being the HERA series. Member States were invited to contribute coastguard boats and personnel for the HERA operations. While there was no obligation, many Member States did so, though each coastguard boat (and some planes were offered as well) operated under their national rules (Carrera 2007).

In 2006 there were approximately 31,000 irregular border crossings to Spain's Canary Islands. The people who individually made up that 31,000 were seeking to arrive in Spain in small boats. On 13 April 2007 the following press release was published: 'Very low numbers of illegal migrants "[are now] arriving to the Canary Islands and more than thousands of human lives saved – that is the outcome of Frontex coordinated operation Hera III", Frontex Executive Director Mr Ilkka Laitinen says as the operation was finishing' (Carrera 2007; Jeandesboz 2008).

'During the two month operation, which started on 12 February, 585 migrants arrived to the islands, about one third of them were interviewed within the operation. Besides, the total of 1167 migrants was diverted back to their points of departure at ports at the West African coast, thus preventing them to risk their lives on the dangerous journey', according to FRONTEX. The question which arises is: did these persons seek entry at a designated border crossing point? We know that most of these points are sea ports, including in the Canary Islands. If they did, were they treated in accordance with the Schengen Borders Code and provided with a written decision refusing them admission to the territory, together with reasons and information regarding their right of appeal? If they were diverted before they arrived at a designated border crossing point, then this ought to have taken place in accordance with Spanish law in so far as the diversion took place within Spanish territorial waters. If the diversion took place in international waters, then the international law of the sea applies, which limits the circumstances in which boats can be intercepted. While there is substantial dispute among legal experts on the law of the sea about this issue (not least because of the political interest of a number of liberal democracies in intercepting boats with suspected foreigners on them before they arrive in the territorial waters of the state), the only justification on which all agree is the right to intercept if lives are at risk. The fact that FRONTEX uses the term 'diversion' rather than 'interception' is because of the sensitivity that the latter term, unless justified in international law, may be equivalent to piracy. If the diversion took place in the territorial waters of a third state then this would need to be in conformity with the laws of that state. If the persons on the boat were nationals of that state and were being diverted from carrying out their normal (fishing) activities in territorial waters, another can of worms about legality is opened.

Of those who, as a result of FRONTEX action, were unable to present themselves at a designated border crossing point – the 1,167 persons of whom the Director spoke on 13 April 2007 – was an individual examination of their application to arrive at a designated Schengen border crossing point made? If so, on what basis was this pre-examination undertaken and were the same rules as apply under the Schengen Borders Code applied to this as well, in particular regarding a written decision and right of appeal? These questions may seem rather simple to some people, badly articulated to a reality which is shown on television regarding the floods of migrants and the inability of the state authorities to deal with them as individuals entitled to a consideration of their singular application and situation (Jorry 2007). Nonetheless, these questions flow from the central concern: how to understand the changing nature of the border and its relationship with law in Europe. What happens to the individual in the tension between border, territory and community, and how does the law work to protect that individual?

Conclusions

The claims of security move in two key directions, collective security and individual security. The security of the individual, for instance security of residence status, is highly visible and particularized, while the claims of collective security form one of the main ways in which the security of the individual is extinguished. The individual as a citizen or foreigner forms the building block of the European system's claim to legitimacy: the citizen as the participant in governance and for whose benefit governance takes place. However, the understanding of the divide between the citizen – the essential participant in (national) community – and the foreigner has become exceptionally complex in Europe and derives from a very wide range of sources. The relationship of the citizen and the state is articulated around claims of security. Though 'security' itself, as a word which expresses some essential content, is much contested – in particular as regards how it works within the relationship of individual, community and state – the determining elements are empowerment and justification. The proliferation of statuses of the individual between citizen and foreigner in Europe can be described by the relationship to claims of exclusion by the state on grounds of security (whether this is territorial exclusion, social exclusion in the form of barring from social security, or other forms and manners of security) and to empowerment through inclusion – becoming a member of the group entitled to claim security as a right. Exclusion is the consequence of the state justification of collective security, which enters into conflict with the individual's claim to empowerment – individual security.

The typology of European inclusion and exclusion, as viewed from the perspective of security and the individual, looks something like this:

- the citizen of the state in Europe: this is a source of security of residence for the individual, through the constitution, reinforced by the international treaty system which no longer permits banishment or exile.

- the citizen of the European Union who is not a national of the state where he or she is living (e.g. the Polish national living and working in Ireland): here, although the individual has the name of citizen of the Union, he or she is still eligible to be expelled (back to Poland for instance); the right of entry, residence, economic activity and protection against expulsion comes from the EC Treaty and is not subject to change by the state acting alone – the state is not sovereign as regards citizens of the Union; expulsion and exclusion are possible only on the grounds of public policy, public security or public health and it is for the state to justify why and how the exclusion or expulsion of the individual should take place;
- the citizen of the Union who is temporally excluded: the case of the nationals of the 2004 and 2007 enlargement of the European Union, not all of whom enjoy the right to take employment in all Member States though they are entitled to reside anywhere in the EU; these restrictions are time-limited;
- the Swiss national (or the Norwegian, Icelander, etc.) in a Member State, who, although not a citizen of the Union and thus a third-country national, enjoys rights equivalent to those of the citizen of the Union;
- the Turkish worker in an EU state: on the basis of the 1963 agreement between the EU and Turkey, Turkish workers are also protected to the same high level as citizens of the Union against expulsion from the Member States;
- the third-country national who has lived lawfully in a Member State for five years or more and is thus entitled to the status of long-term resident third-country national: this third-country national enjoys protection against expulsion equivalent to that of migrant citizens of the Union;
- the third-country national whose country of nationality is on the EU's visa white-list (e.g. US nationals): he or she is only obligatorily excluded from the EU territory on the basis of a positive act by a Member State to include his or her identity in a database of persons to be excluded on security grounds; there is no system to prevent the individual from arriving in the EU, only to refuse admission once he or she is here;
- the third-country national whose country of nationality is on the EU's visa black-list but with which the EU has a visa facilitation agreement in force (e.g. Russian nationals): here the individual is collectively described as a potential security risk of some kind (illegal immigration, criminality, political violence, depending on the state to which he or she belongs) but this presumption of a security risk is then partially neutralized by the visa facilitation agreement which provides for easy, rapid and cheaper issue

of visas for short stays in the EU; the place where the security control takes place is the consulate of the Member State where the application is made; the security reassurance for the EU which 'compensates' for the facilitation of visas is the conclusion of a readmission agreement, whereby states with visa facilitation agreements will take back their citizens when they are expelled from the EU (and usually also agree to take back non-nationals who have arrived in the EU via their state (Trauner & Krause 2008));

- the third-country national whose country is on the EU visa black-list and with which there is no visa facilitation agreement (e.g. Chinese nationals); there is a presumption that these persons pose a security risk, and thus they must obtain a visa at an EU Member State consulate in their country of origin proving that they are not a security risk before they are issued a visa which will allow them to go to the EU;
- the third-country national whose country is on the EU visa black-list and whose country has been specified in the EU visa rules as a country of specific security concern by at least one Member State (Bigo & Guild 2003): here the presumption that the individual is likely to be a security threat is higher than for third-country nationals whose countries are on the visa black-list but not this security threat list.

The different statuses and their variety can be understood as expressions of a security relationship among individuals, communities and states. The various forms of security provide an organizing principle around which territorial and social inclusion and exclusion are drawn. The multiplicity of meanings of security and their contestation can be read through the practices. The proliferation of practices of semi-inclusion, allocation of rights and possibilities indicates that there is no longer any clear and simple line of citizen versus foreigner, nor lines of sovereign borders in Europe. How community can be described through its members finds its sources and expressions in a multiplicity of places – national laws, EU laws (even including international human rights rules) – which are best characterized by their diversity and opaque meanings, effects and justifications.

The relationship of sovereignty, security, borders and people is undergoing substantial change in the EU. There is a fundamental transformation taking place regarding the position of authority and the consequences of that authority for individuals. While the uniforms of the officials who are carrying out border controls have not changed, what they do and where they do it has. The rule of law, a principle deeply embedded in the Member States, requires a new hierarchy in respect of how national order is articulated so as to fulfil the requirements of EU law. Sovereignty, in the form of authority, is migrating away from the territorial borders of the state and instead can be found at work deep within the territory of other states through visa rules, on the high seas and elsewhere. The political argument for the migration of sovereignty is security, but whose security and security in whose name becomes more opaque the farther the exercise of authority moves from its traditional territorial home.

Two key ideas inform this book: finish international political sociology – following the individual rather than the state to understand the meaning of migration for states, the international community and migrants themselves. This enables a critical migration studies approach, which reveals how state power is structured and used, and where and how the possibilities of resistance for the individual are and work. Second, the relationship of security and insecurity is a continuum which permits insecurity to follow the subject – the foreigner, the immigrant – even though the individuals concerned are completely different, have separate trajectories and objectives. In this last chapter, I have brought the two frameworks together by challenging the central notion of migration studies: the border between states which separates those who belong from the others. In so doing I have followed the individual moving, challenging and resisting his or her categorization by the state, both as a foreigner and as a bead on the insecurity continuum necklace.

Notes

Chapter 1 Understanding security and migration in the twenty-first century

1. By reference to the individual, I mean the person struggling for rights – human and legal – nested in the social structures – family, community, society and transnational.
2. See, for instance, the Academy of Migration Studies in Denmark which focuses on migrants and immigration; and the Migration Studies Unit, London School of Economics, which provides a home for scholars working on cross-disciplinary migration issues.
3. A good example of this is the press release of the Bertelsmann Foundation regarding the award of a prize in education for immigration children: www.bertelsmann-stiftung.de/cps/rde/xchg/SID-0A000F0A-CF63108F/bst_engl/hs.xsl/nachrichten_86840.htm.
4. www.immi.gov.au/media/publications/compliance/managing-the-border/pdf/mtb-chapter5.pdf.
5. According to the Australian government, the total population of Kiribati is 88,500: www.ausaid.gov.au/country/country.cfm?CountryId=20.
6. This is also among the reasons why international political sociology provides a useful frame of analysis, as within this discipline the focus on sociology at the international level means that attention is paid to this aspect.

Chapter 2 Migration, citizenship and the state

1. German Federal Ministry of the Interior, www.bmi.bund.de/nn_148264/Internet/Content/Themen/Staatsangehoerigkeit/Einzelseiten/Wichtige__Fragen__und__Antworten__zum__deutschen__Staatsangehoerigkeitsrecht__en.html.
2. See the UK Home Office, www.bia.homeoffice.gov.uk/britishcitizenship/eligibility/.
3. www.bia.homeoffice.gov.uk/britishcitizenship/withdrawingcitizenship/.
4. *LeGrand (Germany* v. *USA)* International Court of Justice 27 June 2001.
5. *Medellin* v. *Texas* US Supreme Court, final judgment: 25 March 2008, www.supremecourtus.gov/opinions/07pdf/06-984.pdf.
6. Aljazeera.net, 30 May 2007. He had been convicted by a military tribunal in Guantánamo Bay and the Australian authorities agreed to detain him for the completion of his sentence, which they did until he was released from prison in Australia on 29 December 2007. His state of health is extremely fragile according to news reports: 'The mental damage from almost six years in Guantánamo limbo will require strong professional and family support, say psychologists who are unsure if Hicks can ever make a complete recovery.' B. Adams, 'Release the First Step in Long Battle', *The New Zealand Herald*, 31 December 2007.
7. These negotiations were accompanied by a judgment of the UK's Court of Appeal in which the second highest court in the UK termed the detention centre in Guantánamo 'a legal black hole'. The case was brought to force the UK authorities to enter into negotiations for the release of the British nationals held in the detention centre. *Abbassi &*

Another v. *Secretary of State for the Foreign and Commonwealth Office and the Secretary of State for the Home Office* [2002] EWCA Civ. 1598.

8 www.reprieve.org.uk/.
9 *Hamdan* v. *Rumsfeld* US Supreme Court judgment 29 June 2006.
10 *Hicks* v. *Ruddock* [2007] FCA 299 (8 March 2007).
11 *Secretary of State for the Home Department* v. *Hicks* Court of Appeal [2006] EWCA Civ. 400.
12 The first decision was on 13 December 2005 and was in favour of David Hicks' claim.
13 Section 20 British Nationality Act 1948; s. 40 British Nationality Act 1981 as amended by the Nationality, Immigration and Asylum Act 2002.
14 *Joyce v. DPP* [1946] AC 347.
15 Paragraph 24.
16 It was only on 20 December 2001 that the UN Security Council, by Resolution 1386 (2001), authorized the establishment of an International Security Assistance Force (ISAF) to help maintain security in Kabul and its surrounding areas.
17 See *Hamdan* v. *Rumsfeld* 126 US 2749 (2006).
18 See the website 'Bring David Hicks Home', www.bringdavidhickshome.org/, visited 23 August 2008.
19 Decided on 12 June 2008, www.scotusblog.com/wp/wp-content/uploads/2008/06/06-1195.pdf, visited 23 August 2008.
20 *Hicks* v. *Ruddock* [2007] FCA 299.
21 The Australian Parliament was provided with a useful note on the subject before the proceedings had finished: www.aph.gov.au/library/pubs/rn/2004-05/05rn33.htm, visited 23 August 2008.

Chapter 3 Migration, expulsion and the state

1 Only non-US nationals can be held at the US detention centre in Guantánamo Bay according to US law (Sands 2008).
2 The core international human rights instruments are now easily available at the UN's website: www2.ohchr.org/english/law/index.htm#core, visited 25 August 2008.
3 'Guatemala Gang Clash Injures 12, *BBC News*, 5 September 2005: 'The gangs, or maras, emerged in Los Angeles and spread to Central America when gang members were deported.'
4 Austria, Belgium, Bulgaria, Cyprus, the Czech Republic, Denmark, Estonia, Finland, France, Germany, Greece, Hungary, Ireland, Italy, Latvia, Lithuania, Luxembourg, Malta, the Netherlands, Poland, Portugal, Romania, Slovakia, Slovenia, Spain, Sweden, the UK. There are also three candidate countries: Croatia, the Former Yugoslav Republic of Macedonia (FYRM) and Turkey. The remaining Western Balkan states are described as potential candidate countries.
5 The EU twenty-seven as well as: Albania, Andorra, Armenia, Azerbaijan, Bosnia & Herzegovina, Croatia, FYRM, Georgia, Iceland, Liechtenstein, Moldova, Monaco, Montenegro, Norway, Russian Federation, San Marino, Serbia, Switzerland, Turkey and Ukraine.
6 C-340/97 *Nazli* [2000] ECR I-957.
7 Three Member States do not participate in this Directive because of the special arrangements they negotiated: Denmark, Ireland and the UK.
8 The 4th Protocol, adopted in 1963, includes two provisions which deal specifically with the rights of nationals and the rights of aliens. Article 3 prohibits the expulsion of nationals and affirms the right of the national to enter the territory of his or her state. Article 4 prohibits the collective expulsion of aliens. This prohibits any measure compelling aliens, as a group, to leave a country, except where such a measure is taken on the basis of a reasonable and objective examination of the particular case of each individual alien

in the group. Protocol 7, adopted in 1984, provides new rights for foreigners on a territory. Article 1 of that Protocol sets out procedural safeguards relating to expulsion of foreigners. It provides that an alien lawfully resident on the territory of a state shall not be expelled except in pursuance of a decision reached in accordance with law. The alien must be permitted to submit reasons against his expulsion and to have his case reviewed and be represented for these purposes before a competent authority. However, it permits expulsion of an individual before the exercise of the rights where necessary in the interests of public order or national security.

9 The Council of Europe keeps an updated list of signatures and ratifications of the ECHR at conventions.coe.int/Treaty/Commun/ListeTableauCourt.asp?MA=3&CM=16&CL=ENG.

10 *Conka* v. *Belgium*, Application no. 51564/99 European Court of Human Rights 5 May 2002.

11 *R. (Al-Skeini)* v. *Secretary of State for Defence (The Redress Trust intervening)* [2007] UKHL 26.

12 *Boultif* v. *Switzerland*, Application no. 54273/00 European Court of Human Rights 2 August 2001.

13 With the addition of clarification from a later case: *Uner* v. *the Netherlands* Application no. 46410/99 European Court of Human Rights 5 July 2005.

Chapter 4 Armed conflict, flight and refugees

1 This is an exception to the general rule in this book that I am only concerned here with migration across international borders.

2 International Committee of Red Cross (ICRC) Fact Sheet 31 October 2002.

3 Ibid.

4 www.crisisgroup.org/home/index.cfm, visited 26 August 2008.

5 UNHCR 2008.

6 Internal Displacement Monitoring Centre 2008.

7 Ibid.

8 UN Doc.E/CN.4/RES/1992/73.

9 The European Commission published a report on the implementation of this Directive: COM(2007)745 final.

10 Article 1(1) 'Any act by which severe *pain* or suffering, whether physical or mental, is intentionally inflicted on a *person* for such purposes as obtaining from him or a third person information or a confession, punishing him for an act he or a third person has committed or is suspected of having committed, or intimidating or coercing him or a third person, or for any reason based on discrimination of any kind, when such pain or suffering is inflicted by or at the instigation of or with the consent or acquiescence of a public official or other person acting in an *official capacity*. It does not include pain or suffering arising only from, inherent in or incidental to lawful sanctions.'

11 *Saadi* v. *Italy*, Application no. 37201/06 European Court of Human Rights 28 February 2008.

Chapter 5 Migration, torture and the complicit state

1 www2.ohchr.org/english/bodies/cat/stat3.htm, visited 14 July 2008.

2 According to the ticking-bomb scenario argument, if, by torturing a person, one would acquire information as to the whereabouts of a ticking bomb which, if it went off, would kill many people, and as a result of that information one was able to find and disarm the bomb, the torture would be justified. For a very good analysis of why the ticking-bomb scenario is a dangerous chimera designed to undermine rule of law see Sands (2008).

3 Once again international law rejects any right of states to expel their own nationals: art.

12(4) of the International Covenant on Civil and Political Rights 1966 states: 'No one shall arbitrarily be deprived of his right to enter his own country.'

4 Communication No. 233/2003 *Agiza* v. *Sweden* 24 May 2005 (Convention against Torture).

5 Communication No. 1416/2005 *Alzery* v. *Sweden* 10 November 2006 (UNHRC).

6 CCPR/C/88/D/1416/2005 Communication No. 1416/2005 *Alzery* v. *Sweden* 10/11/2006 Human Rights Committee paras. 3.8–3.10.

7 CAT/C/34/D/233/2003 Communication No. 233/2003 *Agiza v. Sweden* 24 May 2005 paras. 12.28–12.29.

8 Ibid. para. 3.11.

9 Communication No. 233/2003 *Agiza* v. *Sweden*.

10 Communication No. 1416/2005 *Alzery* v. *Sweden* 10/11/2006 Human Rights Committee.

11 '1. Each State Party shall undertake to prevent in any territory under its jurisdiction other acts of cruel, inhuman or degrading treatment or punishment which do not amount to torture as defined in article 1, when such acts are committed by or at the instigation of or with the consent or acquiescence of a public official or other person acting in an official capacity. In particular, the obligations contained in articles 10, 11, 12 and 13 shall apply with the substitution for references to torture or references to other forms of cruel, inhuman or degrading treatment or punishment.
2. The provisions of this Convention are without prejudice to the provisions of any other international instrument or national law which prohibit cruel, inhuman or degrading treatment or punishment or which relate to extradition or expulsion.'

12 Communication No. 233/2003 *Agiza* v. *Sweden* para. 13.4.

13 The Parliamentary Ombudsman, *A Review of the Enforcement by Security Police of a Government Decision to Expel Two Egyptian Citizens* Adjudication no. 2169-2004 22 March 2005, www.jo.se/Page.aspx?MenuID=106&Language=en&Object, visited 29 January 2007, section 2.4: 'K.J. has stated that the officials at the Ministry of Foreign Affairs told him that during the presentation there was some concern that either the UN Committee against Torture or the European Court of Human Rights would have time to issue a staying order before enforcement could take place.'

14 Committee against Torture, 40th Session, 28 April – 16 May 2008; CAT/C/SWE/CO/5, 4 June 2008.

15 The Parliamentary Ombudsman, *A Review*.

Chapter 6 Migration and data: documenting the non-national

1 DG H 2A, EU Council Document No. 8065/07; the 2008 report is entitled *TE-SAT 2008 EU Terrorism Situation and Trend Report 2008* (The Hague, 2008).

2 This formulation is used by EUROPOL, as well as many other European institutions such as the UK's Intelligence and Security Committee, which defines it as the threat from individuals who claim a religious justification for terrorism. I will not use this term but rather the less emotive one of 'extreme Islamic political violence'.

3 *Framework Decision on Combating Terrorism* (2002/275/JHA).

4 Austria, Belgium, Denmark, France, Germany, Ireland, Italy, Luxembourg, the Netherlands, Poland, Slovakia, Spain, Sweden and the UK.

5 'Foreigners Commit 20 Per Cent of Crime in London Say Police', *Daily Mail*, 14 August 2007.

6 EUROSTAT, *Crime and Criminal Justice*, 19/2008.

7 UN, *International Migration 2006*, No. E.06.XIII.6.

8 This is the result of the citizenship choices which were made when the two states gained independence in the early 1990s. Lithuania chose to accord citizenship on the basis of

presence on the territory, Estonia chose a historic relationship to the state. The result was the inclusion of the Russian ethnic minority which had moved to the area when it was part of the USSR in the case of Lithuania, and the exclusion of this group in the case of Estonia.

9 See the Office of the High Commission for Human Rights, *General Comment No. 17: Rights of the Child (article 24)*, 7 April 1998.
10 *Goodwin & I* v. *UK* European Court of Human Rights 11 July 2002.
11 See, for instance the preamble of the EU Regulation on Visas 539/2001 as amended – recital (5): 'the determination of those third countries whose nationals are subject to the visa requirement, and those exempt from it, is governed by a considered, case-by-case assessment of a variety of criteria relating *inter alia* to illegal immigration, public policy and security, and to the European Union's external relations with third countries, consideration also being given to the implications of regional coherence and reciprocity'.
12 Bolivia, Botswana, Brazil, Lesotho, Malaysia, Mauritius, Namibia, South Africa, Swaziland, Trinidad and Tobago, and Venezuela.
13 Press release, UK Borders Agency, 'Results of Britain's first global visa review', 10 July 2008.
14 European Commission, 'European Union Fact Sheet: Visa Reciprocity', June 2006: http://ec.europa.eu/external_relations/us/sum06_06/docs/visa.pdf, visited 13 August 2008.
15 European Commission, *Report on the Evaluation of the Dublin System*, SEC (2007) 742, 6 June 2007.
16 Council Document 17102/06 of 22 December 2006.
17 Council Document 16982/06 of 20 December 2006.
18 *The Queen on the application of Mr Numieri Mohammed Ali* v. *Secretary of State for the Home Department* CO/1472/2005. The UK authorities conceded liability so there is no written judgment.
19 EDPS Opinion concerning access for consultation of the Visa Information System (VIS) by the authorities of Member States responsible for internal security and by Europol for the purposes of the prevention, detection and investigation of terrorist offences and other serious criminal offences, OJ 2006 No. C 97/6.
20 C-317/04 (*Parliament* v. *Council*) European Court of Justice 30 May 2006.
21 For the documents and analysis see Statewatch, http://database.statewatch.org/searchdisplay.asp, visited 13 August 2008.
22 See chapter 5 on the exchange of information among states resulting in the allocation of suspicions in respect of terrorism.

Chapter 7 Economy and migration

1 For instance the European Union's Lisbon Strategy for Growth and Jobs designed in 2000 reflects this: http://ec.europa.eu/growthandjobs/faqs/background/index_en.htm#bg01, visited 27 August 2008.
2 The Council of Europe published its Vocational Training Projects: Towards Equal Opportunities for Immigrants: Practical Guidelines in 2008 to strengthen cooperation in this area.
3 Preamble, EC Regulation 1612/68 on Freedom of Movement for Workers within the Community.
4 Brussels European Council, 14/15 December 2006, Council Document No. 16879/1/06.
5 A forum where governments of thirty democracies work together to address the economic, social and environmental challenges of globalization, according to its publications. The member countries are: Australia, Austria, Belgium, Canada, the Czech Republic,

Denmark, Finland, France, Germany, Greece, Hungary, Iceland, Ireland, Italy, Japan, Korea, Luxembourg, Mexico, the Netherlands, New Zealand, Norway, Poland, Portugal, the Slovak Republic, Spain, Sweden, Switzerland, Turkey, the UK and the USA.

6 India has 9.43 million citizens working in OECD countries.

7 Mexico has 2.095 million citizens working in OECD countries.

8 European Commission, *Social Protection in the European Union* (Luxembourg 2008).

9 The issue is more complicated as some states export old age benefits to migrant workers who have gone back to their country of origin, but this is usually on the basis of bilateral agreements between states and is by no means universal or even the norm among OECD states.

10 The current EU Directive in force is 2004/38 which still contains this prohibition on exclusion (or indeed expulsion) to serve economic ends in art. 27.

11 European Commission, Employment: http://ec.europa.eu/employment_social/free_movement/enlargement_en.htm, visited 14 August 2008.

12 European Commission, *Communication on Free Movement of Workers*, COM (2002) 694 final.

13 Initial government projections were for about 12,000–15,000 workers per annum to come to the UK. See Home Office memorandum, 24 February 2004, 'Consequences of EU Enlargement', published in House of Commons Home Affairs Committee 2003-4 *House of Commons Papers* 435.

14 See the national reports of the Commission's Network on Free Movement of Workers for 2006: http://ec.europa.eu/employment_social/free_movement/general_information_en.htm, visited 14 August 2008.

15 Home Office (Border & Immigration Agency), Department of Work and Pensions, HM Revenue and Customs, and Department of Communities and Local Government, *Accession Monitoring Report May 2004–December 2007*

16 Home Secretary John Reid, *House of Commons Debates*, 24 October 2006, column 82WS.

17 European Commission, *Communication: The Impact of Free Movement of Workers in the Context of EU Enlargement*, COM (2008) 697.

18 European Commission Staff Working Document, *Monitoring Progress towards the Objectives of the European Strategy for Social Protection and Social Inclusion*, SEC (2008) 2660 final.

19 European Commission, *Communication: The Impact of Free Movement of Workers in the Context of EU Enlargement*, COM (2008) 697.

20 Article 7(2) Regulation 1612/68.

21 Regulation 1408/71.

22 The British NGO, the Child Poverty Action Group, explains the test and its consequences very well: www.cpag.org.uk/cro/wrb/wrb186/reside.htm, visited 14 August 2008.

23 *Zalewska* v. *Department of Social Development* [2007] NICA 17 (9 May 2007).

24 Department of Work and Pensions and Office of National Statistics, *National Insurance Allocations to Overseas Nationals Entering the UK 2006/07*.

25 See the Swedish National Report 2006 on the Free Movement of Workers: http://ec.europa.eu/employment_social/free_movement/docs/sweden_2006_en.pdf, visited 14 August 2008.

26 See EUROSTAT, Statistics on Social Expenditure in Europe: http://epp.eurostat.ec.europa.eu/tgm/table.do?tab=table&init=1&plugin=0&language=en&pcode=tps00098, visited 14 August 2008.

27 A number of attempts have been made by the European Commission to promote a common set of rules of first admission of labour migrants to the Member States but so far nothing has been adopted.

28 Denmark, Ireland and the UK do not participate in this Directive, in accordance with the Protocols which they negotiated regarding the migration competences of the EU.
29 C-127/08 *Metock* European Court of Justice 25 July 2008.
30 Cresencia Cabotaje Motilla, ARC 5375145, Supreme Court of Cyprus, 21 January 2008.

Chapter 8 Foreigners, trafficking and globalization

1 OECD, *Factbook 2007: Economic, Environmental and Social Statistics* (Paris: OCED, 2007).
2 www.wto.org/english/thewto_e/whatis_e/whatis_e.htm, visited 20 August 2008.
3 Ibid.
4 www.wto.org/english/tratop_e/serv_e/mouvement_persons_e/mouvement_persons_e.htm, visited 20 August 2008.
5 The EU Schengen Borders Code, Regulation No. 562/2006, which applies to all persons seeking entry to an EU state (with the exception of Denmark, Ireland and the UK), provides that if an immigration official refuses admission, that decision must be motivated on grounds within the Regulation and give rise to a right of appeal. This is an innovation of the Regulation which was only included as a result of pressure from the European Parliament and at the last minute.
6 www.wto.org/english/tratop_e/serv_e/8-anmvnt_e.htm, visited 21 August 2008.
7 C-113/89 *Rush Portuguesa* European Court of Justice 27 March 1990.
8 These negotiations, called the Doha Round, opened in November 2001. They were suspended in 2006 but recommenced shortly thereafter.
9 See, for instance, the International Confederation of Free Trade Unions statement, 4 April 2003, 'Global Trade Unions State Position for WTO Cancun Meeting': 'All the while, the impact of China's WTO accession on other developing countries, in terms of continual pressure to reduce core labour standards and, all too often, to increase misery and exploitation (particularly of women workers) often in export processing zones, is continuing to worsen.'
10 www.wto.org/english/thewto_e/minist_e/min96_e/wtodec_e.htm#core_labour_standards, visited 20 August 2008.
11 www.wto.org/english/thewto_e/whatis_e/tif_e/bey5_e.htm, visited 20 August 2008.
12 www.unodc.org/unodc/en/treaties/CTOC/countrylist-traffickingprotocol.html.

Chapter 9 Sovereignty, security and borders

1 http://ec.europa.eu/enlargement/potential-candidate-countries/index_en.htm.
2 While immigration controls are excluded, police controls are not. However, a key characteristic of police controls, in comparison with immigration controls, is that normally, in liberal democracies, they must be motivated.
3 C-136/03 *Dörr and Ünal* 2 June 2005, para. 52.
4 European Commission, *Communication on The Next Steps in Border Management in the European Union*, COM (2008) 69 Final.
5 Article 34 Schengen Borders Code.
6 European Commission, *Communication on The Next Steps*.
7 Council Document 10700/07.
8 2006/C 247/01.

Bibliography

Albert, M., D. Jacobson & Y. Lapid 2001, *Identities, Borders and Orders*. Minneapolis: University of Minnesota Press.

Anderson, B. 2006, *Imagined Communities: Reflections on the Origin and Spread of Nationalism* (2nd edn). London: Verso.

Arendt, H. 1970, *On Violence*. San Diego: Harcourt, Brace & Co.

Avant, D. 2006, 'The Implications of Marketized Security for IR Theory: The Democratic Peace, Late State Building and the Nature and Frequency of Conflict', *Perspectives on Politics*, 4, 3 (September), 507–28.

Bagehot, W. [1873] 2007, *The English Constitution*. New York: Cosimo.

Bagshaw, S. 2007, 'The Guiding Principles on Internal Displacement' in R. Cholewinski, R. Perruchoud & E. MacDonald (eds.), *International Migration Law: Developing Paradigms and Key Challenges*. The Hague: Asser Press, pp. 189–202.

Baldaccini, A. 2005, *A Practitioners' Guide to the Reception Conditions Directive*. London: Justice.

Baldaccini, A., & E. Guild 2007, *Terrorism and the Foreigner: A Decade of Tension around the Rule of Law in Europe*. The Hague: Martinus Nijhoff.

Baldaccini, A., E. Guild & H. Toner (eds.) 2007, *Whose Freedom, Security and Justice? EU Immigration and Asylum Law and Policy*. Oxford: Hart.

Bali, S. 2008, 'Population Movement' in P. Williams (ed.), *Security Studies: An Introduction*. London: Routledge, pp. 468–82.

Balzacq, T., & S. Carrera (eds.) 2006, *Security versus Freedom? A Challenge for Europe's Future*. Aldershot: Ashgate.

Barnes R. 2005, 'Of Vanishing Points and Paradoxes: Terrorism and International Humanitarian Law' in R. Burchill, N. White & J. Morris (eds.), *International Conflict and Security Law*. Cambridge: Cambridge University Press, pp. 129–59.

Bayefsky, A. 2001, *UN Human Rights Treaty System: Universality at the Crossroads*. The Hague: Kluwer Law International.

Baylis, E. 2008, 'National Security and Political Asylum' in C. d'Appllonia & S. Reich (eds.), *Immigration, Integration, and Security: America and Europe in Comparative Perspective*. Pittsburgh: University of Pittsburgh Press, pp. 164–80.

Beaudu, G. 2007, 'L'externalisation dans le domaine des visas Schengen', *Cultures & Conflicts*, 68, 85–109.
Beck, U. 1996, *Risk Society: Towards a New Modernity*. London: Sage.
—— 2000, *What is Globalisation?* Cambridge: Polity Press.
Begag, A. 2007, *Ethnicity and Equality: France in the Balance*. Lincoln: University of Nebraska Press.
Begg, M. 2006, *Enemy Combatant: A British Muslim's Journey to Guantanamo and Back*. London: Free Press.
Bigo, D. 2001, 'The Mobius Ribbon of Internal and External Security' in M. Albert, D. Jacobson & Y. Lapid (eds.), *Identities, Borders and Orders*. Minneapolis: University of Minnesota Press, pp 91–116
—— 2002, 'Security and Immigration: Towards a Governmentality of Unease', *Alternatives*, 27, 63–92.
—— 2006, 'Liberty, Whose Liberty? The Hague Programme and the Conception of Freedom' in T. Balzacq & S. Carrera (eds.), *Security versus Freedom? A Challenge for Europe's Future*. Aldershot: Ashgate, pp. 35–44.
Bigo, D., & E. Guild 2003, 'La mise à l'écart des étrangers: la logique du visa Schengen', *Cultures & Conflits* (Spring).
—— 2005, *Controlling Frontiers: Free Movement into and within Europe*. Aldershot: Ashgate.
Bigo, D., & R. J. B. Walker 2007, 'Political Sociology and the Problem of the International', *Millennium*, 35, 3, 725–39.
Boelart-Suominen, S. 2005, 'Non EU Nationals and Council Directive 2003/109/EC on the Status of Third Country Nationals Who are Long Term Residents: Five Paces Forward and Possibly Three Paces Back' *Common Market Law Review*, 42, pp. 1011–52.
Bogusz, B., R. Cholewinski & E. Szyszczak 2004, *Irregular Migration and Human Rights: Theoretical, European and International Perspectives*. The Hague: Martinus Nijhoff.
Bohning, W. R. 1972, *The Migration of Workers in the United Kingdom and Europe*. London: Oxford University Press.
Bommes, M., & A. Geddes 2000, *Immigration and Welfare: Challenging the Borders of the Welfare State*. London: Routledge.
Bonelli, L. 2008, *La France a peur: une histoire sociale de l'insécurité*. Paris: La Découverte.
Born, H., & M. Caparini 2007, *Democratic Control of Intelligence Services: Containing Rogue Elephants*. Aldershot: Ashgate.
Boswell, C. 2000, *EU Enlargement: What Are the Prospects for East–West Migration?* Chatham House Working Paper. London: Chatham House.
Brouwer, E. 2008, *Digital Borders and Real Rights: Effective Remedies for Third Country Nationals in the Schengen Information System*. The Hague: Martinus Nijhoff.
Buzan, B. 1991, *People, States and Fear: An Agenda for International Security*

Studies in the Post-Cold War Era (2nd edn). London: Harvester Wheatsheaf.

Calavita, K. 2005, *Immigrants at the Margins: Law, Race and Exclusion in Southern Europe*. Cambridge: Cambridge University Press.

Carbey-Hall, J. 2008, *The Treatment of Polish and Other A8 Economic Migrants in the European Union Member States*. Warsaw: Bureau of the Commissioner for Civil Rights Protection.

Carlier, J.-Y., & E. Guild 2006, *Avenir de la libre circulation des personnes dans l'EU*. Brussels: Bruylant.

Carrera S. 2007, *The EU Border Management Strategy: FRONTEX and the Challenges of Irregular Immigration in the Canary Islands*. Brussels: CEPS.

—— 2008, *Benchmarking Integration in the EU: Analysing the Debate on Integration Indicators and Moving it Forward*. Berlin: Bertelsmann Foundation.

Castells, M. 2003, *The Information Age: Economy, Society and Culture*, Vol. II: *The Power of Identity* (2nd edn). Oxford: Blackwell.

Castles, S. 2008, *Undertaking Global Migration: A Social Transformation Perspective*. Oxford: IMI.

Castles, S., & M. Miller 2003, *The Age of Migration*. New York: Guilford Press.

Cohen, R. 2006, *Migration and its Enemies: Global Capital Migrant Labour and the Nation State*. Aldershot: Ashgate.

Cohen, S. 2003, *Folk Devils and Moral Panics*. London: Routledge.

Cole, D. 2005, *Enemy Aliens: Double Standards and Constitutional Freedoms in the War on Terrorism*. New York: New Press.

Condinanzi, M., A. Lang & B. Nascimbene 2008, *Citizenship of the Union and Freedom of Movement of Persons*. The Hague: Martinus Nijhoff.

Coolsaet, R. 2008, *Jihadi Terrorism and the Radicalisation Challenge in Europe*. Aldershot: Ashgate.

Cornellius, W., P. Martin & J. Hollifield 1998, *Controlling Immigration: A Global Perspective*. Stanford: Stanford University Press.

Crepeau, F., & D. Nakache 2006, *Forced Migration and Global Processes: A View from Forced Migration Studies*. New York: Lexington Books.

D'Appollonia, C., & S. Reich (eds.) 2008, *Immigration, Integration, and Security: America and Europe in Comparative Perspective*. Pittsburgh: University of Pittsburgh Press.

Dalai Lama 1990, *Freedom in Exile: An Autobiography of the Dalai Lama*. London: Hodder & Stoughton.

Dalby, S. 2002, *Environmental Security*. Minneapolis: University of Minnesota Press.

Deak, I. 2006, 'Scandal in Budapest', *New York Review of Books*, 53, 16 (19 October).

De Bruycker, P. (ed.) 2000, *Les régularisations des étrangers illégaux dans l'Union européenne, Regularisations of illegal immigrants in the European Union*. Brussels : Bruylant.

Deletant, D. [1995] 2006, *Ceausescu and the Securitate: Coercion and Dissent in Romania 1965–1989*. London: Hurst & Co.
Dembour, M. 2006, *Who Believes in Human Rights? Reflections on the European Convention*. Cambridge: Cambridge University Press.
Dieben, T., & D. Dieben 2005, *When Does War Become Crime? Aspects of the Criminal Case against Eric O*. Nijmegen: Wolf.
Dillon, M. 1996, *The Politics of Security: Towards a Political Philosophy of Continental Thought*. London: Routledge.
Douzinas, C. 2000, *The End of Human Rights*. Oxford: Hart.
Duffield, M. 2007, *Global Governance and the New Wars*. London: Zed Books.
—— 2008, 'Global Civil War: The Non-Insured, International Containment and Post-Interventionary Society', *Journal of Refugee Studies*, 21, 145–65.
Edwards, A., & S. Bloomer 2008, *The Transformation of the Peace Process in Northern Ireland: From Terrorism to Democratic Politics*. Dublin: Irish Academic Press.
Ehrenreich, B., & A. R. Hochschild 2002, *Global Woman: Nannies, Maids and Sex Workers in the New Economy*. London: Granta.
Elsen, C. 1997, 'Schengen et la coopération dans les domaines de la justice et des affaires intérieures. Besoin actuels et options futures' in M. den Boer (ed.), *The Implementation of Schengen: First the Widening, Now the Deepening*. Maastricht: EIPA, pp. 5–15.
Etzioni, A. 2004, *From Empire to Community: A New Approach to International Relations*. New York: Palgrave Macmillan.
Faist, T. 2007, *Dual Citizenship in Europe: From Nationhood to Societal Integration*. Aldershot: Ashgate.
Fan, C. 2007, *China on the Move: Migration, the State, and the Household*. London: Routledge.
Faure-Atger, A. 2008 *The Abolition of Internal Border Checks in an Enlarged Schengen Area: Freedom of Movement or a Scattered Web of Security Checks?* Brussels: CEPS.
Fierke, K. 2007, *Critical Approaches to International Security*. Cambridge: Polity.
Follesdal, A. 2001, 'Union Citizenship: Unpacking the Beast of Burden', *Law and Philosophy*, 20, 3, 313–43.
Forbes Martin, S. 2004, *Refugee Women*. New York: Lexington Books.
Fransman, L. 1998, *Fransman's British Nationality Law* (2nd edn). London: Butterworths.
Gearty, C. 2008, *Essays on Human Rights and Terrorism: Comparative Approaches to Civil Liberties in Asia, the EU and North America*. London: Cameron May.
Gellner, E. 1983, *Nations and Nationalism*. Cornell: Cornell University Press.
Gentile, L. 2002, 'New Asylum Regimes or a World without Asylum? The Myth of International Protection' in D. Joly (ed.), *Global Changes in Asylum Regimes: Closing Doors*. Houndmills: Palgrave, pp. 38–47.

Geyer, F. 2008, *Taking Stock: Databases and Systems of Information Exchange in the Area of Freedom, Security and Justice*. Brussels: CEPS.
Gibney, M. 2004, *The Ethics and Politics of Asylum: Liberal Democracy and the Response to Refugees*. Cambridge: Cambridge University Press.
—— 2006, '"A Thousand Little Guantanamos": Western States and Measures to Prevent the Arrival of Refugees' in K. Tunstall (ed.), *Displacement, Asylum, Migration*. Oxford: Oxford University Press.
Giddens, A. 1985, *A Contemporary Critique of Historical Materialism*. Vol. II: *The Nation-State and Violence*. Berkeley and Los Angeles: University of California Press.
Goodwin-Gill, G., & J. McAdam 2007, *The Refugee in International Law*. Oxford: Oxford University Press.
Gortazar, C. 2001, 'Abolishing Border Controls: Individual Rights and Common Control of the EU External Borders' in E. Guild & C. Harlow (eds.), *Implementing Amsterdam: Immigration and Asylum Rights in EC Law*. Oxford: Hart, pp. 121–40.
Gourevitch, P., & E. Morris 2008, *Standard Operation Procedures*. New York: Penguin Press.
Groenendijk, K. 1997, 'Regulating Ethnic Migration: The Case of the Aussiedler', *New Community*, 461–82.
—— 2007, 'The Long-Term Residents Directive, Denizenship and Integration' in A. Baldaccini, E. Guild and H. Toner (eds.), *Whose Freedom, Security and Justice? EU Immigration and Asylum Law and Policy*. Oxford: Hart, pp. 429–50.
Groenendijk, K., T. Strik & R. van Oers 2007, 'De betekenis van de Gezinsherenigingsrichtlijn voor vluchtelingen en andere migranten', *Nieuwsbrief Asiel- en Vluchtelingenrecht*, 17–29.
Groenendijk, K., R. Fernhout, D. Van Dam, R. Van Oers & T. Strik 2007, *The Family Reunification Directive in EU Member States: The First Year of Implementation*. Nijmegen: Wolf Legal Publishers.
Groenendijk, K., E. Guild & S. Carrera 2009, *Integration of Third Country Nationals and Illiberal Practices in the EU*. Houndsmills: Ashgate.
Guild, E. 2001, *Immigration Law in the European Community*. The Hague: Kluwer Law International.
—— 2003, 'International Terrorism and EU Immigration, Asylum and Borders Policy: The Unexpected Victims of 11 September 2001', *European Foreign Affairs Review*, 8, 3 (Autumn), 331–46.
—— 2004, *The Legal Elements of European Identity*. The Hague: Kluwer.
—— 2006, *Security and European Human Rights: Protecting Individual Rights in Times of Exception and Military Action*. Nijmegen: Wolf.
—— 2007a, 'Citizens without a Constitution, Borders Without a State: EU Free Movement of Persons' in A. Baldaccini, E. Guild & H. Toner (eds.). *Whose Freedom, Security and Justice? EU Immigration and Asylum Law and Policy*. Oxford: Hart, pp. 25–56.

—— 2007b, *Inquiry into the EU–US Passenger Name Record Agreement*. Brussels: CEPS.

—— 2008, 'The Uses and Abuses of Counter-terrorism Policies in Europe: The Case of the Lists', *Journal of Common Market Studies*, 46, 1, 173–93.

Guild, E., & A. Baldaccini 2006, *Terrorism and the Foreigner: A Decade of Tension around the Rule of Law in Europe*, The Hague: Brill.

Guild, E., & P. Minderhoud (eds.) 2001, *Security of Residence and Expulsion: Protection of Aliens in Europe*. The Hague: Kluwer Law International.

—— 2006, *Immigration and Criminal Law in the European Union: The Legal Measures and Social Consequences of Criminal Law in Member States on Trafficking and Smuggling in Human Beings*. The Hague: Martinus Nijhoff.

Guittet, E.-M. 2008, 'Military Activities within National Boundaries: The French Case' in D. Bigo & A. Tsoukala (eds.), *Terror, Insecurity and Liberty: Illiberal Practices of Liberal Regimes after 9/11*. Abingdon: Routledge.

Gyulai, G. 2007, *Forgotten without Reason: Protection of Non-refugee Stateless Persons in Central Europe*. Helsinki: Hungarian Helsinki Committee.

Habermas, J. 1992, 'Citizenship and National Identity: Some Reflections on the Future of Europe', *Praxis International*, 12, 1, 1–19.

Hailbronner, K. 1996, *Rückübernahme eigener und fremder Staatsangehöriger, Völkerrechtliche Verpflichtungen der Staaten*. Heidelberg: Springer Verlag.

—— 2007, 'Free Movement of EU Nationals and Union Citizenship' in R. Cholewinski, R. Perruchoud & E. MacDonald (eds.), *International Migration Law*. The Hague: Asser Press, pp. 313–28.

Halleskov, L. 2005, 'The Long Term Residents Directive; A Fulfilment of the Tampere Objective of Near Equality?' *European Journal of Migration and Law*, 7, 2, 181–202.

Hampson, F.-O., J. Daudelin, J. B. Hay & H. Reid (eds.) 2002, *Madness in the Multitude*. Toronto: Oxford University Press.

Hardin, R. (2003), *Liberalism, Constitutionalism and Democracy*. Oxford: Oxford University Press.

Hartung, W. D. 1995, *And Weapons for All*. New York: HarperCollins.

Hathaway, J. 2005, *The Rights of Refugees in International Law*. Cambridge: Cambridge University Press.

Heater, D. 1999, *What is Citizenship?* Cambridge: Polity.

Herman Burgers, J., & H. Danelius 1998, *The UN Convention against Torture: A Handbook*. The Hague: Martinus Nijhoff.

Holsti, K. 1996, *The State, War and the State of War*. Cambridge: Cambridge University Press.

Hussain, R., & N. Blake QC 2003, *Immigration, Asylum and Human Rights*. Oxford: Oxford University Press.

Huysmans, J. 2006, *The Politics of Insecurity, Fear, Migration and Asylum in the EU*. London: Routledge.

Internal Displacement Monitoring Centre (IDMC) 2008, *Internal Displacement: Global Overview of Trends and Developments in 2007*. Geneva: IDMC.
Ishay, M. 2004, *The History of Human Rights: From Ancient Times to the Globalization Era*. Berkeley: University of California Press.
Isin, E., & G. Neilsen 2008, *Acts of Citizenship*. London: Zed Books.
Jabri, V. 1996, *Discourse on Violence: Conflict Analysis Reconsidered*. Manchester: Manchester University Press.
Jackson, J. 1997, *The World Trading System* (2nd edn). Cambridge, MA: MIT Press.
Jacobs, F., & R. White 2006, *The European Convention on Human Rights* (4th edn). Oxford: Oxford University Press.
Jeandesboz, J. 2008, *Reinforcing the Surveillance of EU Borders: The Future Development of FRONTEX and EUROSUR*. Brussels: CEPS.
Joly, D. 2002, *Global Changes in Asylum Regimes: Closing Doors*. Houndmills: Palgrave.
Jones, M. 2006, 'Lies, Damned Lies and Diplomatic Assurances: The Misuse of Diplomatic Assurances in Removal Proceedings', *EJML*, 8, 9–39.
Jorry, H. 2007, *Construction of a European Institutional Model for Managing Operational Cooperation at the EU's External Borders: Is the FRONTEX Agency a Decisive Step Forward?* Brussels: CEPS.
Judah, T. 2000, *Kosovo: War and Revenge*. New Haven: Yale University Press.
Julien-Laferrière F. 2003, 'Le débat sur la double peine, regards sur l'actualité', *La Documentation Française*, 288 (February).
Kalin, W. 2000, 'Guiding Principles on Internal Displacement, Annotations' ASIL study: www.asil.org/pdfs/study_32.pdf 2000, visited 20 August 2008.
Kalin, W., L. Muller & J. Wyttenbach 2004, *The Face of Human Rights*. Geneva: Lars Muller Publishing.
Kanstroom, D. 2007, *Deportation Nation: Outsiders in American History*. Cambridge, MA: Harvard University Press.
Kaufman, S. 2006, 'Symbolic Politics or Rational Choice? Testing Theories of Extreme Ethnic Violence', *International Security*, 30, 4, (Spring), 45–86.
Kerr, R. 2008, *The Military on Trial: The British Army in Iraq*. Nijmegen: Wolf Legal Publishers.
King, R., & R. Black 1997, *Southern Europe and the New Migrations*. Brighton: Sussex Academic Press.
Kneebone, S., & F. Rawelings-Sanaei 2007, *New Regionalism and Asylum Seekers*. New York: Bergham Books.
Krause, K., & M. Williams 2003, *Critical Security Studies Concepts and Cases*. London: Routledge.
Kurnaz, M. 2007, *Five Years of My Life: An Innocent Man in Guantanamo*. Houndmills: Palgrave.
Kyle, D., & R. Koslowski (eds.) 2001, *Global Human Smuggling: Comparative Perspectives*. Baltimore: Johns Hopkins University Press.

Kymlicka, W. 1995, *Multicultural Citizenship: A Liberal Theory of Minority Rights*. Oxford: Oxford University Press.

Lambert, H. 2001, *The Position of Aliens in Relation to the European Convention on Human Rights*. Strasbourg: Council of Europe.

Lanz, D. 2008, 'Subversion or Reinvention? Dilemmas and Debates in the Context of UNHCR's Increasing Involvement with IDPs', *Journal of Refugee Studies*, 21, 192–209.

Loescher, G. 1993, *Beyond Charity: International Cooperation and the Global Refugee Crisis*. Oxford: Oxford University Press.

Lund Petersen, K. 2008, 'Terrorism: When Risk Meets Security', *Alternatives*, 33, 173–90.

Madood, T. 2007, *Multiculturalism*. Cambridge: Polity.

Martin, D. 1995, *La libre circulation des personnes dans l'Union européenne*. Brussels: Bruylant.

Martin, D. A., & K. Hailbronner (eds.) 2003, *Rights and Duties of Dual Nationals – Evolution and Prospects*. The Hague: Kluwer Law International.

Martin, P., M. Abella & C. Kuptsch 2006, *Managing Labor Migration in the Twenty-first Century*. Ann Arbor: Yale University Press.

Marty, D. 2006, *Alleged Secret Detentions in Council of Europe Member States*. Strasbourg: Council of Europe, 22 January 2006.

Mathieu, L. 2006, *La double peine: histoire d une lutte inachevé*. Paris: Dispute.

Meloni, A. 2005, *Visa Policy within the European Union Structure*. Berlin: Springer.

Mertens, T. 2008, 'Cosmopolitanism and Citizenship: Kant against Habermas', *European Journal of Philosophy*, 4, 3, 328–47.

Minderhoud, P. 2006a, 'The "Other" EU Security: Social Protection', *European Journal of Social Security*, 8, 4, 361–80.

Minderhoud, P. 2006b, 'Social Security Rights of Third Country Nationals under EU Law and under the European Convention of Human Rights' in A. Böcker, T. Havinga, P. Minderhoud & H. van de Put (eds.), *Migratierecht en Rechtssociologie, gebundeld in Kees' studies. Migration Law and Sociology of Law, Collected Essays in Honour of Kees Groenendijk*. Nijmegen: Wolf Legal Publishers, 239–48.

Mitsilegas, V. 2001, 'Defining Organised Crime in the European Union: The Limits of European Criminal Law in an Area of Freedom, Security and Justice', *European Law Review* (December), 565–81.

—— 2007, 'Border Security in the European Union: Towards Centralised Controls and Maximum Surveillance' in A. Baldaccini, E. Guild & H. Toner (eds.), *Whose Freedom, Security and Justice? EU Immigration and Asylum Law and Policy*. Oxford: Hart, pp. 359–94.

Moir, L. 2005, 'Towards the Unification of International Humanitarian Law?' in R. Burchill, N. White & J. Morris (eds.), *International Conflict and Security Law*. Cambridge: Cambridge University Press, pp. 108–28.

Ruhs, M., & P. Martin 2008, 'Numbers vs Rights: Trade-offs and Guest Worker Programs', *International Migration Review*, 42, 1, 249–65.
Ryan, B. 2003, 'The Common Travel Area between Britain and Ireland', *Modern Law Review*, 64, 6, 831–54.
—— 2009, 'The Integration Agenda in British Migration Law' in E. Guild & S. Carrera (eds.), *Integration of Third Country Nationals and Illiberal Practices in the EU*. Houndsmills: Ashgate.
Sadiq, K. 2008, *Paper Citizens: How Illegal Immigrants Acquire Citizenship in Developing Countries*. Oxford: Oxford University Press.
Sales, L. 2007, *Detainee 002: The Case of David Hicks*. Melbourne: Melbourne University Press.
Salter, M. 2003, *Rights of Passage: The Passport in International Relations*. Boulder: Lynne Reiner.
Sands, P. 2008, *Torture Team: Deception, Cruelty and the Compromise of Law*. London: Allen Lane.
Sassen, S. 2006, *Cities in a World Economy*. London: Sage.
Scheinin, M., T. Orlin & A. Roasas (eds.) 2000, *The Jurisprudence of Human Rights: A Comparative Interpretive Approach*. Turku: Abo Akademie.
Sheppard, M. 2008, *The Untold Story of Omar Khadr, Guantanamo's Child*. Mississauga: Wiley.
Sikuta, J., & E. Hubalkova 2007, *The European Court of Human Rights: Case Law of the Grand Chamber*. Amsterdam: TMC Asser.
Smith, M., & A. Favell 2006, *The Human Face of Global Mobility*. Piscataway, NJ: Transaction Publishers.
Soguk, N. 2007, 'Border's Capture: Insurrectional Politics, Border-Crossing Humans and the New Political' in P. J. Rajaram & C. Grundy-Warr (eds.), *Borderscapes: Hidden Geographies and Politics at Territory's Edge*. Minneapolis: University of Minnesota Press, pp. 283–308.
Stafford Smith, C. 2007, *Bad Men: Guantanamo Bay and the Secret Prisons*. London: Phoenix.
Stiglitz, J. 2002, *Globalization and its Discontents*. New York: W. W. Norton & Co.
Strange, S. 1996, *Retreat of the State: The Diffusion of Power in the World Economy*. Cambridge: Cambridge University Press.
Tangseefa, D. 2007, '"Temporary Shelter Areas" and the Paradox of Perceptibility: Imperceptible Naked-Karens in the Thai-Burmese Border Zones' in P. J. Rajaram & C. Grundy-Warr (eds.) *Borderscapes: Hidden Geographies and Politics at Territory's Edge*. London: University of Minnesota Press, pp. 231–62.
Thym, D. 2008, 'Respect for Private and Family Life under Article 8 ECHR in Immigration Cases: A Human Right to Regularize?' *International and Comparitive Law Quarterly*, 57, 87–112.
Tilly, C. 1975, *The Formation of Nation States in Western Europe*. Princeton: Princeton University Press.

Mole, N. 2007, *Asylum and the European Convention on Human Rights*. Strasb
Council of Europe.

Morsink, J. 1999, *The Universal Declaration of Human Rights: Origins, Draftin
Intent*. Philadelphia: Pennsylvania University Press.

Nascimbene, B. (ed.) 1996, *Nationality Laws in the European Union*. Lon
Milan: Butterworths, Giuffrè.

Noiriel, G. 2001, *Nations, migrations et pouvoir d'état*. Paris: Édition Berlin, 2

Noortmann, M. 2005, *Enforcing International law: From Self Help to Self Conta
Regimes*. Aldershot: Ashgate.

OECD 2008, *A Profile of Immigration Populations in the 21st Century: Data
OECD countries*. Paris: OECD.

Peers, S. 2006, *EU Justice and Home Affairs Law*. Oxford: Oxford Univer
Press.

Phuong, C. 2005, *The International Protection of Internally Displaced Pers
Cambridge: Cambridge University Press.

Pinder, J., & S. Usherwood 2007, *The European Union: A Very Short Introduct
Oxford: Oxford University Press.

Pollard, N., M. Latorre & D. Sriskandarajah 2008, *Floodgates or Turnsti
Post-EU Enlargement Migration Flows to (and from) the UK*. London: Institute
Public Policy Research.

Potemkina, O. 2003, 'Some Ramifications of Enlargement on the EU–Rus
Relations and the Schengen Regime', *European Journal of Migration and La*
1, 1.

Pozo, S. (ed.) 2007, *Immigrants and Their International Money Flows*. Kalamazo
W. E. Upjohn Institute.

Preuss, U. 1998, 'Constitutionalism – Meaning, Endangerment, Sustainabilit
in S. Saberwal, & H. Sievers (eds.), *Rules, Laws Constitutions*. New Del
Sage, pp. 172–87.

Prunier, G. 1995, *The Rwanda Crisis: History of a Genocide*. New York: Columb
University Press.

Pugh, M., & N. Cooper 2002, *Security Sector Transformation in Post-Confli
Societies*. Conflict, Security and Development. London: Centre for Defenc
Studies, King's College.

Radin, M.-J. 1996, *Contested Commodities: The Trouble with Trade in Sex
Children, Body Parts and Other Things*. Cambridge, MA: Harvard Universit
Press.

Rajaram, P. J., & C. Grundy-Warr (eds.) 2007, *Borderscapes: Hidden Geographie
and Politics at Territory's Edge*. Minneapolis: University of Minnesota Press.

Rose, D. 2004, *Guantanamo*. London; Faber and Faber.

Rubio-Marin, R. 2000, *Immigration as a Demcratic Challenge*. Cambridge:
Cambridge University Press.

Ruhs, M., & B. Anderson 2006, *Semi Compliance in the Migrant Labour Market*.
Centre on Migration, Policy and Society, Working Paper No 30. Oxford.

Torpey, J. 2000, *The Invention of the Passport: Surveillance, Citizenship and the State*. Cambridge: Cambridge University Press.

Toth, J. 2006, 'Relations of Kin–State and Kin–Minorities in the Shadow of the Schengen Regime', *Regio*, 18–46.

Toyota, M. 2007, 'Ambivalent Categories: Hill Tribes and Illegal Migrants in Thailand' in P. J. Rajaram & C. Grundy-Warr (eds.), *Borderscapes: Hidden Geographies and Politics at Territory's Edge*. Minneapolis: University of Minnesota Press, pp. 91–118.

Trauner, F., & I. Krause 2008, *EC Visa Facilitation and Readmission Agreements: Implementing a New EU Security Approach in the Neighbourhood*. CASE 363 / 2008. Warsaw: Centre for European Policy Studies.

Tridimas, T. 2007, *The General Principles of EU Law*. Oxford: Oxford University Press.

Underhill, G. 1998, *Industrial Crisis and the Open Economy Politics, Global Trade and the Textile Industry in the Advanced Economies*. Houndmills: Palgrave.

Van Selm, J., & E. Guild 2005, *International Migration and Security: Immigrants as an Asset or Threat?* London: Routledge.

Vargas, V. 2003, 'Feminism, Globalisation and the Global Justice and Solidarity Movement', Cultural Studies 17, 6, 905–20.

Verdun, A., & O. Croci 2005, *The European Union in the Wake of Eastern Enlargement*. Manchester: Manchester University Press.

Vertovec, S., & R. Cohen 2002, *Conceiving Cosmopolitanism*. Oxford: Oxford University Press.

Vink, M. 2005, *Limits of European Citizenship: European Integration and Domestic Immigration Policies*. Houndmills: Palgrave.

Waever, O. 1995, 'Securitization and Desecuritization' in R. Lipschutz (ed.), *On Security*. New York: Columbia University Press, pp. 46–86.

Waever, O., B. Buzan, M. Kelstrup & P. Lemaitre 1993, *Identity, Migration and the New Security Agenda in Europe*. New York: St Martin's Press.

Walker, R. J. B. 2009, *After the Global: Before the World*. London: New York: Routledge.

Weale, A., & M. Nentwich 1998, *Political Theory and the European Union: Legitimacy, Constitutional Choice and Citizenship*. London: Routledge.

Weber, M. 1964, *The Theory of Social and Economic Organization*, trans A. M. Henderson & T. Parsons. New York: Free Press.

Weiler, J. H. H. 1985, 'Alternatives to Withdrawal from International Organisations: The Case of the European Economic Community', *Israel Law Review*, 20, 282.

Weiner, M. 1997, *The Global Migration Crisis*. Boulder: Westview Press.

Williams, P. (ed.) 2008, *Security Studies: An Introduction*. London: Routledge.

Worthington, A. 2007, *The Guantanamo Files, The Stories of the 774 Detainees in America's Illegal Prison*. London: Pluto Press.

WTO 2007, *Trade Profiles 2007*. Geneva: WTO.
Zizek, S. 2008, *Violence*. London: Profile Books.
Zolberg, A., & P. Benda 2001, *Global Migrants; Global Refugees*. New York: Bergham Books.

Index